Praise for Apple Delights Cookbook

A Collection of Apple Recipes
Cookbook Delights Series

…"With 2,500 varieties of apples grown in the United States and 500,000 bushels of apples produced each in Washington State alone, it is no wonder that Whispering Pine Press International, Inc. has included *Apple Delights Cookbook* in the Delights Cookbook Series. Delightful, mouthwatering dishes like *Apple Sage Pork Chops* or *Applesauce Glazed Chicken* and desserts like *Scandinavian Apple Cake* or *Apple Huckleberry Crisp*, in addition to unique side dishes like *Apple Autumn Harvest Soup* and *Apple and Green Chili Salad* promise to delight the palate and fire your imagination. This book has something scrumptious for all seasons and occasions.

Included in this tantalizing book are tidbits and informational sections that will delight and entertain your guests with witty and factual information about apples and their history, cultivation, and much more. This must-have book will keep you reading and discovering delicious apple dishes for many years to come."…

Mary Scripture
Graphic Designer

…"*Apple Delights* is one of the most practical cookbooks to come across my desk. It's a 'guidebook' for those who really enjoy eating one of the Northwest's most precious commodities.

Praise for Apple Delights Cookbook

A Collection of Apple Recipes
Cookbook Delights Series

This collection of recipes, both old and new, covers a full range of ways to cook, bake, and blend this high-fiber fruit into your daily diet. I find the apple folklore fascinating and the cultivation information helpful. I particularly like the recipes for *Apple Pecan Sage Stuffing* and *Apple Butter made Easy in Crock-Pot.* And, it wasn't until I read this book that I learned that there are many ways to make apple crisp—one of my favorite desserts!

Apple Delights is now a permanent asset to my cookbook collection, and I've even given away a few copies as gifts."...

Kimberly Carter
Publicist

..."Apples are one of the best-known fruits around the world. Throughout literature, this colorful fruit has captured the imagination of artists, poets, and storytellers alike. Now, *Apple Delights Cookbook* can do the same for your kitchen. You will truly be inspired by the wealth of information, poetry, and more than 240 recipes contained in the pages of this book. With this book you will have fun inspiring others with your newfound delicacies."...

Ed Archambeault
Spokane, WA

Praise for Apple Delights Cookbook

A Collection of Apple Recipes
Cookbook Delights Series

…"*Apple Delights Cookbook* is a great cookbook because it not only includes over 240 recipes, but it also contains information and facts on nutrition, health, and cultivation to support the recipes. Reading the 'Did You Know' facts is fascinating, and the poetry by the author is an added extra feature that you won't find included in other cookbooks. *Apple Delights* is definitely a great value because it is packed with rich information. It makes an interesting book to read as well as a resourceful cookbook with delicious-tasting recipes arranged for easy use. I highly recommend this book to give as a gift."…

Dr. James G. Hood
Editor

Apple Delights Cookbook

A Collection of Apple Recipes
Cookbook Delights Series

Karen Jean Matsko Hood

Current and Future Cookbooks

By Karen Jean Matsko Hood

DELIGHTS SERIES

Almond Delights
Anchovy Delights
Apple Delights
Apricot Delights
Artichoke Delights
Asparagus Delights
Avocado Delights
Banana Delights
Barley Delights
Basil Delights
Bean Delights
Beef Delights
Beer Delights
Beet Delights
Blackberry Delights
Blueberry Delights
Bok Choy Delights
Boysenberry Delights
Brazil Nut Delights
Broccoli Delights
Brussels Sprouts Delights
Buffalo Berry Delights
Butter Delights
Buttermilk Delights
Cabbage Delights
Calamari Delights
Cantaloupe Delights
Caper Delights
Cardamom Delights
Carrot Delights
Cashew Delights
Cauliflower Delights
Celery Delights
Cheese Delights
Cherry Delights
Chestnut Delights
Chicken Delights
Chili Pepper Delights
Chive Delights
Chocolate Delights
Chokecherry Delights
Cilantro Delights
Cinnamon Delights
Clam Delights
Clementine Delights
Coconut Delights
Coffee Delights
Conch Delights
Corn Delights
Cottage Cheese Delights
Crab Delights
Cranberry Delights
Cucumber Delights
Cumin Delights
Curry Delights
Date Delights
Edamame Delights
Egg Delights
Eggplant Delights
Elderberry Delights
Endive Delights
Fennel Delights
Fig Delights
Filbert (Hazelnut) Delights
Fish Delights
Garlic Delights
Ginger Delights
Ginseng Delights
Goji Berry Delights
Grape Delights
Grapefruit Delights
Grapple Delights
Guava Delights
Ham Delights
Hamburger Delights
Herb Delights
Herbal Tea Delights
Honey Delights
Honeyberry Delights
Honeydew Delights
Horseradish Delights

Huckleberry Delights
Jalapeño Delights
Jerusalem Artichoke Delights
Jicama Delights
Kale Delights
Kiwi Delights
Kohlrabi Delights
Lavender Delights
Leek Delights
Lemon Delights
Lentil Delights
Lettuce Delights
Lime Delights
Lingonberry Delights
Lobster Delights
Loganberry Delights
Macadamia Nut Delights
Mango Delights
Marionberry Delights
Milk Delights
Mint Delights
Miso Delights
Mushroom Delights
Mussel Delights
Nectarine Delights
Oatmeal Delights
Olive Delights
Onion Delights
Orange Delights
Oregon Berry Delights
Oyster Delights
Papaya Delights
Parsley Delights
Parsnip Delights
Pea Delights
Peach Delights
Peanut Delights
Pear Delights
Pecan Delights
Pepper Delights
Persimmon Delights
Pine Nut Delights
Pineapple Delights
Pistachio Delights
Plum Delights

Pomegranate Delights
Pomelo Delights
Popcorn Delights
Poppy Seed Delights
Pork Delights
Potato Delights
Prickly Pear Cactus Delights
Prune Delights
Pumpkin Delights
Quince Delights
Quinoa Delights
Radish Delights
Raisin Delights
Raspberry Delights
Rhubarb Delights
Rice Delights
Rose Delights
Rosemary Delights
Rutabaga Delights
Salmon Delights
Salmonberry Delights
Salsify Delights
Savory Delights
Scallop Delights
Seaweed Delights
Serviceberry Delights
Sesame Delights
Shallot Delights
Shrimp Delights
Soybean Delights
Spinach Delights
Squash Delights
Star Fruit Delights
Strawberry Delights
Sunflower Seed Delights
Sweet Potato Delights
Swiss Chard Delights
Tangerine Delights
Tapioca Delights
Tayberry Delights
Tea Delights
Teaberry Delights
Thimbleberry Delights
Tofu Delights
Tomatillo Delights

Tomato Delights
Trout Delights
Truffle Delights
Tuna Delights
Turkey Delights
Turmeric Delights
Turnip Delights
Vanilla Delights
Walnut Delights
Wasabi Delights
Watermelon Delights
Wheat Delights
Wild Rice Delights
Yam Delights
Yogurt Delights
Zucchini Delights

CITY DELIGHTS

Chicago Delights
Coeur d'Alene Delights
Great Falls Delights
Honolulu Delights
Minneapolis Delights
Phoenix Delights
Portland Delights
Sandpoint Delights
Scottsdale Delights
Seattle Delights
Spokane Delights
St. Cloud Delights

FOSTER CARE

Foster Children Cookbook
  and Activity Book
Foster Children's Favorite
  Recipes
Holiday Cookbook for
  Foster Families

GENERAL THEME DELIGHTS

Appetizer Delights
Baby Food Delights
Barbeque Delights
Beer-Making Delights
Beverage Delights

Biscotti Delights
Bisque Delights
Blender Delights
Bread Delights
Bread Maker Delights
Breakfast Delights
Brunch Delights
Cake Delights
Campfire Food Delights
Candy Delights
Canned Food Delights
Cast Iron Delights
Cheesecake Delights
Chili Delights
Chowder Delights
Cocktail Delights
College Cooking Delights
Comfort Food Delights
Cookie Delights
Cooking for One Delights
Cooking for Two Delights
Cracker Delights
Crepe Delights
Crockpot Delights
Dairy Delights
Dehydrated Food Delights
Dessert Delights
Dinner Delights
Dutch Oven Delights
Foil Delights
Fondue Delights
Food Processor Delights
Fried Food Delights
Frozen Food Delights
Fruit Delights
Gelatin Delights
Grilled Delights
Hiking Food Delights
Ice Cream Delights
Juice Delights
Kid's Delights
Kosher Diet Delights
Liqueur-Making Delights
Liqueurs and Spirits Delights
Lunch Delights

Marinade Delights
Microwave Delights
Milk Shake and Malt Delights
Panini Delights
Pasta Delights
Pesto Delights
Phyllo Delights
Pickled Food Delights
Picnic Food Delights
Pizza Delights
Preserved Delights
Pudding and Custard Delights
Quiche Delights
Quick Mix Delights
Rainbow Delights
Salad Delights
Salsa Delights
Sandwich Delights
Sea Vegetable Delights
Seafood Delights
Smoothie Delights
Snack Delights
Soup Delights
Supper Delights
Tart Delights
Torte Delights
Tropical Delights
Vegan Delights
Vegetable Delights
Vegetarian Delights
Vinegar Delights
Wildflower Delights
Wine Delights
Winemaking Delights
Wok Delights

GIFTS-IN-A-JAR SERIES

Beverage Gifts-in-a-Jar
Christmas Gifts-in-a-Jar
Cookie Gifts-in-a-Jar
Gifts-in-a-Jar
Gifts-in-a-Jar Catholic
Gifts-in-a-Jar Christian
Holiday Gifts-in-a-Jar
Soup Gifts-in-a-Jar

HEALTH-RELATED DELIGHTS

Achalasia Diet Delights
Adrenal Health Diet Delights
Anti-Acid Reflux Diet Delights
Anti-Cancer Diet Delights
Anti-Inflammation Diet Delights
Anti-Stress Diet Delights
Arthritis Diet Delights
Bone Health Diet Delights
Diabetic Diet Delights
Diet for Pink Delights
Fibromyalgia Diet Delights
Gluten-Free Diet Delights
Healthy Breath Diet Delights
Healthy Digestion Diet Delights
Healthy Heart Diet Delights
Healthy Skin Diet Delights
Healthy Teeth Diet Delights
High-Fiber Diet Delights
High-Iodine Diet Delights
High-Protein Diet Delights
Kidney Health Diet Delights
Lactose-Free Diet Delights
Liquid Diet Delights
Liver Health Diet Delights
Low-Calorie Diet Delights
Low-Carb Diet Delights
Low-Fat Diet Delights
Low-Sodium Diet Delights
Low-Sugar Diet Delights
Lymphoma Health Support Diet Delights
Multiple Sclerosis Healthy Diet Delights
No Flour No Sugar Diet Delights
Organic Food Delights
pH-Friendly Diet Delights
Pregnancy Diet Delights
Raw Food Diet Delights
Sjögren's Syndrome Diet Delights

Soft Food Diet Delights
Thyroid Health Diet Delights

HOLIDAY DELIGHTS

Christmas Delights, Vol. I-II
Easter Delights
Father's Day Delights
Fourth of July Delights
Grandparent's Day Delights
Halloween Delights
Hanukkah Delights
Labor Day Weekend Delights
Memorial Day Weekend
    Delights
Mother's Day Delights
New Year's Delights
St. Patrick's Day Delights
Thanksgiving Delights
Valentine Delights

HOOD AND MATSKO FAMILY FAVORITES

Hood and Matsko Family
    Appetizers Cookbook
Hood and Matsko Family
    Beverages Cookbook
Hood and Matsko Family
    Breads and Rolls
    Cookbook
Hood and Matsko Family
    Breakfasts Cookbook
Hood and Matsko Family
    Cakes Cookbook
Hood and Matsko Family
    Candies Cookbook
Hood and Matsko Family
    Casseroles Cookbook
Hood and Matsko Family
    Cookies Cookbook
Hood and Matsko Family
    Desserts Cookbook
Hood and Matsko Family
    Dressings, Sauces, and
    Condiments Cookbook
Hood and Matsko Family
    Ethnic Cookbook

Hood and Matsko Family
    Jams, Jellies, Syrups,
    Preserves, and Conserves
Hood and Matsko Family
    Main Dishes Cookbook
Hood and Matsko Family,
    Pies Cookbook
Hood and Matsko Family
    Preserving Cookbook
Hood and Matsko Family
    Salads and Salad Dressings
Hood and Matsko Family
    Side Dishes Cookbook
Hood and Matsko Family
    Vegetable Cookbook
Hood and Matsko Family,
    Aunt Katherine's Recipe
    Collection, Vol. I-II
Hood and Matsko Family,
    Grandma Bert's Recipe
    Collection, Vol. I-IV

HOOD AND MATSKO FAMILY HOLIDAY

Hood and Matsko Family
    Favorite Birthday Recipes
Hood and Matsko Family
    Favorite Christmas Recipes
Hood and Matsko Family
    Favorite Christmas Sweets
Hood and Matsko Family
    Easter Cookbook
Hood and Matsko Family
    Favorite Thanksgiving
    Recipes

INTERNATIONAL DELIGHTS

African Delights
African American Delights
Australian Delights
Austrian Delights
Brazilian Delights
Canadian Delights
Chilean Delights
Chinese Delights

Czechoslovakian Delights
English Delights
Ethiopian Delights
Fijian Delights
French Delights
German Delights
Greek Delights
Hungarian Delights
Icelandic Delights
Indian Delights
Irish Delights
Italian Delights
Korean Delights
Mexican Delights
Native American Delights
Polish Delights
Russian Delights
Scottish Delights
Slovenian Delights
Swedish Delights
Thai Delights
The Netherlands Delights
Yugoslavian Delights
Zambian Delights

REGIONAL DELIGHTS
Glacier National Park Delights
Northwest Regional Delights
Oregon Coast Delights
Schweitzer Mountain
  Delights
Southwest Regional
  Delights
Tropical Delights
Washington Wine Country
  Delights
Wine Delights of Walla
  Walla Wineries
Yellowstone National Park
  Delights

SEASONAL DELIGHTS
Autumn Harvest Delights
Spring Harvest Delights
Summer Harvest Delights
Winter Harvest Delights

SPECIAL EVENTS DELIGHTS
Birthday Delights
Coffee Klatch Delights
Super Bowl Delights
Tea Time Delights

STATE DELIGHTS
Alaska Delights
Arizona Delights
Georgia Delights
Hawaii Delights
Idaho Delights
Illinois Delights
Iowa Delights
Louisiana Delights
Minnesota Delights
Montana Delights
North Dakota Delights
Oregon Delights
South Dakota Delights
Texas Delights
Washington Delights

U.S. TERRITORIES DELIGHTS
Cruzan Delights
U.S. Virgin Island Delights

MISCELLANEOUS COOKBOOKS
Getaway Studio Cookbook
The Soup Doctor's Cookbook

BILINGUAL DELIGHTS SERIES
Apple Delights, English-
  French Edition
Apple Delights, English-
  Russian Edition
Apple Delights, English-
  Spanish Edition
Huckleberry Delights,
  English-French Edition

Huckleberry Delights,
English-Russian Edition
Huckleberry Delights,
English-Spanish Edition

CATHOLIC DELIGHTS SERIES

Apple Delights Catholic
Coffee Delights Catholic
Easter Delights Catholic
Huckleberry Delights
Catholic
Tea Delights Catholic

CATHOLIC BILINGUAL DELIGHTS SERIES

Apple Delights Catholic,
English-French Edition
Apple Delights Catholic,
English-Russian Edition
Apple Delights Catholic,
English-Spanish Edition
Huckleberry Delights
Catholic, English-Spanish
Edition

CHRISTIAN DELIGHTS SERIES

Apple Delights Christian
Coffee Delights Christian
Easter Delights Christian
Huckleberry Delights
Christian
Tea Delights Christian

CHRISTIAN BILINGUAL DELIGHTS SERIES

Apple Delights Christian,
English-French Edition
Apple Delights Christian,
English-Russian Edition
Apple Delights Christian,
English-Spanish Edition
Huckleberry Delights
Christian, English-
Spanish
Edition

FUNDRAISING COOKBOOKS

Ask about our fundraising
cookbooks to help raise
funds for your organization.

The above books are also available in bilingual versions. Please contact Whispering Pine Press International, Inc., for details.

Please note that some books are future books and are currently in production. Please contact us for availability date. Prices are subject to change without notice.

The above list of books is not all-inclusive. For a complete list please visit our website or contact us at:

Whispering Pine Press International, Inc.
Your Northwest Book and Gift Company
507 N. Sullivan Road Suite LL-5
Spokane Valley, WA 99037-8576 USA
Phone: (509) 928-8700 | Fax: (509) 922-9949
Publisher Websites: www.whisperingpinepress.com www.whisperingpinepressbookstore.com
Blog: www.whisperingpinepressblog.com
Email: sales@whisperingpinepress.com

Apple Delights Cookbook

A Collection of Apple Recipes
Cookbook Delights Series

Karen Jean Matsko Hood

Published by:

Whispering Pine Press International, Inc.
Your Northwest Book and Gift Company

507 N. Sullivan Road Suite LL-5,
Spokane Valley, WA 99037-8576 USA
Phone: (509) 928-8700 | Fax: (509) 922-9949
Websites: www.whisperingpinepress.com
www.whisperingpinepressbookstore.com
Blog: www.whisperingpinepressblog.com
Email: sales@whisperingpinepress.com

SAN 253-200X
Printed in the U.S.A.

Published by Whispering Pine Press International, Inc.
507 N. Sullivan Road Suite LL-5
Spokane Valley, Washington 99037-8576 USA

For sales outside the United States, please contact the
Whispering Pine Press International, Inc., International
Sales Department.

Book and Cover Design by Artistic Book and Web Design
c/o Artistic Design Service, Inc.
507 N. Sullivan Road, Suite LL-6
Spokane Valley, WA 99037-8576 USA
www.artisticdesignservice.com

Library of Congress Number (LCCN): pending

Hood, Karen Jean Matsko

   Title: Apple Delights Cookbook: A Collection of Apple Reci-
pes: Cookbook Delights Series

       p.   cm.

ISBN: 978-1-59649-402-2   case bound
ISBN: 978-1-59210-542-7   perfect bound
ISBN: 978-1-59649-231-8   spiral bound
ISBN: 978-1-930948-88-4   3-ring binder
ISBN: 978-1-59434-799-3   large print edition
ISBN: 978-1-59210-695-0   comb bound
ISBN: 978-1-59210-697-4   printable cd
ISBN: 978-1-59649-060-4   E-PDF
ISBN: 978-1-59210-360-7   E-PUB
ISBN: 978-1-59434-858-7   E-PRC

First Edition: January 2013
1. Cookery (Apple)   1. Title

Apple Delights Cookbook

A Collection of Apple Recipes
Cookbook Delights Series

Gift Inscription

To: _____

From: _____

Date: _____

Special Message: _____

_____

_____

_____

_____

_____

_____

_____

*It is always nice to receive a personal note to
create a special memory.*

www.whisperingpinepress.com
www.whisperingpinepressbookstore.com
www.appledelights.com

Dedication

To my husband and best friend, Jim.

To our seventeen children: Gabriel, Brianne Kristina and her husband Moulik Kothari, Marissa Kimberly, Janelle Karina and her husband Paul Turcotte, Mikayla Karlene, Kyler James, Kelsey Katrina, Corbin Joel, Caleb Jerome, Keisha Kalani Hiwot, Devontay Joshua, Kianna Karielle Selam, Rosy Kiara, Mercedes Katherine, Jasmine Khalia Wengel, Cheyenne Krystal, and Anna Kaylee.

To my brother, Stephen, and his wife, Karen.

To my husband's ten siblings: Gary, Colleen, John, Dan, Mary, Ray, Ann, Teresa, Barbara, Agnes, and their families.

In loving memory of my mom, who passed away in 2007; my dad, who passed away in 1976; and my sister, Sandy, who passed away due to multiple sclerosis in 1999.

To Sandy's three sons: Monte, Bradley, and Derek. To Monte's wife, Sarah, and their children: Liam, Alice, Charlie, and Samuel. To Bradley's wife, Shawnda, and their children: Anton, Isaac, and Isabel.

To our foster children (past and present): Krystal, Sara, Rebecca, Janice, Devontay Joshua, Mercedes Katherine, Zha'Nell, Makia, Onna, Cheyenne Krystal, and Onna Marie, our future foster children, and all foster children everywhere.

To the Court Appointed Special Advocate (CASA) Volunteer Program in the judicial system which benefits abused and neglected children.

To the Literacy Campaign, dedicated to promoting literacy throughout the world.

Acknowledgements

I would like to acknowledge all those individuals who helped me during the time I wrote this book. I appreciate all the time and effort they put into this project.

I owe deep gratitude and profound thanks to my husband, Jim, for giving freely of his time and encouragement during this project. Also, I owe thanks to my children Gabriel, Brianne Kristina and her husband Moulik Kothari, Marissa Kimberly, Janelle Karina and her husband Paul Turcotte, Mikayla Karlene, Kyler James, Kelsey Katr1ina, Corbin Joel, Caleb Jerome, Keisha Kalani Hiwot, Devontay Joshua, Kianna Karielle Selam, Rosy Kiara, Mercedes Katherine, Jasmine Khalia Wengel, Cheyenne Krystal, and Onna Marie. They all inspire my writing.

I wish to thank Beverly Koerperich for her assistance in typing this manuscript for publication. Thanks also to the entire team at Artistic Design Service, Inc. and Artistic Book and Web Design for all of their help with this book.

I could not have completed the project without them.

A great many thanks are due to my family, all of whom were very supportive during the time it took to complete this project. Their patience and support are greatly appreciated.

xviii

Apple Delights Cookbook

Table of Contents

Apple Delights Cookbook

A Collection of Apple Recipes
Cookbook Delights Series

Introduction

Living in the heart of Washington brings great appreciation for the apple farmers and their crops. Did you know that Washington is the top apple-producing state in the nation?

Apple orchards are beautiful! Daily, we enjoy the beauty of the apple trees and the many stories they have inspired. Many of us can remember the nostalgic Americana stories of Johnny Appleseed and his quest to plant apple orchards all over the eastern and Midwestern United States.

Apples are indeed a tasty and delicious food in all forms. Apples come in a large variety of flavorful fruit in all colors, sizes, and textures. The fruit is great for cooking and nutritious to eat by itself.

Apples have an interesting history of facts and folklore. Their blossoms are beautiful, and the fruit is delicious to eat cooked or raw. It is no wonder that apple tree cultivation quickly spread from Rome to England and then to the United States from east to west.

Some of this apple folklore is included in this book. As a poet, I also found it enjoyable to color this cookbook with poetry so that readers could savor the metaphorical richness of the apple as well as its literal flavor. Also included in this *Apple Delights Cookbook* are some articles on history, cultivation and botanical information, and interesting facts about apples.

The *Cookbook Delights Series* would not be complete without *Apple Delights Cookbook*, because apples are such a common and popular American fruit. We hope you enjoy reading it as well as trying out all the recipes. The cookbook is organized in convenient alphabetical sections to assist you in finding recipes related to the type of cooking you need: appetizers and dips; beverages; breads and rolls; breakfasts; cakes; candies; cookies; desserts; dressings, sauces, and condiments; jams, jellies, and syrups; main dishes; pies; preserving; salads; side dishes; soups; and wines and spirits.

Enjoy your reading about apples, but most importantly, have fun with those you care about while you are cooking.

Following is a collection of recipes gathered and modified to bring you *Apple Delights Cookbook: A Collection of Apple Recipes, Cookbook Delights Series* by Karen Jean Matsko Hood.

Apple Delights Cookbook

A Collection of Apple Recipes
Cookbook Delights Series

Apple Botanical
Classification

Botanical Classification

The botanical classification of the apple is *Rosaceae*; it is a member of the rose family. Roses and apples are related because their flowers share a five-petal pattern. Pome is derived from the Latin *pomum*, meaning "fruit." The scientific name *malus* comes from the Latin word for apple and ultimately from the archaic Greek *malon*. The apple was first assigned to the genus *Pyrus* along with pears and quinces, but it was later separated into its own genus.

Apples are the best example of the pome (fleshy fruit). A pome is an accessory fruit that has five or more carpels (pockets containing seeds). Apples have five carpels, each generally containing 2 seeds, depending on fertilization, although there are a few varieties that can produce more seeds per carpel.

The apple tree is a small deciduous tree with a broad, often densely twiggy crown. The leaves are alternately arranged, a simple oval shape with an acute tip and serrated margin, slightly downy below, 2 to 5 inches long, and 1 to 2½ inches broad on a ¾- to 2-inch petiole (stem). The flowers are produced in spring with the leaves. They are white and are usually tinged pink at first. The fruit matures in autumn and is typically 2 to 3½ inches in diameter.

It is difficult to establish when apples were first domesticated. The earliest evidence discovered so far goes back to the 10th century B.C. from a site in Israel. That area was so dry, that for apples to grow, they would have had to have been cultivated and irrigated. Remains of apples have been found in archaeological sites dating back as far as Neolithic times. This would indicate that wild apples were being eaten by man from the earliest times. Our domestic apple, a combination of at least four wild species (*Malus sylvestris, M. pumila, M. dasyphylla,* and *M. sieversii)* is a hybrid.

Apple Cultivation and Gardening

Apple Cultivation and Gardening

To start your own apple trees, it is best to purchase rootstock from a reputable nursery. These plants will be from two to four years old.

One plant is generally selected for its roots. This plant is called the stock or rootstock. The scion (the plant grafted on) is selected for its leaves, stems, flowers, or fruit. In stem grafting a dormant side bud of one plant is grafted onto the stem of the rootstock. When it has fused, it is encouraged to grow by cutting off the stem above this new bud. Successful grafting takes place when the vascular tissues of the two plants connect.

Seedling apples are different from their parents, sometimes radically. Most new apple cultivars originate as seedlings, which either arise by chance or are bred by deliberately crossing cultivars with promising characteristics. The words "seedling," "pippin," and "kernel" in the name of an apple cultivar suggest that it originated as a seedling. Apples can also form bud sports (mutations on a single branch). Some bud sports turn out to be improved strains of the parent cultivar. Some differ sufficiently from the parent tree to be considered new cultivars.

Rootstock sold to homeowners wanting just a few trees is generally from standard seedlings or semi-dwarf rootstock. The standard seedlings produce a full-size tree, while the semi-dwarf rootstock produces a smaller tree. Dwarf trees tend to sustain more damage from cold and wind. High-density orchards using full-dwarf trees support them with posts or trellises.

After you plant your trees, semi-dwarf varieties will need to grow for three to five years and standard trees will need to grow for four to ten years before they will produce quantities of fruit. It is very important to train limbs and nip off buds growing in the wrong places during this growing time so that the tree will grow in such a way that it will be strong enough to carry the load of a good harvest.

Apples must be cross-pollinated to develop fruit. Check with the nursery where you purchase your trees to find out which trees will be compatible with the ones you want to grow. If you only have one tree, you might gather some bouquets of crab apple blossoms, put them in buckets, and place them near your blooming tree for pollination.

Inadequate pollination will result in fruit that drops when it is marble sized, fruit that is small, misshapen, and slow to ripen, and fruit that has few seeds. Well pollinated apples will have seven to ten seeds. Apples with fewer than three seeds will fall off the tree in the early summer. Poor pollination can result when there are not enough pollinators or enough pollen. Poor weather at pollination time can also result in a poor crop.

A late frost can destroy the apple blossoms, so in the northern hemisphere it is best not to plant trees on a south facing slope. This will discourage early blooming which would leave the tree vulnerable to a late frost. If your tree is blooming and you have a frost that is not too severe, you can wet the tree with water spray before the morning sun hits the flowers. This may save the blossoms. You can evaluate how much damage you sustained from frost by checking the blossoms 24 hours later. If the pistils are black, the blossoms will not produce fruit.

The cooling effect of a body of water nearby helps to slow the spring warmup and keeps the tree from flowering too early. Cool, humid spring weather can be a disadvantage, though, since it might increase the possibility of fungal diseases, especially apple scab. If a body of water is not available, plant on a north slope.

Apples tend to bear every other year. When the tree carries a large crop, the fruit needs to be thinned or the tree may have very few flowers the following year. If thinned properly, the tree will produce a good crop every year.

Apple trees have blooms in groups of five. The first one to open is called the king bloom. Of the five blossoms, this one will produce the best fruit. When the next three blossoms open, thin out two of them so that the remaining one can produce good fruit. It does not matter which two of the three blooms you remove. If the final blossom of the five is the only one that sets fruit, the crop will not be spectacular, but it will help reduce sucker growth.

Some trees, if left unpruned, will get large. This allows them to bear more fruit, but it makes harvest much more difficult. Soil conditions do not have much effect on trees, but they do require good drainage.

Apple trees are affected by fungal and bacterial diseases as well as insect pests. Commercial orchards generally have an aggressive chemical spray program so they can have healthy trees, high yields, and high-quality fruit.

If you choose to spray your trees, never spray when the tree is in bloom because you do not want to kill the pollinators. If you are going to be using insecticides, do not grow plants on the ground near the trees that attract bees. The bees visiting these plants could be affected by the insecticides.

Some of the worst diseases affecting apple trees are fireblight, which is bacterial, and apple scab, black spot, and Gymnosporangium rust, which are fungal. The worst insect problem is the plum curculio. Some of the others are the apple maggot and the codling moth.

Apple scab manifests as dull black or grey-brown lesions on the tree leaves, buds, or fruits. It generally shows up on the undersides of leaves and the fruit. It rarely kills the host plant, but it can reduce yields and quality.

Mice and deer can damage young trees by eating the soft bark. Placing a sheath of wire mesh around young trees helps protect them.

Growing apples organically is difficult, although it can be done. Spraying a light coating of kaolin clay on the apples provides a barrier to some insects and helps reduce sun scald.

Apple trees make a great choice for learning to grow and cultivate in your back yard. These trees will provide you and your family years of enjoyment as well as delicious fruit.

Apple Delights Cookbook

A Collection of Apple Recipes
Cookbook Delights Series

Apple Facts

Apple Facts

Apples are a versatile fruit and can be made into many different courses, from appetizers to soups and main dishes to desserts. Most fresh apples are harvested from July through December, so take advantage of the fresh ripened fruit, and plan menus to incorporate these nutritious fruits. Some late varieties of apples, such as the Granny Smith, are harvested from January through April.

When purchasing apples, look for ones that have not been waxed. Farmers' markets are the best place to buy apples without paraffin. If your budget allows, seek out fruit grown in orchards without pesticides, even though these are difficult to find. They are more expensive, but many feel the long-term health effects may be worth it, although there is not enough long-term research available.

Apples keep best and longest when refrigerated. Non-refrigerated apples can become soft in a few days depending on the variety. Try to purchase apples at farmers' markets and ask how freshly picked they are. Some grocery stores have a fresh section where apples are kept cool; this is the best choice for keeping apples fresh longer. For the highest quality, apples should be firm and without blemishes.

Always wash apples thoroughly before eating or cutting to reduce intake of pesticide residues or bacterial contaminants that result from handling. Be careful when cutting fruits because it is easy to carry pesticides from the skin into the inside fruit with one cut of the knife.

It is suggested that you peel off the skin, if the fruit is waxed, to avoid eating any of the paraffin coating. To prevent cut apples from turning brown because of oxidation, toss them with citrus juices such as the juices of oranges, lemons, or limes.

If you enjoy cooking historical dishes, you can try this apple dumpling, created in 1849 by Eliza Action. She peeled and cored apples, filled the cavities with fruits and spices, and wrapped the apples in her favorite pastry. Each apple was then wrapped in a handmade cloth and boiled. This method led to the baked version so popular today.

Apple Delights Cookbook

A Collection of Apple Recipes
Cookbook Delights Series

Apple Folklore

Apple Folklore

The apple played a central role in many Greek stories. In one, Eris, the Goddess of discord, was angered because she had not been invited to the wedding of a fellow god and goddess. She threw a golden apple among the guests with this inscription, "For the fairest." According to this myth, the discord she caused eventually led to the Trojan War.

In another myth, Atlanta refused to marry unless a suitor could defeat her in a race. One suitor, Milanion, won her hand by dropping three golden apples, which had been given to him by Venus, the Goddess of love, during the race. Atlanta stopped to pick them up, losing the race, and so became his wife.

In Celtic myth, apples were considered fruit from another world. Numerous stories speak of otherworldly women carrying off heroes found sleeping beneath apple trees. The apple was also an emblem of fruitfulness and sometimes a means to immortality.

Swiss folklore tells us that William Tell, using a crossbow, shot an apple from his son's head. This act defied a tyrannical ruler and brought freedom to his people.

Irish folklore claims that if a woman peels an apple into one continuous ribbon and throws it over her shoulder, it will land in the shape of the initials of her future husband.

According to another popular legend, Isaac Newton, when he saw an apple fall from its tree, was inspired to conclude that a similar "universal gravitation" attracted the moon toward the earth as well.

The apple tree is the central tree of heaven to the Iroquois Indians.

In the United States, Denmark, and Sweden, a polished apple is a traditional gift for a teacher. During the 16th to 18th centuries, teachers were poorly paid, so parents would compensate the teacher by providing food. Since apples were a very common crop, students would often give teachers baskets of apples. When wages increased, the quantity of apples was toned down to a single fruit.

Apple Delights Cookbook

A Collection of Apple Recipes
Cookbook Delights Series

Apple History

Apple History

From the very beginning, the apple has been associated with the fall of Adam and Eve in the Garden of Eden. The fruit referred to was quite likely not an apple, but nevertheless, it is the fruit that has been written about in association with this story. Apples appear in many religious traditions, often as a mystical and forbidden fruit, but one of the problems with identifying apples in religion, mythology, and folktales is that the word "apple" was used as a generic term for all fruit, other than berries but including nuts, as late as the 17th century.

From at least as far back as the Neolithic period, evidence has been found of apple use. Both the Greeks and the Romans cultivated apples. In the first century B.C., when the Romans conquered England, the art of apple cultivation came with them. Apple orchards and brewers are mentioned as far back as the 8th century by Charlemagne. South America and Mexico learned of apples through the Spaniards when they arrived there. The Pilgrims planted apple trees in 1629 in the Massachusetts Bay Colony. As the pioneers moved west, they took apple trees with them, and Indians planted trees using seeds given to them by white settlers.

The apple tree may be the earliest tree to be cultivated, and apples are still an important crop in cooler climates. Apples can be stored for months and still retain most of their nutritive value. Winter apples, harvested in late autumn and stored at temperatures just above freezing, have been a significant food in Europe and Asia for thousands of years.

There are more than 7,500 known varieties (called cultivars) of apples. The world's largest collection of apple varieties is at the National Fruit Collection in England. There are different varieties available for subtropical and temperate climates. Apple trees are not grown in tropical climates because they must be chilled for a certain number of hours each winter to produce normal spring growth and blossoms.

Desired qualities in commercially produced apples include soft but crisp flesh, colorful skin, no russeting (a brown, corky, netlike condition on the skin), ease of shipping, prolonged storage ability, high yields, disease resistance, "Red Delicious" apple shape, a long stem, and flavor.

Older varieties can often be oddly shaped, have a variety of textures and colors, and be russeted, but many of them have a better flavor than most modern varieties. Older varieties also many times have low yield, are not as disease resistant, and do not store or ship well. There are a few varieties that are still grown commercially, but most are grown by home gardeners or farmers who sell directly to local markets.

Most cultivars produce dessert apples (for eating fresh), but some are grown specifically as cooking apples or for producing cider. The astringency and tartness of cider apples produces a rich-flavored cider, but makes the apples less palatable for eating fresh. Dessert apples do not make a flavorful cider because of their sweetness. Tastes in apples change continually over time, and different people prefer different varieties. Washington State was known for its Red Delicious apple for many years, but some now consider it inferior to varieties like Gala and Fuji because of its mild flavor and softer texture.

A history of apples would not be complete without mentioning Johnny Appleseed. Born in 1774 as John Chapman, Johnny Appleseed was a pioneer nurseryman and a missionary. Although the popular image of Johnny Appleseed has him spreading apple seeds randomly, that is not the case. What he did was to plant nurseries instead of orchards, building fences around them to protect them from wildlife and livestock. He would then leave these nurseries in the care of a neighbor who would sell the trees on shares. Johnny would return every year or so and tend the nurseries.

Sir Isaac Newton is also connected with the apple. The story goes that it was an apple he saw drop from a tree that caused him to discover the laws of gravitation and motion.

Apples have been associated with love, beauty, luck, health, comfort, pleasure, wisdom, temptation, sensuality, sexuality, virility, and fertility. They are such a part of our lives that we have many popular sayings or phrases that include apples. The protuberance on a man's throat began being called an Adam's apple because it was thought it was caused by a piece of the forbidden fruit that Adam swallowed.

The term "apple eater" is used for a person who is easily led astray, again referring back to the Garden of Eden.

The phrase "apple of my eye" dates back to ancient Greece and Rome when people thought the pupil of the eye was a global object, like the apple. The pupil of the eye was also viewed as the window into the treasured secrets within us, thus the "apple of my eye" was someone treasured or beloved.

The phrase "apple polisher" is associated with giving a polished apple to the teacher. A child whose math skills were not what they should be would try to distract the teacher with a shiny apple.

New York City received the nickname "The Big Apple." This really had nothing to do with apples, but with jazz. Manhattan became known in the 1930s and 1940s for having "lots of apples on the tree," meaning there were lots of places to play jazz.

"Upper crust" is a phrase that is associated with apple pie. In early America times were tough, so to save on ingredients, pies were made with only a bottom crust. The wealthier people could afford to have a bottom as well as an upper crust on their pies, so they became known as "upper crust."

As you can see, the apple has a long and varied past. There is not room here to cover it all, so we encourage you to learn more about this delicious fruit's history, as well as to enjoy its flavor.

Apple Delights Cookbook

A Collection of Apple Recipes
Cookbook Delights Series

Apple Nutrition and Health

Apple Nutrition and Health

We have all heard the old adage, "An apple a day will keep the doctor away." Although it will take more than an apple each day to keep you healthy, it is certainly a step in the right direction. Apples are delicious and low in calories. They are easy to carry with you for a snack. Apples are also a natural mouth freshener, and they are still relatively inexpensive.

Apples are a source of soluble and insoluble fiber. Soluble fiber such as pectin helps to prevent cholesterol buildup in the lining of the walls of blood vessels. This helps to reduce the incidence of atherosclerosis and heart disease. The insoluble fiber provides bulk in the intestinal tract, helping to move food quickly through the digestive system, which may help reduce the incidence of colon cancer.

It is a good idea to eat apples with their skin. Almost half of the vitamin C content is just underneath the skin. Vitamin C, as well as a host of other antioxidant compounds in apples, may reduce the risk of cancer by preventing DNA damage. Eating the skin will increase insoluble fiber content.

Contamination from pesticides has been linked to an increasing number of diseases. Pesticides are generally found on the outside of fruits and vegetables. Washing or peeling before eating may reduce pesticide intake, but peeling will also reduce the intake of beneficial nutrients.

Eating apples can help remove trapped food and clean between the teeth, but excessive consumption could cause the erosion of tooth enamel over time from the malic acid contained in the apple.

Apple juice has a significant concentration of phenolics thought to help protect from many diseases associated with aging, including heart disease and cancer. Aside from other obvious fruit vitamins like vitamin C, apple juice also contains the mineral nutrient boron, which is thought to promote healthy bones.

There are hundreds of varieties of apples on the market today. Depending on which one you choose, apples can be tart or sweet, soft and smooth, or crisp and crunchy. With all these attributes, we should all be eating an apple a day!

Apple Delights Cookbook

A Collection of Apple Recipes
Cookbook Delights Series

Poetry

A Collection of Poetry with Apple Themes

Table of Contents

Page

Fallen Apples

Remember that special October day?
The air was cold and crisp.
The sky was azure blue,
punctuated with autumn's auburn tones.

Crunchy McIntosh, crispy Jonathans,
and tart Grannies
savored by the morsel.
Piquant cider spiced
to perfection,
Transparents saved for sauce.

Green orchard grasses wave in
plumes as we walk over clumps
between barren spots of soil.
Rotting apples lay upon the

ground. Time has come and
gone. Neglected,
bruised, battered
and worn,
no one wants these fallen apples.
Our calico children

frolic in the fall day.
They do make
delightful cider,
even bruised.

Karen Jean Matsko Hood ©2012
Published in *Apple Delights Cookbook*, 2012
By Whispering Pine Press International, Inc., 2012

Homemade Apple Pie

Remember mom's homemade apple pie?
That firm flaky crust baked just so?
Lattice-top checkers, juice oozes
through, escaping squares,

peppered with cinnamon. Fragrant
apple slices, layered in glass,
steam puffs from open crisscross,
as mom smiles and we know
                    all is good.

Karen Jean Matsko Hood ©2012
Published in *Apple Delights Cookbook*, 2012
By Whispering Pine Press International, Inc., 2012

Apple Tree

There I sit, beside the old apple tree,
magnificent under the sun . . .
The apple tree that is. Rings of wood

one by one, stack upon the other,
grown thick with age,
dry and wrinkled over time . . .
The trunk that is. Green leaves

drop to the ground, a piece at a time,
for mother earth to accept to
nourish the rich loam
that blankets the roots . . .
Of the apple tree, of course.

Snowflakes come and dust the bark,
bare and naked, without leaves.
Proud it stands with arms stretched out . . .
The tree that is.

Then we feast on the sight
of the canvas that moves,
the still of night, painted bright . . .
The apple tree that is.

Karen Jean Matsko Hood ©2012
Published in *Apple Delights Cookbook*, 2012
By Whispering Pine Press International, Inc., 2012

Red Apple

There hangs on the branch of the tree,
a giant apple – red and shiny under the sun.

The apple of advice there waits to speak.
Finally, the wisdom of the fruit talks.

Notice the world around you, it begins.
Breathe in the view around you.

Did you notice the beautiful petals
of the blossom that formed me?

The gift package of energy yellow
that flew to pollinate my blossoms?

Enjoy the lighthearted orchard grass
as it snaps below my tired branches.

Hear to notice, to appreciate . . .
the gift of life. Love the

earth and share its gifts.
Give something of ourselves to others.

Make a difference in the world.
    The reminder of the apple.

Karen Jean Matsko Hood ©2012
Published in *Apple Delights Cookbook*, 2012
By Whispering Pine Press International, Inc., 2012

Apple Crates

Apple box crates:
>> Beds or tables,
>>> Furniture of the Ritz,
>>>> Or storage of the migrant.

Workers in the fields
>> Or thoughtful slaves?
>>> Rough hewn boards build
>>>> Apple crates for export.

Cottage décor and art nouveau lines torn pockets.
>> Apple crates stacked with pride
>>> By calloused leather hands
>>>> Seen by sunken eyes.

Feast or famine; red or green,
>> Brown hands rugged for the lilies.
>>> Blossoms unfolding
>>>> Or wandering weeds?

Karen Jean Matsko Hood ©2012
Published in *Apple Delights Cookbook*, 2012
By Whispering Pine Press International, Inc., 2012

Apple Delights

Nostalgic memories of apples' fragrant
blossom on the branches. Red skins,
bright yellow, spring green,
arboreal bouquets.

Grandma bakes the pies
McIntosh, Golden Delicious,
among Paula Reds.
Don't forget the Spicy Gravenstein,

or the tart Granny Smith,
or the Yellow Transparent
tree that grew in my backyard
when I was a kid.

Warm apple strudel,
fragrant, with fresh
cinnamon sprinkles.
Perfect decoration for the slices.

Warm apple cider
on the stove, aromatic
with spices that flavor,
juicy fruit, ripened
flawless from the sun.

Apple Delights.

Karen Jean Matsko Hood ©2012
Published in *Apple Delights Cookbook*, 2012
By Whispering Pine Press International, Inc., 2012

Grandma's Apple Pie

Remember that old-fashioned apple pie
that grandma used to bake?
Hand rolled lard crust,
lattice top baked just right.
Sprinkles of cinnamon and sugar,
perfect proportions on golden,
baked crust, warm and fragrant.
Grandma used to tell the stories,
the ones about picking the apples,
tart and crisp, from her
favorite backyard apple trees.
We would get
to taste the fruits
of grandma's labor
in her old-fashioned
apple pie . . . the
one I miss so much.

Karen Jean Matsko Hood ©2012
Published in *Apple Delights Cookbook*, 2012
By Whispering Pine Press International, Inc., 2012

Apple Season

Remember those times around the apple tree,
the American symbol, warm as apple pie?
Apple seedlings struggled to become the
largest apple tree, the focus of our tiny orchard.

We did worry for a while about that
little seedling. Would it ever grow?
I was told, wait for the roots,
my child. The roots must grow deeper,
to make it strong, they explained.

Not so patiently, I waited. Then it
happened. Year by year, the apple tree
unfolded. Layer of bark upon bark,
strengthened that trunk.

Buds formed branches in the
most artistic arrangement in the
vase of the trunk. Limb by limb,
nothing symmetrical. Always a surprise.

Finally, after what seemed a lifetime,
spring blossoms unfurl,
perfectly designed. Fragile, yet strong,
delicate apple blossoms expand on fragrant wood.

Such a gift that surpasses my dream. A gift that waits
to invite honeybees to blossoms
that share sweet nectar and greet
the morning dew.

Karen Jean Matsko Hood ©2012
Published in *Apple Delights Cookbook*, 2012
By Whispering Pine Press International, Inc., 2012

Applewood

Dry, sweet applewood burns at fireside,
sweetens still night air
as a circle of friends
watches the puffs of smoke that
skip to the clouds.

Karen Jean Matsko Hood ©2012
Published in *Apple Delights Cookbook*, 2012
By Whispering Pine Press International, Inc., 2012

Apple Types

Apple Types

Baldwin: The Baldwin is a winter apple, bright red, good quality, and easily shipped. For many years is was the most popular apple in New England and New York. It is said to have originated from a chance seedling around 1740. The Baldwin was first known as the Butters or Woodpecker apple. It has fallen out of favor, and very little of this apple is commercially grown today, even though it is an excellent apple for cider.

Braeburn: The Braeburn has red, vertical streaks in its skin. The intensity of its color varies with different varieties. It has a sweet and tart flavor combination. It exports well, so it is popular with fruit growers. Harvest is in late April through mid October. The Braeburn was named after an area in New Zealand, even though it was first grown by an Englishman.

Cameo®: The Cameo was discovered by chance in a Dryden, Washington, orchard in 1987. It may be a cross between a Golden Delicious and a Red Delicious, but no one is sure. Its skin is creamy orange and red striped, with firm, crisp flesh, and an aromatic flavor. It resists browning, so it works well on fruit trays and in salads.

Cortland: The Cortland is the result of a cross between a McIntosh and a Ben Davis. It is sweeter that the McIntosh, has a very white flesh, and is a wonderful dessert apple.

Crispin: Mutsu was the original name of this apple, which reflects its Japanese heritage. Renamed Crispin in the late 1960s, this apple is yellow when ripe and is very juicy and crisp. It makes excellent cider and sauce and is a good eating apple. It is harvested in late October and is available through February.

Fuji: The Fuji apple was developed in Japan in the late 1930s. It was brought to market in 1962. The Fuji is a cross between the Red Delicious and the old Virginia Ralls Genet. The result of that cross was an apple that was crispier and sweeter than many other varieties. Even without refrigeration, the Fuji keeps longer than other apples. It can last 5 to 6 months under refrigeration. An unrivaled favorite in Japan, it is gaining popularity in the United States.

Gala: The Gala has a mild, sweet flavor and soft flesh, making it an excellent eating apple. It is generally small, and its skin is red and greenish or yellow-green. The Gala was developed in New Zealand in the 1920s and is a cross between the Golden Delicious and the Kidd's Orange Red. It is grown September through June.

Golden Delicious: This apple is large, yellow skinned, and is very sweet. It bruises and shrivels easily, so it needs careful handling. The Golden Delicious is a favorite for salads, applesauce, and apple butter. It is harvested from autumn through winter and is available year round.

Granny Smith: The Granny Smith originated in Australia in 1868 from a chance seedling. It is thought to be from a cross between the European Wild Apple and a domestic apple. That would make it a hybrid. Granny Smiths are light speckled green in color and can have a pink blush. They are crisp, tart, juicy apples and are good for cooking and eating. They work well in salads because they do not brown as quickly as most other apple varieties. Granny Smiths grow best in areas with milder weather because they need a longer growing season. Their harvest begins in August, but they are available year round.

Honeycrisp: This apple, developed by the University of Minnesota, is juicy, crisp, and sweet. It is a cross between the Macoun and the Honeygold. It is good for snacking, sauce, and salads.

Idared: The Idared is the result of a cross between the Jonathan and Wagener apple varieties. It was introduced in 1942. Its skin is a bright red, the flesh is firm, and it is tangy like the Jonathan. Since it holds its shape well when cooked, the Idared is a good choice for baking, frying, or in pies.

Jonagold: A cross between the Jonathan and the Golden Delicious apple, the Jonagold is good both eaten fresh and in cooking. It is sweet, tart, crisp, and juicy. One of Europe's most preferred eating apples, the Jonagold's skin is yellow with a red blush.

Jonathan: A medium-sized, round apple, bright red, and striped with yellow, the Jonathan's flesh is juicy, tender, and pleasantly tart with a spicy tang. It was discovered in the 1920s in Woodstock, New York. The Jonathan blends well with other apples to make sauce and is an excellent pie apple. It is generally available from September through April.

McIntosh: The McIntosh is one of the most popular apples. It is both sweet and tart, juicy and crisp, and has a red and green skin. It is well suited for applesauce, cider, and pies, as well as eating. Unpeeled, it makes a pink applesauce.

Pink Lady®: Originally known as Cripp's Pink, the Pink Lady is a cross between the Golden Delicious and Lady Williams. It has firm, crisp, white flesh and a tangy-tart, sweet flavor. The bright pink color of the Pink Lady's skin is brought on by crisp fall nights. It is one of the last apples to be harvested, with harvest starting in mid October. Pink Lady is a registered trademark of Brandt's Fruit Trees, Inc.

Red Delicious: The Red Delicious is the most widely grown variety of apple in the world. It has firm, white or cream-white flesh that is juicy, aromatic, and sweet tasting. It is best eaten raw because of its thick skin. Originally called Delicious, the name was changed to Red Delicious when the Golden Delicious was discovered.

Rhode Island Greening: The Rhode Island Greening is an old variety. It was developed in Rhode Island in 1650. This apple is large, juicy, firm, and crisp, making it an excellent cooking apple. Harvest is from late October to early November with availability through March.

Red Rome: The Red Rome, also known as the Rome Beauty, originated in Ohio in 1816. It is excellent for baking, because its firm, greenish white flesh holds its shape and its rich flavor is enhanced in the baking process. The Red Rome is round and has a dark red, solid-colored skin. It is available nearly year round.

Yellow Transparent: The Yellow Transparent is also sometimes called the White Transparent. Its flesh is white, fine-grained, tender, and juicy. One of the first varieties to ripen, it is harvested in July and early August. It is very good for drying, freezing, juice, wine, sauces, and cooking. It does not store well.

Twenty Ounce: Also known as Cayuga Red Streak, this heirloom variety was a favorite because of its large size and cooking qualities. It is tender but firm, tart, and juicy, making it excellent for pies, sauce, and baking. It is harvested in September and October.

Winesap: The Winesap is a small apple with deep red skin. Its greenish yellow flesh is coarse, juicy, and firm. The Winesap is an all-purpose apple that keeps its flavor in sauces and pies. It keeps well and is available from November through May.

York Imperial: The York Imperial was developed in the 1820s in York County, Pennsylvania. It has also been called the "Imperial of Keepers" because of how well it holds up in storage. It has also earned the designation of an "antique apple," which only apples that have been raised for more than 180 years can be labeled. This apple is still being grown on orchards and farms across the country, and is only available at some orchards and roadside stands. The York Imperial is medium to large in size and is crisp, firm, and juicy. It is recognizable by its lopsided shape. It is a good baking and cooking apple and is harvested in October.

Apple Delights Cookbook

A Collection of Apple Recipes
Cookbook Delights Series

RECIPES

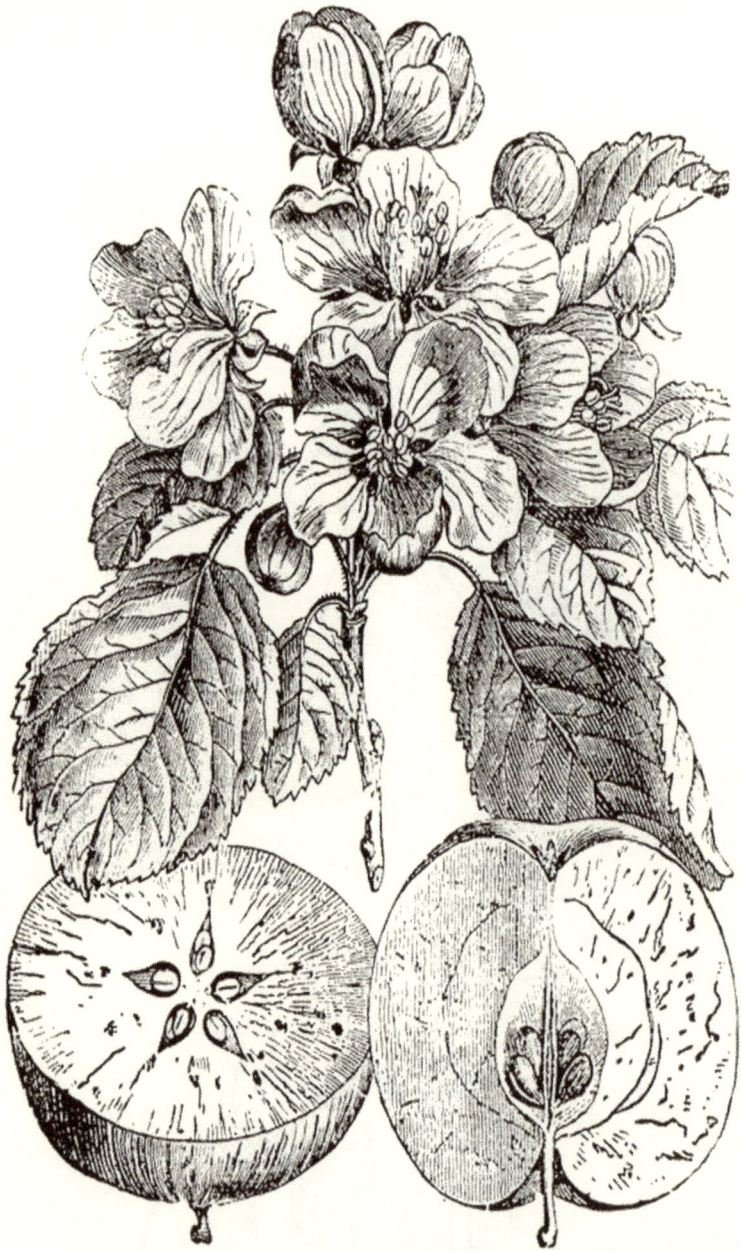

Apple Delights Cookbook

A Collection of Apple Recipes
Cookbook Delights Series

Appetizers and Dips

Table of Contents

Page

Did You Know? . . .

Did you know that the Iroquois Indians believe the apple tree is the central tree of heaven?

Apple Cinnamon Chips

My children love dried apple chips. They are a delicious snack or really handy for their lunch pails. Try making them from various types of apples.

Ingredients:

- 2 c. unsweetened apple juice
- 1 cinnamon stick (3-in. length)
- 3 fresh red apples, cored, sliced ¼ inch thick

Directions:

1. Preheat oven to 250 degrees F.
2. In large skillet or pot, combine apple juice and cinnamon stick; bring to low boil while preparing apples.
3. Drop unpeeled apple slices into boiling juice; blanch 1 to 2 minutes or just until slices begin to appear translucent and lightly golden; do not overcook.
4. With slotted spatula remove apple slices from juice and place on paper towels; pat dry.
5. Arrange slices on narrow slotted wire racks, being sure none overlap; place racks on middle shelf in oven.
6. Bake for 40 minutes or until apple slices are lightly browned and almost dry to touch.
7. Remove from oven and let chips cool on racks completely before serving.
8. May be stored in airtight container up to 6 weeks.

Did You Know? . . . .

Did you know that apples are about 85 percent water?

Apple Snacks

Here is a nutritious snack that everyone will enjoy. It is delicious with the combination of apples, peanut butter, and honey.

Ingredients:

2   fresh apples, cored, cut into 12 wedges
½   c. chunky peanut butter
2½ Tbs. honey
½   tsp. ground cinnamon
12   graham cracker squares
      lemon juice

Directions:

1. Preheat oven to 350 degrees F.
2. Dip apple wedges in lemon juice to prevent browning; place on nonstick baking sheet.
3. Cover loosely with foil, and bake just until apples are tender and hold their shape; do not overbake.
4. Remove from oven; drain and cool apples on paper towels.
5. In small bowl combine peanut butter, honey, and cinnamon; use additional peanut butter if too runny.
6. Spread layer of peanut butter mixture on each cracker, and lay 6 singly on plate.
7. Place 2 apple wedges on top of one peanut butter-covered cracker, and cover with additional cracker to serve.

Yields: 6 servings.

Did You Know? . . . .

Did you know that apple trees belong to the rose family?

Apple Dip

Enjoy this easy and quickly made caramel-like dip with slices of apples for a healthy snack! Be creative.

Ingredients:

    8   oz. cream cheese, softened
    ½   c. brown sugar, firmly packed
    1   Tbs. vanilla extract
    ¼   c. dried apples, minced fine

Directions:

1. In medium mixing bowl combine cream cheese, brown sugar, and vanilla.
2. Mix well until brown sugar has been completely blended into cream cheese and vanilla; add finely minced dried apples.
3. If mixture is too runny, add small amount of brown sugar to mixture; if too thick, add small amount of vanilla.

Yields: 4 servings.

Caramelized Apple Bites

You will want to make plenty of these delicious appetizers so everyone with a sweet tooth can get their fill!

Ingredients:

    20   individual caramels, unwrapped, chopped
    6   Tbs. light corn syrup
    6   fresh apples, peeled, cored, cut into chunks

Directions:

1. Place caramels and corn syrup in top of double boiler.
2. Heat and stir until melted; cool to warm.
3. Place apples in medium bowl; pour caramel syrup over top and toss until coated.
4. Allow to cool completely.
5. Arrange on large plate and serve with wooden picks.

Yields: 12 servings.

Feta, Apple, and Pimiento Blend

This makes an interesting, colorful appetizer spread with a nutritious blend of fruit, vegetables, and cheese.

Ingredients:

1½ Granny Smith apples, peeled, cored, chopped
1   med. carrot, peeled, shredded
4   oz. diced pimientos, drained
8   oz. Feta cheese, crumbled
½   c. sour cream
¼   c. black olives, pitted, finely chopped
1   Tbs. parsley, chopped

Directions:

1. In medium bowl combine apples, carrot, and pimientos; mix well.
2. Add cheese and sour cream; blend well.
3. Chill until ready to serve.
4. Serve on small sliced bagels, quartered pita rounds, or crackers.
5. Sprinkle with chopped olives and parsley.

Apple Sausage Snack Rolls

These snack rolls are easy to make and very flavorful. They are good served cold or with your favorite crackers, pita bread, or just inside your favorite sandwich roll.

Ingredients:

    1 lb. turkey sausage
    2 c. diced apples
    2 c. dry bread crumbs
    1 sm. onion, diced

Directions:

1. On wax paper, roll out turkey sausage into rectangle ½ inch thick.
2. Combine apples, bread crumbs, and onion; spread over meat.
3. Start from long edge and roll as for jellyroll, using wax paper for guide in rolling; cover and chill in refrigerator for 2 hours.
4. Preheat oven to 350 degrees F.
5. Remove from refrigerator and slice into ½-inch-thick rounds; place on cookie sheets.
6. Bake for 20 minutes or until lightly browned.
7. Remove from oven; place on paper towel-covered wire rack to cool.
8. When ready to serve, place on serving dish, and heat for 30 seconds in microwave or in oven at 350 degrees F. for 1 minute, just until warm.
9. Serve with small dipping bowl of salsa.

Did You Know? . . . .

Did you know that a Granny Smith is the apple used on labels for Apple Records?

Apple Turkey Rolls

This tasty turkey roll can be served as an appetizer or as a main dish.

Ingredients:

  1 lb. ground turkey
  2 c. fresh apples, peeled, cored, diced
  2 c. bread crumbs
  ½ tsp. sage
  ½ tsp. poultry seasoning
  1 sm. onion, diced
  ½ c. cheddar cheese, grated

Directions:

  1. Preheat oven to 350 degrees F.
  2. On wax paper flatten out ground turkey into rectangle ½ inch thick.
  3. Combine apples, bread crumbs, sage, poultry seasoning, and onion; spread over meat.
  4. Start from long edge and roll as for jellyroll, using wax paper for guide in rolling.
  5. Place in 13 x 9 x 2-inch baking dish or cookie sheet.
  6. Bake for 45 minutes.
  7. During last 10 minutes of baking, sprinkle grated cheddar cheese over top of roll and finish baking.
  8. Cool before slicing and place on serving platter; reheat if preferred warm for serving.
  9. Serve with salsa of choice for dipping.
  10. This can also be made into meatballs instead of a roll.

Did You Know? . . . .

Did you know that the apple blossom is the state flower of Arkansas and Michigan?

Creamy Smoked Trout with Apple and Horseradish on Crisp Brown Bread

This recipe can be made even easier by preparing the toast points two hours ahead. Store them in an airtight container at room temperature. For a vegetarian dish, substitute tofu marinated in lapsang souchong tea for the smoked trout.

Ingredients:

11 oz. smoked trout (about 3 fillets), coarsely flaked
1   med. Granny Smith apple, peeled, cored, cut into matchstick-size strips
1   c. finely chopped celery (about 2 stalks)
¼   c. finely chopped fresh chives
½   c. sour cream
½   c. mayonnaise
1½ Tbs. fresh lemon juice
1   Tbs. (or more) finely grated, peeled, fresh horseradish or prepared horseradish sauce
1   loaf thinly sliced pumpernickel bread, lightly toasted, cut into triangles
    salt and pepper to taste

Directions:

1. Mix trout, apple, celery, and chives in large bowl to blend.
2. Whisk sour cream, mayonnaise, lemon juice, and 1 tablespoon horseradish in small bowl to blend.
3. Fold horseradish mixture gently into trout mixture (do not break up trout).
4. Season to taste with salt, pepper, and more horseradish if desired.
5. Can be made 1 day ahead; cover and refrigerate.
6. Transfer trout mixture to serving bowl and place on platter.
7. Surround with toast points and serve.

Yields: 12 servings.

Turkey Apple Quesadillas

This recipe makes a tasty appetizer with the delicious combination of apples, turkey, and cheese.

Ingredients:

3   Tbs. butter
3½ fresh apples, peeled, cored, coarsely grated
1   tsp. chipotle in adobo, finely chopped, to taste
8   flour tortillas (6-inch)
1   c. cheddar cheese or cheese blend
4   oz. smoked turkey or chicken, chopped
2   green onions, thinly sliced
    sour cream
    green onion, finely sliced or slivered
    salsa

Directions:

1. Heat butter in nonstick skillet until foamy; add grated apple and chipotle.
2. Cook, stirring, about 3 minutes or until apples are crisp tender.
3. Remove apple mixture from skillet and set aside to cool slightly; wipe skillet with paper towel.
4. Place 4 flour tortillas on work surface.
5. Sprinkle each tortilla with 2 tablespoons of cheese, ¼ of the turkey, 3 tablespoons apple mixture, ¼ of green onion, and another 2 tablespoons of cheese; cover each with a tortilla.
6. In dry skillet over medium heat, brown quesadillas one at a time, about 3 minutes on each side, turning carefully, until cheese is melted and tortillas are crisp and lightly browned.
7. Cut each quesadilla into triangles; place on serving dish.
8. Place small bowl of sour cream and small dish of chopped onion or salsa on the side for guests to add to their quesadilla wedge.

Yields: 8 to 12 servings

Ham and Melon Apple Chutney on Cornbread Rounds

This appetizer has a wonderful presentation and is easy to make.

Ingredients for cornbread rounds:

⅔ c. yellow cornmeal
⅓ c. all-purpose flour
2 Tbs. sugar
½ tsp. baking powder
½ tsp. salt
5 Tbs. unsalted butter, melted, cooled
2 Tbs. milk
1 lg. egg

Ingredients for topping:

2 Tbs. (about) Dijon mustard
¼ lb. sliced, cooked Virginia or Black Forest ham, cut into 1½ x ⅓-inch strips
½ c. Melon Apple Chutney (recipe page 175)

Directions for cornbread rounds:

1. Preheat oven to 350 degrees F.; place rack in center of oven.
2. Whisk together cornmeal, flour, sugar, baking powder, and salt in bowl.
3. Whisk together butter, milk, and egg in small bowl, then add to cornmeal mixture and stir just until combined.
4. Spread (or pat out) batter in very thin, even layer in well-greased 13 x 9 x 2-inch metal baking pan.
5. Bake until firm and pale golden, 20 to 25 minutes.
6. Cut out 24 rounds from hot cornbread with 1½-inch round cookie cutter; transfer rounds to rack to cool.

7. Reserve remaining cornbread for another use.
8. Cornbread rounds can be made 1 day ahead, cooled, and kept in airtight container at room temperature.

Directions for topping:

1. Spread each round with thin layer of mustard.
2. Top with a few strips of ham and about 1 teaspoon chutney.

Yields: 24 hors d'oeuvres.

Fruit Bites with Shrimp and Herbed Cheese

Here is a quick appetizer you can have ready in fifteen minutes.

Ingredients:

1 lg. container garlic and herb seasoned cheese (12 oz.)
6 oz. tiny, cooked, peeled shrimp
3 fresh, firm apples, cored, cut into thin wedges
3 fresh, firm, ripe pears, cored, cut into thin wedges

Directions:

1. Preheat oven to 425 degrees F.
2. Place cheese and shrimp in ovenproof bowl; mix well.
3. Bake about 8 minutes or just until mixture becomes bubbly.
4. Remove from oven and place bowl on platter; surround with apple and pear wedges with wooden picks on the side for dipping fruit.

Yields: 8 to 10 servings.

Sausage and Apple Appetizers

Your company and family together will enjoy these tasty, flavorful tidbits for a great get-together.

Ingredients:

2	Tbs. butter
1	lg. onion, chopped
½	c. apple jelly (recipe page 186)
½	c. brown sugar, firmly packed
2	lb. smoked sausages, cocktail size
3	fresh apples, peeled, cored, sliced
1	Tbs. cornstarch
2	Tbs. warm water

Directions:

1. In large skillet melt butter over medium-high heat.
2. Add onion and sauté, stirring constantly, until onion is golden.
3. Stir in apple jelly and brown sugar; add sausages and reduce heat to medium-low.
4. Cook, stirring occasionally, for 10 minutes; mixture will begin to thicken slightly.
5. Add apples; toss and cook for a few minutes or just until apples are crisp-tender; remove and drain both apples and sausage on paper towels.
6. Combine cornstarch with water and stir into mixture in pan; cook until mixture thickens.
7. Arrange apples and sausage on serving platter with wooden picks; place thickened mixture in small bowl alongside for dipping.

Yields: 30 appetizers.

Sesame Seed Fruit Appetizers

Here is an unusual appetizer that your guests will rave about for a long time to come! This recipe makes plenty for all to enjoy!

Ingredients for fruit:

> 75 bite-size pieces of fruit: peaches, bananas, oranges, apples, pineapple, kiwi, etc.
> 1 c. cornstarch
> ¼ c. butter

Ingredients for dip:

> 1 c. maple or fruit-flavored syrup
> 2 tsp. toasted sesame seeds

Directions for fruit:

> 1. Blot fruit on paper towel, then roll several pieces of fruit in cornstarch; sauté in butter until lightly browned.
> 2. Drain pieces on absorbent paper; repeat until all fruit is done.

Directions for dip:

> 1. Heat syrup to boiling; place in small serving bowl.
> 2. Place sesame seeds in separate bowl.
> 3. Serve fruit on large tray with picks.
> 4. Spear and dip pieces of fruit in syrup, then into sesame seeds.

Yields: 15 to 20 servings.

Delicious Apple Spread Tray

This spread is easily prepared and is great served with crackers, pita bread, or slices of French bread.

Ingredients:

3	fresh apples, cored, sliced into ½-inch rings
1	Tbs. caraway seeds
3	oz. cream cheese, softened
½	c. butter, softened
½	c. cottage cheese
½	tsp. bottled hot pepper sauce
¼	c. green onion, finely chopped
1	sm. clove garlic, minced
2	full ½-inch slices cooked ham
	lemon juice

Directions:

1. Dip freshly sliced apples into lemon juice to prevent browning; drain on paper towel.
2. Process caraway seeds in blender or food processor; add cream cheese, butter, and cottage cheese, blending well.
3. Stir in pepper sauce, onion, and garlic to taste; blend well.
4. Place spread in serving bowl; chill in refrigerator for several hours or overnight.
5. Cut each slice of ham into 1½ x 3-inch strips.
6. When ready to serve, place spread in small bowl on serving platter, arrange sliced apples and ham strips around edge, and provide wooden picks on the side.
7. May be served with additional crackers or breads.

Apple Delights Cookbook

A Collection of Apple Recipes
Cookbook Delights Series

Beverages

Table of Contents

Page

Did You Know? . . .

Did you know that reputedly the world's largest collection of apple cultivars is housed at the National Fruit Collection in England?

Apple Banana Malt

This double-fruit malt is delicious as well as nutritious. Your children will love it.

Ingredients:

- 1 whole banana
- ½ c. chopped apple
- 2 scoops vanilla ice cream
- 2 c. milk
- 2 tsp. dry malt
  banana or apple slices for garnish

Directions:

1. Combine banana and apple in blender; blend until smooth.
2. Add ice cream, milk, and malt; blend well.
3. Pour into chilled glasses, and serve with apple or banana slices on top as garnish.

Yields: 4 servings.

Apple Berry Drink

Looking for a different beverage? Try this combination of apple juice blended with berries.

Ingredients:

- 2 c. apple juice, chilled
- ½ c. frozen blueberries
- ½ c. frozen strawberries
- 12 ice cubes

Directions:

1. Blend apple juice and berries together in blender for 40 seconds.
2. Add ice cubes 2 at a time, cover, and blend until smooth.
3. Pour into chilled tall glasses to serve.

Yields: 4 to 6 servings.

Apple Frost

This is an easy recipe for a quick drink. Use your favorite type of apple and your choice of ice cream or yogurt. Enjoy!

Ingredients:

½ c. apple juice or cider
2 c. red apples, unpeeled, chopped
1 tsp. ground cinnamon
1 tsp. crystallized ginger, finely chopped
1 qt. vanilla ice cream or frozen yogurt
   apple slices dipped in lemon juice for garnish

Directions:

1. Place juice or cider in blender; add apples and blend until chunky.
2. Add cinnamon, ginger, and ice cream, blending on medium speed until smooth; stop blender as needed to scrape down sides of container.
3. To serve, pour into chilled glasses immediately, and garnish with apple slice, if desired.

Yields: 6 to 8 servings.

Apple Cider Tea

This makes a warm, spicy, and fragrant combination for tea drinkers and hot apple cider fans alike.

Ingredients:

8   c. apple cider
2   c. water
4   Tbs. lemon juice
¼   c. brown sugar, firmly packed
1   cinnamon stick
1   tsp. whole cloves
½   tsp. whole allspice
2   tea bags

Directions:

1. In 3-quart saucepan combine apple cider, water, lemon juice, and brown sugar.
2. Place cinnamon stick, cloves, and allspice in cheesecloth square and close bag with tie; add to mixture.
3. Place over medium heat until mixture starts to boil.
4. Reduce heat and simmer 10 minutes.
5. Remove from heat and add tea bags to hot mixture.
6. Cover and let steep 5 minutes; remove spices and tea bags.
7. Serve hot in warmed mugs.

Yields: 8 to 10 servings.

Did You Know? . . . .

Did you know that one of the oldest apples in the United States may be the Roxbury Russet (1640)?

Apple Cinnamon Iced Tea

This tea is perfect for early fall when the weather is still warm enough for you to want something cold to drink.

Ingredients:

- 2 qt. water
- ¼ c. loose black tea leaves or 8 standard tea bags
- 2 lemons, thinly sliced
- 2 med. crisp apples, cut into thin wedges
- 1 lg. stick cinnamon
  sugar to taste

Directions:

1. Bring water to a boil in teakettle.
2. Put tea leaves in deep, heatproof bowl or large teapot.
3. As soon as water begins to boil, pour over tea leaves; stir and let steep 4 minutes.
4. Put lemons, apples, and cinnamon stick in pitcher.
5. Strain tea through fine wire-mesh sieve or coffee filter over fruit.
6. Let steep at least 10 minutes before serving.
7. Sweeten to taste and serve over ice.

Yields: 10 servings.

Did You Know? . . . .

Did you know that at the end of the 1800s, 7,000 named apple varieties were grown in the United States and that now 6,800 of them are extinct?

Apple Slush Punch

Try this delicious recipe for a refreshing and cooling slush drink on a hot summer day.

Ingredients:

2   c. apple cider or juice
½   c. sugar
2   c. applesauce (recipe page 169)
6   Tbs. frozen orange juice concentrate, undiluted
3   Tbs. lemon juice
¼   c. grenadine syrup
5   c. lemon-lime soda
    fresh strawberries for garnish

Directions:

1. In 3-quart saucepan heat apple juice and sugar, stirring occasionally, until dissolved.
2. Remove from heat and stir in applesauce, orange juice, lemon juice, and grenadine syrup; blend well and cool completely.
3. Place in covered container and freeze until fairly firm, about 4 to 6 hours.
4. To serve, thaw mixture at room temperature about 10 minutes.
5. Portion into punch cups or tall glasses, and fill with lemon-lime soda.
6. Garnish with strawberries, if desired.

Yields: 10 to 12 servings.

Did You Know? . . . .

Did you know that there is a small amount of cyanide in apple seeds?

Apple Cider with Lemonade

This cold drink is great for those who enjoy tangy lemons and mint. It is also a soothing drink served warm during the cold and flu season.

Ingredients:

¼ c. chopped fresh mint
¾ c. sugar
3 c. water
4 c. apple cider
1 c. frozen lemonade concentrate, thawed, undiluted

Directions:

1. In small saucepan combine mint, sugar, and water; place over medium heat.
2. Cook, stirring occasionally, until mixture starts to boil.
3. Reduce heat and simmer 15 minutes.
4. Remove from heat and cool.
5. Strain cooled mint mixture into 2-quart pitcher.
6. Add cider and lemonade concentrate.
7. Chill and serve over ice cubes, or try it warm.

Yields: 8 servings.

Did You Know? . . . .

Did you know that the Apple Wassail is a traditional form of wassailing practiced in cider orchards of Southwest England during the winter? The ceremony is said to "bless" the apple trees to produce a good crop in the forthcoming season.

Apple Raspberry Iced Tea

This combination of tea and apple juice makes a most refreshing drink.

Ingredients:

½ c. apple juice
1½ c. raspberry-flavored herbal tea
½ c. carbonated water
    honey to sweeten (optional)
    ice cubes
    raspberries for garnish
    apple slices for garnish

Directions:

1. Mix juice and tea together; sweeten with honey if desired.
2. Pour mixture over ice in 2 tall glasses.
3. Fill with carbonated water.
4. Garnish with fresh raspberries and apple slices.

Yields: 2 servings.

Apple Cider Ice Cream Soda

Ice cream sodas bring fond memories to all. This combination adds extra flavor.

Ingredients:

4 c. apple cider
1 qt. vanilla ice cream or frozen yogurt
2 c. lemon-lime soda

Directions:

1. For each serving, pour ½ cup apple cider into chilled glass.
2. Add about ½ cup ice cream.
3. Pour ¼ cup lemon-lime soda over ice cream.
4. Place straw in glass and serve immediately.

Yields: 8 to 10 servings.

Apple Raspberry Hot Cider

This is a tasty alternative to the classic hot apple cider. The red raspberry juice adds an attractive color and a different flavor.

Ingredients:

10 c. apple cider or apple juice
1 c. frozen raspberry juice concentrate, thawed
1 c. water
1 cinnamon stick

Directions:

1. Combine juices, water, and cinnamon in nonreactive 4-quart saucepan.
2. Heat over medium heat, stirring occasionally, until mixture starts to simmer.
3. Reduce heat and simmer 20 minutes more.
4. Remove from heat and remove cinnamon stick.
5. When ready to serve, pour into warmed mugs.

Yields: 10 to 12 servings.

Apple Yogurt Milkshake

This makes an easy apple shake for those who prefer yogurt to ice cream.

Ingredients:

2   c. vanilla yogurt
⅛   c. sugar
¼   c. honey
1   c. frozen apple juice concentrate, thawed
3½ c. milk

Directions:

1. In blender combine yogurt, sugar, honey, and apple juice concentrate; blend well.
2. Place in container or tray, and freeze until almost solid.
3. Remove from freezer and return to blender; add milk and blend quickly just until smooth.
4. Pour into chilled glasses and serve immediately.

Yields: 6 to 8 servings.

Red Apple Milkshake

This is truly a delicious and refreshing shake made with nutritious fresh apples. It is so easy to make.

Ingredients:

1   fresh red apple, peeled, cored, chopped
2   c. cold skim milk
2   Tbs. sugar
    fresh mint leaves for garnish

Directions:

1. Place apple, skim milk, and sugar in blender; blend until smooth.
2. Pour into chilled glasses; serve immediately.
3. Garnish with mint if desired.

Yields: 2 servings.

Cold Apple Cider Punch

Try this refreshing spicy, citrus, and apple punch. It is great for autumn or winter parties.

Ingredients:

    2 qt. apple cider
    2 c. orange juice
    1 c. lemon juice
    1 c. water
    1 stick cinnamon
    1 tsp. whole cloves

Directions:

1. Combine cider, orange juice, and lemon juice in large saucepan.
2. Heat just until hot; do not boil.
3. Add water, cinnamon, and cloves; continue to heat for 5 minutes, until hot.
4. Remove from heat, remove cinnamon stick, and chill in refrigerator; strain to remove cloves.
5. To serve, pour into chilled glasses.

Yields: 12 servings.

Apple Walnut Ice Cream Soda

The walnuts and ginger add a unique texture to this classic ice cream soda.

Ingredients:

½   c. apple cider
2   c. red apples, unpeeled, chopped
1¼ tsp. ground cinnamon
½   tsp. crystallized ginger, finely chopped
1   qt. vanilla ice cream
¼   c. walnuts, chopped
     apple slices dipped in lemon juice for garnish

Directions:

1. Place cider, chopped apples, cinnamon, and ginger in blender container.
2. Cover and blend on medium speed until smooth, stopping blender several times to scrape down container sides.
3. Add ice cream to blender mixture, and blend until smooth.
4. Add nuts; blend only until mixed.
5. Serve immediately in chilled glasses with apple slice garnish, if desired.

Yields: 6 servings.

Did You Know?....

Did you know that apples must cross-pollinate to develop fruit?

Apple Delights Cookbook

A Collection of Apple Recipes
Cookbook Delights Series

Breads and Rolls

Table of Contents

Page

Did You Know? . . .

Did you know that every McIntosh apple has a direct lineage to a single tree discovered in 1811 by John McIntosh on his farm in Dundela, a hamlet located in Dundas County in the Canadian province of Ontario, near Morrisburg?

Anytime Apple Carrot Muffins

This combination of apples, carrots, and nuts makes a great, moist muffin.

Ingredients:

3	c. all-purpose flour
1	c. whole-wheat flour
2	c. sugar
2	tsp. baking soda
2	tsp. baking powder
1	tsp. ground cinnamon
¼	tsp. ground nutmeg
⅔	c. plain yogurt
½	c. orange juice
½	c. maple syrup
6	egg whites
⅓	c. canola oil
1½	Tbs. vanilla extract
2	tsp. dried orange peel
4	c. carrots, grated
4	c. fresh apples, cored, chopped fine
¾	c. walnuts, chopped

Directions:

1. Preheat oven to 375 degrees F.
2. In mixing bowl blend flours, sugar, baking soda, baking powder, cinnamon, and nutmeg.
3. In separate bowl mix together yogurt, orange juice, maple syrup, egg whites, oil, and vanilla; blend well.
4. Stir liquid mixture into dry ingredients, mixing just until moistened; do not overmix.
5. Gently fold in orange peel, carrots, apples, and nuts.
6. Spoon batter into paper-lined or nonstick muffin tins, filling ⅔ full.
7. Bake for 23 to 25 minutes or until tops spring back when lightly touched.
8. Remove from oven and lift out onto wire rack to cool.

Apple Bread with Whole-Wheat Flour

This is a good recipe for those who enjoy the wholesome flavor and nutrition of whole wheat.

Ingredients:

    2¾ c. whole-wheat flour
    2   tsp. ground cinnamon
    1   tsp. baking soda
    ½   tsp. baking powder
    ¼   c. applesauce (recipe page 169)
    ¼   c. corn syrup
    1½ c. sugar
    4   egg whites
    1   tsp. vanilla extract
    3   c. apples, peeled, cored, coarsely chopped

Directions:

1. Preheat oven to 350 degrees F.
2. In large bowl sift together flour, cinnamon, soda, and baking powder.
3. In medium bowl combine applesauce, corn syrup, sugar, egg whites, vanilla, and apples; stir into flour mixture just until blended.
4. Divide mixture between 2 greased and floured 8 x 4-inch bread pans.
5. Bake for 40 to 45 minutes or until wooden pick inserted in center comes out clean.
6. Remove from oven, let stand for 10 minutes, then turn out onto wire rack to cool.
7. When completely cooled, slice to serve.

Yields: 2 loaves.

Apple Butter Pecan Bread

There is no need to chop the apples for this bread. Use tasty apple butter instead for a quicker version of this delicious treat.

Ingredients:

½ c. butter, softened
1 c. brown sugar, firmly packed
1 egg
¾ c. buttermilk
2 tsp. baking soda
2 c. all-purpose flour
1 tsp. ground cinnamon
1 tsp. ground nutmeg
1 tsp. ground allspice
½ tsp. ground cloves
¼ c. apple butter (recipe page 230)
1 c. pecans

Directions:

1. Preheat oven to 350 degrees F.
2. Cream together butter, sugar, and egg.
3. Combine buttermilk and soda; add to creamed mixture and set aside.
4. In large bowl sift together flour and spices.
5. Add liquid mixture to flour; stir just to moisten.
6. Gently fold in apple butter and pecans; spoon into greased and floured 9 x 5 x 3-inch loaf pan.
7. Bake for 1 hour or until wooden pick inserted in center comes out clean.
8. Remove from oven, cool in pan for 5 minutes, then turn out onto wire rack to cool completely before slicing to serve.

Apple Buttermilk Bread

This quick bread is especially suited to breakfast. Make it the night before for best flavor.

Ingredients:

    1½ c. all-purpose flour
    1   c. whole-wheat flour
    ½   c. natural bran cereal
    1   tsp. baking soda
    ½   tsp. baking powder
    ¼   tsp. ground ginger
    1⅓ c. buttermilk
    ¾   c. sugar
    ¼   c. vegetable oil
    1   lg. egg
    1   tsp. grated orange zest
    2   Gala or Golden Delicious apples, cored, chopped

Directions:

1. Preheat oven to 350 degrees F.
2. Combine flours, bran cereal, soda, baking powder, and ginger; set aside.
3. In large bowl combine buttermilk, sugar, oil, egg, and orange zest; blend well.
4. Add flour mixture to buttermilk mixture, stirring just until combined; gently fold in apples.
5. Spoon into greased and floured 9 x 5-inch loaf pan.
6. Bake for 45 to 50 minutes or until wooden pick inserted in center comes out clean.
7. Remove from oven and cool in pan 10 minutes, then turn out onto wire rack to cool completely before slicing to serve.

Yields: 1 loaf.

Apple Cinnamon Yogurt Muffins

This is another great apple muffin with spicy cinnamon in the recipe.

Ingredients:

- 3   c. all-purpose flour
- 1¾ c. sugar, divided
- 3½ tsp. baking powder
- ½   tsp. salt
- ½   tsp. grated orange zest
- ¼   tsp. ground nutmeg
- 1   c. butter, divided
- 1   c. Braeburn or Golden Delicious apples, grated
- 1   c. vanilla yogurt
- 2   lg. eggs, beaten
- 1   tsp. ground cinnamon

Directions:

1. Preheat oven to 350 degrees F.; grease 24 muffin pan cups (3-inch) or line with paper liners.
2. In large bowl combine flour, 1 cup sugar, baking powder, salt, orange zest, and nutmeg.
3. With pastry blender or fork, cut in ¾ cup butter until mixture is crumbly.
4. In medium bowl combine apple, yogurt, and eggs; add to flour mixture, stirring just until combined.
5. Spoon batter into prepared muffin cups, and bake for 20 to 25 minutes or until centers spring back when gently pressed.
6. Cool muffins in pan 5 minutes; remove from pan and cool until able to handle.
7. Meanwhile, melt remaining ¼ cup butter.
8. In small bowl combine remaining ¾ cup sugar and cinnamon.
9. To serve, brush tops of muffins with butter and roll top in cinnamon-sugar mixture before placing on serving dish.

Yields: 24 muffins.

Apple Molasses Muffins

Strewn with apple bits, these moist and tender muffins also boast the goodness of molasses.

Ingredients:

- 2   c. all-purpose flour
- ¼ c. sugar
- 1   Tbs. baking powder
- 1   tsp. ground cinnamon
- ¼ tsp. salt
- 1   Fuji apple, peeled, cored, finely chopped
- ½ c. milk
- ¼ c. molasses
- ¼ c. vegetable oil
- 1   lg. egg

Directions:

1. Preheat oven to 450 degrees F.
2. In large bowl combine flour, sugar, baking powder, cinnamon, and salt; add apple and stir to coat.
3. In small bowl beat together milk, molasses, oil, and egg.
4. Combine with dry ingredients; mix just until blended.
5. Spoon into lightly greased 3-inch muffin pan cups, filling ¾ full.
6. Bake 5 minutes, then reduce heat to 350 degrees F.
7. Bake 12 to 15 minutes longer or until centers of muffins spring back when gently pressed.
8. Cool in pan for 10 minutes before removing to wire rack to cool.
9. Serve cooled or warm with butter.

Apple Oat Bran Muffins

Low in cholesterol and saturated fat, these muffins are much healthier for all than the average store-bought variety.

Ingredients:

¾ c. all-purpose flour
¾ c. whole-wheat flour
1½ tsp. ground cinnamon
1 tsp. baking powder
½ tsp. baking soda
¼ tsp. salt
1 c. buttermilk
½ c. oat bran
¼ c. brown sugar, firmly packed
2 Tbs. vegetable oil
1 lg. egg
1½ c. apples, peeled, cored, finely chopped

Directions:

1. Preheat oven to 375 degrees F.
2. In large bowl combine flours, cinnamon, baking powder, soda, and salt.
3. In medium bowl beat buttermilk, oat bran, brown sugar, oil, and egg until blended.
4. Stir buttermilk mixture into flour mixture just until combined; gently fold in apples.
5. Spoon batter into greased 12-muffin tin, filling each cup ¾ full.
6. Bake for about 20 minutes or until tops spring back when lightly touched.
7. Remove from oven and lift out onto wire rack to cool, or serve while warm.

Yields: 12 muffins.

Apple Pie Bread

For those of you without bread machines, this is the same bread as Apple Pie Filling Bread Recipe for Bread Machines. It is just as tasty and fragrant!

Ingredients:

3   c. all-purpose flour
4   tsp. baking powder
1   tsp. salt
1   tsp. ground cinnamon
1   tsp. ground cloves
1   c. sugar
1   egg
2   Tbs. oil
1½ c. milk
1½ c. apples, unpeeled, cored, diced

Directions:

1. Preheat oven to 350 degrees F.
2. Sift together flour, baking powder, salt, cinnamon, and cloves; set aside.
3. Cream together sugar, egg, and oil until well blended.
4. Add milk alternately with flour mixture to creamed ingredients just until moistened.
5. Gently fold in apples; spoon into greased and floured 9 x 5-inch loaf pan.
6. Bake for 1 hour and 20 minutes or until wooden pick inserted in center comes out clean.
7. Remove from oven, let stand for 10 minutes, then turn out onto wire rack to cool before slicing to serve.

Yields: 1 loaf.

Chocolate Apple Bread

It is the chocolate in this apple bread that makes it special for both adults and children.

Ingredients for topping:

2 Tbs. sugar
¼ tsp. ground cinnamon
¼ c. walnuts, finely chopped

Ingredients for bread:

2 c. all-purpose flour
½ tsp. baking powder
½ tsp. baking soda
¾ tsp. ground cinnamon
¼ tsp. ground nutmeg
½ c. butter, softened
1 c. sugar
2 eggs
1 tsp. vanilla extract
2 Tbs. buttermilk
1¼ c. apples, chopped
¾ c. walnuts, finely chopped
¾ c. semisweet chocolate chips

Directions for topping:

1. In small bowl mix sugar, cinnamon, and walnuts.
2. Set aside.

Directions for bread:

1. Preheat oven to 350 degrees F.
2. In medium bowl sift together flour, baking powder, soda, cinnamon, and nutmeg.
3. In separate large bowl cream butter and sugar; add eggs and vanilla and mix well.
4. Gradually beat flour mixture into creamed mixture alternately with buttermilk.
5. Fold in apples, walnuts, and chocolate chips.
6. Pour into greased and floured 9 x 5 x 3-inch loaf pan; sprinkle with topping.

7. Bake for 50 to 60 minutes or until wooden pick inserted in center comes out clean.
8. Remove from oven and cool in pan for 15 minutes.
9. Loosen edges from pan sides with knife, and gently shake loaf from pan onto side.
10. Place on wire rack to cool completely before slicing to serve.

Yields: 1 loaf.

Apple Rhubarb Bread

Apple and rhubarb make a great combination in this moist bread.

Ingredients:

1½ c. apples, unpeeled, cored, chopped
1½ c. rhubarb, finely chopped
1¼ c. walnuts, chopped
1½ c. sugar
½ c. canola oil
1   tsp. vanilla extract
4   eggs
3   c. all-purpose flour
3½ tsp. baking powder
1   tsp. ground cinnamon

Directions:

1. Preheat oven to 350 degrees F.
2. Combine apples, rhubarb, nuts, sugar, oil, vanilla, and eggs in large bowl.
3. Sift together flour, baking powder, and cinnamon; stir into fruit mix, blending well.
4. Spoon into greased and floured 9 x 5 x 3-inch loaf pan.
5. Bake for 50 to 60 minutes or until wooden pick inserted in center comes out clean.
6. Remove from oven and cool 10 minutes; loosen sides of loaf from pan, and turn out onto wire rack.
7. Cool completely before slicing to serve.

Yields: 1 large loaf.

Whole-Wheat Apple Muffins

Not only are these muffins tasty, but they are also nutritious and low-sugar.

Ingredients:

 1   c. all-purpose flour
 1   c. whole-wheat flour
 ¼   c. sugar
 1   tsp. baking powder
 ⅛   tsp. ground allspice
 1   c. milk
 ⅓   c. oil
 1   egg, beaten
 1   c. finely chopped Golden Delicious apple
 ½   c. chopped nuts (optional)

Directions:

1. Preheat oven to 400 degrees F.
2. Combine flours, sugar, baking powder, and allspice.
3. Beat together milk, oil, and egg until well blended.
4. Add liquid ingredients to flour mixture; blend only until moistened.
5. Gently fold in apples and nuts; spoon into 12 greased muffin cups, filling ¾ full.
6. Bake about 30 minutes or until wooden pick inserted near center comes out clean.
7. Remove from oven, and lift out onto wire rack to cool; serve while warm or leave until cooled completely.

Yields: 12 muffins.

Apple Walnut Bread

For your family, this is a really special bread with the wonderful taste of walnuts for their enjoyment.

Ingredients:

- 2 c. all-purpose flour
- 1 tsp. baking powder
- ½ tsp. baking soda
- 1¼ tsp. ground cinnamon
- ¼ tsp. salt
- ½ c. butter, softened
- 1 c. sugar
- 2 eggs
- 1 tsp. vanilla extract
- 1¼ c. apples, shredded
- 1 c. walnuts, chopped

Directions:

1. Preheat oven to 350 degrees F.
2. Sift together flour, baking powder, soda, cinnamon, and salt.
3. In large bowl beat butter, sugar, eggs, and vanilla until creamy.
4. Blend flour mixture into creamed batter; stir just until moistened.
5. Gently fold in apples and nuts; spoon into greased and floured 9 x 5-inch bread pan.
6. Bake for 50 to 60 minutes or until wooden pick inserted in center comes out clean.
7. Remove from oven, let stand for 10 minutes, then turn out onto wire rack to cool before slicing to serve.

Yields: 1 large loaf.

Apple Cinnamon Bread

This scrumptious apple bread has a crunchy cinnamon topping. Serve it warm with butter, or enjoy a cold slice with a glass of milk.

Ingredients for bread:

½ c. butter, softened
1 c. sugar
2 eggs
1 tsp. vanilla extract
2 Tbs. milk
2 c. all-purpose flour
½ tsp. salt
1 tsp. baking soda
¾ c. nutmeats, chopped
2 c. fresh apples, peeled, cored, chopped fine

Ingredients for topping:

2 Tbs. butter
2 Tbs. all-purpose flour
2 Tbs. sugar
1 Tbs. ground cinnamon

Directions for bread:

1. Preheat oven to 350 degrees F.
2. Cream together butter, sugar, and eggs.
3. Add vanilla and milk, blending well; set aside.
4. Sift together flour, salt, and baking soda.
5. Blend liquid mixture with flour mixture, stirring just until moistened; gently fold in apples and nuts.
6. Spoon into greased and floured 9 x 5 x 3-inch pan.

Directions for topping:

1. Blend together butter, flour, sugar, and cinnamon until of a coarse texture; sprinkle evenly over batter in pan.
2. Bake for 1 hour or until wooden pick inserted in center comes out clean.
3. Remove from oven, and cool on wire rack before removing from pan.

Yields: 1 large loaf.

Apple Delights Cookbook

A Collection of Apple Recipes
Cookbook Delights Series

Breakfasts

Table of Contents

Did You Know? . . . .

Did you know that even though we think of apple pie as a symbol of America, it has been traced back as far as fourteenth century England?

Apple and Cinnamon Oatmeal Pancakes

The Granny Smith apples are a must in these light and tasty pancakes.

Ingredients:

1¼ c. buttermilk, divided
⅔ c. quick-cooking rolled oats (not instant)
1 lg. egg, lightly beaten
2 Tbs. light brown sugar, firmly packed
⅔ c. peeled, grated, firmly packed, Granny Smith apple, excess juice squeezed out
6 Tbs. all-purpose flour
6 Tbs. whole-wheat flour
1 tsp. baking soda
½ tsp. salt
1 tsp. ground cinnamon
2 Tbs. vegetable oil plus additional for griddle maple syrup

Directions:

1. In bowl whisk together 1 cup buttermilk and oats; let stand for 15 minutes.
2. In large bowl whisk together egg, brown sugar, and apple.
3. Stir in flours, soda, salt, cinnamon, 2 tablespoons oil, oats mixture, and remaining ¼ cup buttermilk; combine batter well.
4. Heat griddle over moderate heat until hot enough to make drops of water scatter over surface.
5. Brush with oil, and drop batter by half-filled ¼-cup measures onto it.
6. Cook pancakes for 1 to 2 minutes on each side or until golden and cooked through.
7. Serve with maple syrup.

Yields: 2 to 3 servings (twelve 4-inch pancakes).

Apple Berry Breakfast Crisp

This delicious crisp makes a great breakfast treat that the whole family will enjoy.

Ingredients for topping:

- 1 c. old-fashioned rolled oats, uncooked
- ½ c. brown sugar, firmly packed
- ⅓ c. butter, melted
- 2 Tbs. all-purpose flour

Ingredients for filling:

- 4 med. apples, peeled, cored, sliced thin
- 2 c. blueberries, fresh or frozen (or sliced strawberries)
- ¼ c. brown sugar, firmly packed
- ¼ c. frozen orange juice concentrate, thawed
- 2 Tbs. all-purpose flour
- 1 tsp. ground cinnamon

Directions for topping:

1. Combine oats, brown sugar, butter, and flour in small bowl, and blend until crumbly.
2. Set aside.

Directions for filling:

1. Preheat oven to 350 degrees F.
2. Combine apples, berries, brown sugar, orange juice, flour, and cinnamon, stirring until fruit is evenly coated.
3. Spoon mixture into buttered 8-inch square glass baking dish.
4. Sprinkle topping evenly over fruit.
5. Bake for 30 to 35 minutes or until apples are tender.
6. Remove from oven, and serve warm with cream or plain yogurt if desired.

Apple Breakfast Bread

This sweet bread is great for breakfast or lunch. It is delicious with butter and honey or just plain.

Ingredients:

2   c. all-purpose flour
4   tsp. baking powder
2   tsp. brown sugar
4   Tbs. butter
2   c. raisins, chopped
¾   c. milk
1   egg, beaten
4   apples, peeled, cored, thinly sliced
3   Tbs. butter, melted
1½ tsp. ground cinnamon
3   Tbs. brown sugar

Directions:

1. Preheat oven to 400 degrees F.
2. Sift together flour, baking powder, and sugar.
3. Cut in butter, then add raisins.
4. Combine milk and egg; add sufficient amount to dry ingredients to make stiff dough, mixing thoroughly.
5. Spoon into greased and floured 13 x 9 x 2-inch baking pan; brush with melted butter.
6. Arrange apple slices in rows on top of dough, allowing edges to overlap; brush apples with more melted butter.
7. Mix together cinnamon and brown sugar; sprinkle over top of apples.
8. Bake for 20 minutes or until apples are tender.
9. Remove from oven and cool on wire rack before cutting into squares to serve.

Yields: 12 to 14 servings.

Apple French Toast

The cooked apples on French toast make a delicious and attractive breakfast presentation.

Ingredients:

    2 firm apples, peeled, cored, sliced thin
    1 c. apple juice
    2 Tbs. cold water
    2 tsp. cornstarch
    ¼ tsp. ground cardamom
    4 lg. eggs, beaten
    ¾ tsp. vanilla extract
    8 slices bread

Directions:

1. In small pot combine apple slices and apple juice; cover and cook just until crisply tender.
2. With slotted spoon remove apple slices and reserve.
3. Combine water, cornstarch, and cardamom; whisk into apple juice in pot.
4. Heat mixture to boiling and cook, stirring until thickened and syrupy; remove from heat and set aside.
5. Heat large, nonstick skillet over medium heat.
6. In wide, shallow bowl whisk eggs and vanilla well.
7. Dip 2 bread slices in egg mixture to coat both sides; cook in skillet until golden brown on both sides.
8. Remove to serving plate; arrange apple slices on top of French toast, and drizzle with reserved syrup.
9. Repeat with remaining egg mixture and bread slices.

Did You Know? . . . .

Did you know that more than half of all apples are eaten fresh?

Apple Fritters

This recipe was given to me by my mother and has been passed on through the generations. These are great rolled in confectioners' sugar or cinnamon and sugar. I can still remember eating them for a special breakfast treat as a child, and years later, I enjoy serving them to my family as a special treat during the apple season.

Ingredients:

    2 c. sifted all-purpose flour
    2 tsp. baking powder
    ½ c. sugar
    2 Tbs. oil
    2 eggs, well beaten
    1 c. milk
    3 fresh apples of choice, peeled, cored, finely chopped
       oil for frying
       confectioners' sugar
       sugar
       ground cinnamon

Directions:

1. Sift together flour, baking powder, and sugar.
2. Beat together oil and eggs; add milk.
3. Blend into flour mixture, mixing thoroughly.
4. Gently fold in apples just until combined.
5. Drop by ample teaspoonfuls into hot oil (400 degrees F.); fry to golden brown, turning once.
6. Drain on paper towels until lukewarm.
7. Roll in your choice of confectioners' sugar, sugar, or cinnamon and sugar. (Our family likes all three.)

Did You Know? . . . .

Did you know that in 1730 the first apple nursery was opened in Flushing, New York?

Apple Sausage Breakfast Ring

This is a delicious breakfast dish that can be made ahead and is perfect for a leisurely breakfast or brunch. Fill the center of the ring with scrambled eggs right before serving, and the meal is complete!

Ingredients:

2   lb. lean, unflavored bulk sausage
2   lg. eggs
1½ c. club or butter crackers, crushed
¼   c. milk
1   apple, peeled, cored, chopped fine
½   c. onion, minced
      scrambled eggs

Directions:

1. Combine sausage, eggs, crackers, and milk in medium mixing bowl, blending well.
2. Add apple and onion, and press into ring mold lined with wax paper or plastic wrap.
3. Chill overnight.
4. Preheat oven to 300 degrees F.
5. Unmold, remove paper, and place onto baking sheet with raised edges.
6. Bake for 1 hour.
7. Remove from oven, fill with scrambled eggs, and serve while hot.

Did You Know? . . . .

Did you know that the Cortland apple was developed in 1898? It was named for Cortland County, New York, near where it was developed.

Breakfast Apple Citrus Compote

This refreshing fruit compote is easy to make ahead.

Ingredients:

    2   c. tart apples, peeled, cored, sliced
    1½ c. pitted prunes
    1½ c. orange juice
    2   Tbs. honey
    2   Tbs. lemon juice
    ¾   tsp. ground cinnamon
    2   naval oranges, peeled, sectioned, halved
    2   pink grapefruit, peeled, sectioned, halved
        mint sprigs for garnish

Directions:

1. In large saucepan combine apples, prunes, and orange juice; bring to a boil, reduce heat, and simmer just until apples are crisp tender, about 10 minutes.
2. Remove from heat; stir in honey, lemon juice, and cinnamon.
3. Cover and chill completely in refrigerator; stir in oranges and grapefruit.
4. When ready to serve, spoon fruits with their liquid into serving dishes; garnish with mint sprigs.

Yields: 8 to 10 servings.

Did You Know? . . . .

Did you know that the apple crop in the United States totals about 5 million tons each year and has a wholesale value of over $1.3 billion?

Breakfast Kabobs

Many of my family members enjoy the festive nature of kabobs, and they make an eye-catching presentation for guests, also. Apples and pork sausage make an attractive breakfast or addition to your brunch menu.

Ingredients:

    2 c. water
    2 Tbs. lemon juice
    2 lg. Golden Delicious apples
    1 lb. kielbasa or breakfast sausages
    1 bunch fresh sage (optional)
       vegetable oil cooking spray

Directions:

1. Preheat oven to 400 degrees F.
2. Lightly coat baking sheet with vegetable oil cooking spray.
3. In small bowl combine water and lemon juice.
4. Core apples, cut lengthwise into quarters, then cut each quarter into 4 wedges.
5. Soak slices in lemon water 1 minute; drain on paper towels.
6. Cut kielbasa diagonally into 24 oval slices, ½ inch thick.
7. On wooden or metal skewers, alternately thread 4 slices of apple and 3 slices of kielbasa (through skin), beginning and ending with apple.
8. Place kabobs on lightly oiled baking sheet, and roast 15 to 20 minutes, turning occasionally, or until apple slices soften and kielbasa browns.
9. Set on bed of sage leaves, if desired, and serve.

Golden Yogurt Coffee Cake

One of my daughters really enjoys coffee cake, and this is a tasty variation of this popular cake.

Ingredients for cake:

- 1   Tbs. butter, melted
- 1   Tbs. brown sugar, firmly packed
- ½   tsp. ground cinnamon
- 2   Golden Delicious apples, peeled, cored, sliced
- 2   c. all-purpose flour
- 1   tsp. baking powder
- 1   tsp. baking soda
- ½   tsp. salt
- ½   c. sugar
- ½   c. butter
- ½   c. milk
- 2   eggs
- 8   oz. plain yogurt

Ingredients for streusel:

- ¼   c. brown sugar, firmly packed
- 1   Tbs. butter, melted
- 1   Tbs. all-purpose flour
- 1   tsp. ground cinnamon
- ¼   c. walnuts or pecans, chopped

Directions for cake:

1. Grease bottom of 13 x 9 x 2-inch baking pan with melted butter.
2. Mix together brown sugar, cinnamon, and apples; arrange in layer on bottom of pan.
3. Sift together flour, baking powder, baking soda, salt, and sugar; cut in butter.
4. Mix together eggs, milk, and yogurt; stir into flour mixture, blending well.

5. Pour over apple mixture.
6. Top with streusel topping.

Directions for streusel:

1. Preheat oven to 375 degrees F.
2. Combine brown sugar, butter, flour, cinnamon, and chopped walnuts or pecans.
3. Blend together until mixture becomes crumbly.
4. Sprinkle over cake before baking.
5. Bake for about 25 minutes or until wooden pick inserted near center comes out clean.
6. Remove from oven, let stand for 10 minutes, then cut into squares to serve.

Yields: 12 to 14 servings.

Sausages with Baked Apples

This recipe is a unique combination which can be served for breakfast, as a main dish served with fresh buns and condiments, or as an attractive side dish.

Ingredients:

1 lb. sausage, links or ground
4 lg. tart apples, unpeeled, cored

Directions:

1. Cook sausage until done and drain off fat; place on serving dish and keep warm.
2. Cut apples in medium-thick slices, leaving skins on.
3. Fry in sausage drippings just until tender crisp; keeping whole slices.
4. Place around cooked sausage on serving dish.
5. Keep hot until ready to serve.
6. Try serving with fresh biscuits and scrambled eggs for a really satisfying meal.

Golden Apple Oatmeal

Our family really enjoys hot oatmeal in the morning, and this recipe has a few tasty additions.

Ingredients:

- 1   Golden Delicious apple, peeled, cored, diced
- 1   c. apple juice
- ½ c. water
- ½ tsp. ground cinnamon
- ½ tsp. ground nutmeg
- ⅔ c. quick-cooking rolled oats, uncooked

Directions:

1. Combine apples, juice, water, cinnamon, and nutmeg in medium saucepan.
2. Over medium heat, bring ingredients to a boil, stir in rolled oats, and cook for 1 minute longer.
3. Remove from heat, cover, and let stand several minutes before serving.
4. Delicious served with butter and brown sugar or milk. Try it both ways.

Yields: 2 servings.

Did You Know? . . . .

Did you know that nearly 100 varieties of apples are grown commercially in the United States, but a total of 15 popular varieties accounted for almost 90 percent of 2006 production?

High-Protein Breakfast Cookies

These cookies are great to have on hand for a quick breakfast or to take along on the mornings you are rushing out the door.

Ingredients:

⅔ c. butter, softened
⅓ c. brown sugar, firmly packed
1 egg
1 tsp. vanilla extract
½ tsp. ground cinnamon
¾ c. all-purpose flour
½ tsp. baking powder
½ tsp. salt
1½ c. oatmeal
1 c. shredded cheddar cheese
¾ c. raisins
1 c. chopped apple

Directions:

1. Preheat oven to 375 degrees F.
2. Cream butter and sugar.
3. Thoroughly mix in egg and vanilla.
4. Stir in cinnamon, flour, baking powder, and salt.
5. Add oatmeal, cheese, and raisins; mix well.
6. Stir in chopped apple.
7. Drop by large spoonfuls onto ungreased baking sheet.
8. Bake for 15 minutes.
9. Remove to racks to cool.
10. Store in tightly covered containers in refrigerator or freezer.

Pan-Grilled Sausages with Apples and Onions

Serve this tasty sausage, apple, and onion dish with potato pancakes for a hearty breakfast.

Ingredients:

    3 Tbs. butter, divided
    4 fully cooked sausages (13 oz. total)
    1 med. onion, sliced
    1 med. tart apple, peeled, cored, sliced
    ½ c. apple cider or apple juice
    ½ c. chicken broth
    2 Tbs. chopped fresh sage
    2 Tbs. fresh lemon juice
       salt and pepper

Directions:

1. Melt 1 tablespoon butter in large skillet over medium heat.
2. Add sausages and cook until beginning to brown, turning occasionally, about 5 minutes.
3. Add onion and apple to sausages in pan; cook until onion and apple are tender and brown, stirring often, about 5 minutes.
4. Add apple cider, broth, and chopped sage; increase heat to high, and stir until liquid is slightly reduced, about 2 minutes.
5. Stir in lemon juice; season to taste with salt and pepper.
6. Using slotted spoon, transfer onion and apple to 2 plates, dividing equally; top with sausages.
7. Whisk remaining 2 tablespoons butter into cider mixture.
8. Season sauce to taste with salt and pepper.
9. Drizzle over sausages and serve.

Yields: 2 servings.

Apple Delights Cookbook

A Collection of Apple Recipes
Cookbook Delights Series

Cakes

Table of Contents

Did You Know? . . . .

Did you know that the legend of William Tell appears first in the 15th century in two different versions?

Apple Buttermilk Cake

This delicious cake combines buttermilk with apples. The crumb topping is a flavorful bonus. Your family will be sure to enjoy this cake!

Ingredients for cake:

2 c. all-purpose flour
2 tsp. baking powder
½ tsp. salt
¼ c. butter, softened
½ c. sugar
½ c. brown sugar, firmly packed
1 lg. egg
½ c. buttermilk
2½ c. apples, peeled, cored, finely chopped
1 tsp. grated lemon zest
lemon frozen yogurt (optional)

Ingredients for topping:

⅓ c. all-purpose flour
⅓ c. brown sugar, firmly packed
½ tsp. ground cinnamon
¼ c. butter
⅓ c. blanched almonds, chopped

Directions for cake:

1. Preheat oven to 375 degrees F.
2. Sift together flour, baking powder, and salt.
3. In large bowl cream together butter, sugars, and egg.
4. Add buttermilk and flour mixture alternately to creamed mixture just until blended.
5. Fold in apples and lemon zest.
6. Spread batter in greased and floured, 9-inch square baking pan.

Directions for topping and assembly:

1. Combine flour, sugar, cinnamon, and butter until crumbly, then stir in almonds.

2. Sprinkle mixture over top of cake batter in pan.
3. Bake for 35 to 40 minutes or until wooden pick inserted in center comes out clean.
4. Remove from oven and place on wire rack to cool before cutting into squares.
5. Try serving with lemon frozen yogurt.

Yields: 12 servings.

Marinated Apple Cake

This is a different cake that is so easy to make. Simply marinate the first seven ingredients for 1½ hours, then add the rest of the ingredients.

Ingredients:

1	c. oil
2	c. sugar
2	tsp. ground cinnamon
3	eggs, beaten
3	tsp. vanilla extract
1½	c. nuts, chopped
4	fresh apples, peeled, cored, chopped
3	c. all-purpose flour
2	tsp. baking soda
	confectioners' sugar

Directions:

1. Mix together oil, sugar, cinnamon, eggs, vanilla, nuts, and apples; let stand for 1½ hours.
2. Preheat oven to 350 degrees F.
3. Sift together flour and baking soda; add to marinated mixture and mix well.
4. Bake in greased tube pan 1 hour or until done.
5. Remove from oven, let stand for 10 minutes, then turn out onto wire rack to cool.
6. When completely cooled, dust with confectioners' sugar before slicing to serve.

Apple Cake with Maple-Walnut Cream Cheese Frosting

This is not an easy recipe, but it is well worth the effort. The frosting is the crowning touch on this moist and delicious cake.

Ingredients for cake:

    1   lb. tart apples (about 2 med.), peeled, cored, diced
    ¼   c. water
    2½ c. plus 1 Tbs. all-purpose flour, divided
    2   tsp. baking soda
    1½ tsp. ground cinnamon
    ½   tsp. salt
    ¼   tsp. ground nutmeg
    ¼   tsp. ground cloves
    1   c. dried currants
    1   c. walnuts or pecans (about 4 oz.), toasted, chopped
    2   c. sugar
    1   c. unsalted butter, room temperature
    1   Tbs. brandy or bourbon (optional)
    1½ tsp. vanilla extract
    4   lg. eggs

Ingredients for frosting:

    1   c. unsalted butter, room temperature
    1   c. dark brown sugar, firmly packed
    2   pkg. cream cheese (8 oz. each), room temperature
    ½   c. pure maple syrup
    ¼   tsp. maple flavoring
    2   c. walnuts or pecans, toasted, chopped

Directions for cake:

1. Butter and flour three 9-inch-diameter cake pans with 1½-inch-high sides.
2. Combine apples and water in small saucepan.

3. Cover and simmer over medium-low heat until apples are tender, about 20 minutes; cool.
4. Preheat oven to 350 degrees F.
5. Sift 2½ cups flour and next 5 ingredients into medium bowl.
6. Toss currants with remaining 1 tablespoon flour in small bowl to coat; mix in nuts.
7. Using electric mixer, beat sugar, butter, brandy, and vanilla in large bowl until blended.
8. Beat in eggs one at a time.
9. Beat in flour mixture; stir in apples, currants, and nuts.
10. Divide batter among prepared pans.
11. Bake until cake springs back when touched near center, about 20 minutes.
12. Cut around pan sides to loosen cakes; turn out onto racks and cool.

Directions for frosting:

1. Using electric mixer, beat butter and sugar in large bowl until blended.
2. Beat in cream cheese then maple syrup and flavoring.
3. Chill until beginning to firm, about 20 minutes.

Directions for assembly:

1. Place 1 cake layer on platter; spread with ¾ cup frosting.
2. Top with second layer; spread with ¾ cup frosting.
3. Top with third layer; spread 1 cup frosting in thin layer over cake; chill 15 minutes.
4. Spread remaining frosting over cake.
5. Press 2 cups walnuts halfway up sides of cake.
6. Chill until frosting is set, at least 30 minutes.
7. Can be made 1 day ahead; cover and keep chilled.
8. Let stand at room temperature 1 hour before serving.

Yields: 8 to 10 servings.

Apple Cinnamon Cake

This recipe produces a wonderfully moist cake, and the nuts give it added flavor. It freezes extremely well.

Ingredients:

        3   lg. eggs, beaten
        1½   c. sugar
        ¾   c. vegetable oil
        2   c. all-purpose flour
        1½   Tbs. ground cinnamon
        1   tsp. baking soda
        ½   tsp. salt
        3   apples, peeled, cored, sliced
        ½   c. nuts, chopped
             whipped cream or ice cream

Directions:

1. Preheat oven to 325 degrees F.
2. In large bowl blend eggs, sugar, and oil.
3. Sift together flour, cinnamon, baking soda, and salt; blend into egg mixture until well combined.
4. Stir in apples and nuts.
5. Spread batter into greased and floured 8-inch square pan.
6. Bake for 65 to 70 minutes or until wooden pick inserted in center comes out clean.
7. Remove from oven, and cool on wire rack before cutting into squares to serve.
8. Serve warm, topped with whipped cream or ice cream if desired.

Yields: 12 servings.

Apple Coconut Cake

The combination of coconut and lots of nuts makes this a moist and flavorful apple cake.

Ingredients:

- 3 eggs
- 1 c. sugar
- ½ c. oil
- 2 tsp. vanilla extract
- 3 c. all-purpose flour
- 1 tsp. baking powder
- 1 tsp. baking soda
- ½ tsp. salt
- 1½ c. chopped apples
- 1½ c. coconut
- 1 c. chopped walnuts
  whipped cream or vanilla ice cream

Directions:

1. Preheat oven to 350 degrees F.
2. Beat eggs, sugar, oil, and vanilla until creamy and light in texture.
3. Sift together flour, baking powder, baking soda, and salt; add to creamed mixture and beat well.
4. Fold in apples, coconut, and walnuts.
5. Spoon into greased 13 x 9 x 2-inch cake pan.
6. Bake for 40 minutes or until wooden pick inserted in center comes out clean.
7. Remove from oven, let stand 10 minutes, then cut into squares to serve.
8. Serve warm, topped with whipped cream or ice cream.

Apple Rum Bundt Cake

Rum adds extra flavor to the apples and pecans in this easy-to-make, attractive cake. It is great with a scoop of ice cream or a dollop of sweetened whipped cream.

Ingredients:

2   eggs
1   c. sugar
1   c. brown sugar, firmly packed
1¼   c. canola oil
1   tsp. vanilla extract
1   Tbs. rum
2   c. all-purpose flour
1   tsp. baking soda
1   tsp. ground cinnamon
½   tsp. salt
1¼   c. chopped pecans
4   c. chopped apples
1   pt. whipping cream
1   tsp. brown sugar

Directions:

1. Preheat oven to 350 degrees F.
2. Beat eggs well, then add sugars, oil, vanilla, and rum; beat until creamy.
3. Sift together flour, soda, cinnamon, and salt; mix until well blended.
4. Combine creamed ingredients with dry ingredients; beat until creamy.
5. Fold in nuts and apples; spoon into buttered and sugared bundt pan.
6. Bake for 1 hour; add 15 minutes for a crispy crust.
7. Remove from oven, let stand for 10 minutes, then turn out onto wire rack to cool.
8. When cooled, dust with confectioners' sugar.
9. Just before serving, whip cream until almost stiff; add brown sugar and beat until creamy.
10. Top each serving with a dollop of whipped cream.

Yields: 12 to 14 servings.

Jewish Apple Cake

This moist cake with cinnamon and sugar between the layers is always a favorite.

Ingredients:

2½ c. sugar, divided
4   eggs
2½ tsp. vanilla extract
1   c. canola oil
3   c. all-purpose flour, sifted
3   tsp. baking powder
1¼ c. nuts, chopped
3   c. apples, finely chopped
1   Tbs. ground cinnamon

Directions:

1. Preheat oven to 350 degrees F.
2. Mix together 2 cups sugar, eggs, vanilla, and oil on high speed of electric mixer, beating for 10 minutes.
3. Sift together flour and baking powder; add to sugar mixture, mixing well.
4. Grease and lightly flour bundt pan; pour ⅓ of batter into pan.
5. Combine nuts and apples and sprinkle half over batter.
6. Mix together cinnamon and remaining ½ cup sugar; sprinkle half over nuts and apples.
7. Add another ⅓ of batter; top with remaining nuts and apples, and sprinkle with remaining sugar and cinnamon.
8. Add last ⅓ of batter over top, and bake for 1 hour and 15 minutes or until wooden pick inserted near center comes out clean.
9. If cake begins to brown too much, cover with foil and continue baking.
10. Remove from oven, let stand 10 minutes in pan, then turn out onto wire rack to cool.
11. When cooled completely, dust with confectioners' sugar or frost with a drizzle icing.

Yields: 12 servings.

Apple Loaf Cake

Here is an easy-to-make, delicious loaf cake recipe that you might want to double so that you have extra in the freezer for a quick snack or dessert when in a hurry.

Ingredients:

2   Tbs. butter
1   c. sugar
1½ tsp. vanilla extract
1   egg, beaten
1   c. all-purpose flour
¾   tsp. ground cinnamon
½   tsp. ground nutmeg
1   tsp. baking soda
3   c. apples, diced

Directions:

1. Preheat oven to 350 degrees F.
2. Cream together butter, sugar, vanilla, and egg until light and fluffy.
3. Sift together flour, spices, and baking soda; stir into creamed mixture just until well blended.
4. Fold in apples, and stir just enough to mix in.
5. Spoon dough into greased and floured 9 x 5-inch pan.
6. Bake for 35 to 40 minutes or until wooden pick inserted in center comes out clean.
7. Remove from oven, let stand in pan for 10 minutes, then turn out onto wire rack to cool before slicing.

Did You Know? . . . .

Did you know that extremely sweet apples with barely any acid flavor are popular in Asia and India?

Easy Apple Cake

This is one of those recipes you will want to double, since it is so easy to make.

Ingredients:

½ c. all-purpose flour
½ c. sugar
1 tsp. baking powder
1 tsp. ground cinnamon
¼ tsp. ground nutmeg
3 med. apples, peeled, cored, chopped
⅓ c. raisins
1 egg, slightly beaten
1 tsp. vanilla extract
Sweetened Whipped Cream (recipe page 155)

Directions:

1. Preheat oven to 350 degrees F.
2. Sift together flour, sugar, baking powder, cinnamon, and nutmeg in medium bowl.
3. Add apples and raisins to dry mixture, stirring lightly to coat.
4. Combine egg and vanilla in small bowl; add to dry ingredients, stirring only until moistened.
5. Spoon mixture into greased 9-inch pie pan.
6. Bake for 30 minutes or until golden brown.
7. Remove from oven and cool on wire rack.
8. When ready to serve, top with whipped cream.

Yields: 6 to 8 servings.

Glazed Apple Cake

The glaze keeps this cake moist, adding to its delicious taste.

Ingredients:

- 3 med. apples, peeled, cored, sliced into rings
- ½ c. fresh lemon juice
- ¾ c. sugar
- 1 c. butter, softened
- 3 c. all-purpose flour
- 1 c. milk
- 2 tsp. ground cinnamon
- 1 tsp. baking powder
- 2 tsp. vanilla extract
- 3 lg. eggs
- ¾ c. pecans, chopped
- 2 med. fresh apples, peeled, cored, chopped
- 3 Tbs. apple jelly (recipe page 186)

Directions:

1. Preheat oven to 350 degrees F.
2. Cut apple rings in half and toss with lemon juice; drain on paper towels and set aside.
3. In large bowl with mixer on high speed, beat sugar and butter until light and fluffy.
4. Reduce mixer speed to low and add flour, milk, cinnamon, baking powder, vanilla, and eggs; beat until just blended.
5. Increase speed to medium and beat 3 minutes.
6. With rubber spatula, gently fold in pecans and chopped apples.
7. Spread batter evenly into greased and floured 13 x 9 x 2-inch baking pan.
8. Arrange apple slices on top of batter.
9. In small saucepan over medium heat, melt apple jelly; with pastry brush, spread jelly over apple slices.
10. Bake for 45 to 50 minutes or until cake tester comes out clean.
11. Remove from oven, and cool on wire rack before cutting into squares to serve.

Yields: 12 servings.

Old-Fashioned Applesauce Cake

This cake reminds me of my dad since he always liked it so much. This particular cake is made in a tube pan and is delicious sprinkled with confectioners' sugar or cinnamon.

Ingredients:

1¾ c. walnuts, coarsely chopped
1¾ c. raisins
3½ c. all-purpose flour, divided
2 tsp. baking soda
¼ tsp. salt
1½ tsp. ground cinnamon
1 tsp. ground cloves
1 tsp. ground ginger
¼ tsp. ground nutmeg
1 c. butter, softened
2 c. sugar
2 lg. eggs
2 c. applesauce (recipe page 169)
 confectioners' sugar

Directions:

1. Preheat oven to 350 degrees F.
2. Dredge nuts and raisins in ½ cup flour; set aside.
3. Sift together remaining flour, soda, salt, and spices.
4. Cream butter, sugar, and eggs until light and fluffy.
5. Add dry ingredients, alternating with applesauce, to creamed ingredients.
6. Fold in nuts and raisins with dredged flour.
7. Spoon batter into greased and floured 9-inch tube pan.
8. Bake for 1 hour and 25 minutes or until cake feels springy and has pulled away from sides.
9. Remove from oven, and turn out onto wire rack to cool.
10. When ready to serve, dust with confectioners' sugar and slice.

Yields: 12 to 14 servings.

Scandinavian Apple Cake

This is a moist, spicy cake with plenty of nuts. Scandinavians value the patience of waiting one week for the flavors to blend.

Ingredients:

    2   c. all-purpose flour
    2   tsp. baking soda
    2½ tsp. ground cinnamon
    2   tsp. ground allspice
    1   c. sugar
    ⅔ c. butter, melted
    2   eggs, beaten
    3   tsp. vanilla extract
    1   tsp. cardamom
    4   lg. tart apples, peeled, cored, chopped
    1½ c. nuts, chopped

Directions:

1. Preheat oven to 350 degrees F.
2. Sift together flour, baking soda, cinnamon, and allspice.
3. Combine sugar, butter, eggs, vanilla, and cardamom; add to dry ingredients, stirring just until blended.
4. Gently fold in apples and nuts; spoon into 2 greased and floured 9-inch square cake pans.
5. Bake for 45 to 50 minutes or until wooden pick inserted near center comes out clean.
6. Remove from oven, let stand for 10 minutes, then turn out onto wire rack to cool.
7. Wrap and refrigerate for 1 week to blend flavors before serving; keeps up to 3 months frozen.

Apple Delights Cookbook

A Collection of Apple Recipes
Cookbook Delights Series

Candies

Table of Contents

Page

Did You Know? . . .

Did you know that apples were brought to North America with colonists in the 1600s? The first apple orchard on the North American continent was said to be near Boston in 1625.

Aplets

This delicious apple-walnut candy was developed in Washington state in 1918. It is considered a Northwest delicacy.

Ingredients:

- 1 c. grated Red or Golden Delicious apples
- 2 c. sugar
- 2 Tbs. unflavored gelatin
- 5 Tbs. cold water
- 1/8 tsp. rose culinary essence or 1 Tbs. rose flower water
- 1 c. finely chopped walnuts
  confectioners' sugar

Directions:

1. Note: Culinary rose essence can be found in Asian or Indian grocery and spice stores. If you are unable to find culinary essence or rose water, substitute 1 tablespoon lemon juice.
2. Butter 8-inch square pan.
3. In large saucepan over medium heat, combine apples and sugar.
4. Bring to a boil; boil 1 minute, stirring constantly.
5. Turn heat to low and simmer another 30 minutes, stirring occasionally; remove from heat.
6. In small bowl combine gelatin and water; add to apple and sugar mixture, stirring constantly until dissolved.
7. Add rose culinary essence and walnuts; stir until well blended.
8. Pour into prepared pan; cool at least 2 hours but preferably overnight.
9. With oiled knife, cut into 1-inch squares, then roll in confectioners' sugar.
10. Store, covered, in refrigerator.

Yields: 64 candy squares.

Apple Butterscotch Candies

This is a wonderfully light and airy candy with a delicious butterscotch coating over chewy apple centers.

Ingredients:

- 1 lb. brown sugar, firmly packed
- 1 c. water
- 4 Tbs. distilled white vinegar
- 3 Tbs. light corn syrup
- ½ tsp. baking soda
- 16 oz. butterscotch baking chips
- 2 Tbs. shortening

Directions:

1. Mix together sugar, water, vinegar, and syrup in heavy 4-quart saucepan; heat mixture, stirring with wooden spoon, until sugar has dissolved and syrup has melted.
2. Bring to a boil, cover, and boil for 3 minutes; remove lid and boil until temperature reaches 285 degrees F. on candy thermometer.
3. Remove from heat and stir in baking soda, mixing well to allow bubbles to subside a little.
4. Pour hot mixture into 8-inch, lightly buttered pan, and leave until just beginning to set; mark into squares with lightly oiled knife.
5. Leave to set completely, then cut or break into pieces.
6. Combine chips and shortening in 2-quart glass bowl; microwave on high for 2 minutes to melt, stirring well.
7. Remove from microwave, cool slightly, and dip candy pieces, covering completely; let cool on wax paper.
8. Wrap each piece in wax paper and twist ends; store in airtight container.

Apple Gumdrops

These delicious old-fashioned gumdrops can be made right in your own home where the children can have fun helping.

Ingredients:

    1 c. sugar
    1 c. light corn syrup
    ¾ c. apple cider
    1 pkg. powdered fruit pectin
    ½ tsp. baking soda
    2 drops red food coloring (optional)
       sugar
       vegetable oil

Directions:

1. Line 9 x 5 x 3-inch loaf pan with aluminum foil; brush with oil.
2. Heat sugar and corn syrup to boiling in small saucepan over medium heat, stirring constantly, until sugar is dissolved.
3. Bring to a boil and cook without stirring to 280 degrees F. on candy thermometer or until small amount of mixture dropped in cold water forms a hard ball.
4. Place apple cider, pectin, and baking soda in pan over medium heat; bring to boiling, remove from heat, and add to sugar mixture.
5. Stir in food coloring and let stand 2 minutes; skim off foam.
6. Pour mixture into loaf pan; cover and let stand at room temperature 24 hours.
7. Remove cover, and cut into 1-inch squares with sharp knife dipped in sugar, or you can cut gumdrops

into different shapes with a cutter, just as you would cookies.
8. Roll squares in sugar and let stand at room temperature 1 hour; repeat rolling and standing.
9. Store gumdrops in airtight container.

Caramel Apple Bites

These are delicious caramel candies with the wonderful taste of apples added. They are so easy to make.

Ingredients:

2 Tbs. butter
⅓ c. light corn syrup
40 caramel candies, unwrapped
1 c. dried apples, chopped
⅔ c. walnuts, finely chopped
3 c. crispy rice cold cereal

Directions:

1. Melt butter in large saucepan; add corn syrup and caramel candies.
2. Cook over low heat, stirring constantly, until caramels are just melted.
3. Remove from heat and add apples, nuts, and cereal; stir until completely coated.
4. Spread mixture on wax paper or buttered baking sheet; cool slightly.
5. Cut into bite-size pieces; cool thoroughly.
6. May be kept in refrigerator or up to 1 month in airtight container.

Yields: 16 servings.

Apple Nut Nuggets

Fruit and nut nugget candy rolled in confectioners' sugar is a very popular candy in the Northwest. This candy can be made at home as a real treat. This is a favorite candy of one of my daughters.

Ingredients:

1½ c. apple purée, divided
2   env. unflavored gelatin
2   c. sugar
¼   tsp. almond extract
1   c. walnuts, chopped
    confectioners' sugar

Directions:

1. Sprinkle gelatin over ½ cup of apple purée; set aside to soften.
2. Combine sugar and remaining apple purée in medium saucepan.
3. Bring to a boil over moderate heat, stirring constantly; add softened gelatin mixture and continue stirring.
4. Boil mixture for 15 to 20 minutes longer.
5. Remove from heat, and stir in almond extract and nuts.
6. Pour into greased 8 x 8-inch pan; cool to room temperature then refrigerate overnight.
7. Cut into 1 x 1-inch pieces; remove from pan and roll in confectioners' sugar.
8. Allow to stand 2 to 3 days before serving or placing in an airtight container to store.

Apple Raisin Squares

Apples and raisins are always good together, and this candy combines those delicious flavors.

Ingredients:

- 3   c. sugar
- 1   c. evaporated milk
- ½   tsp. almond flavoring
- 1   c. dried apples, chopped
- 1   c. white raisins
- confectioners' sugar
- chopped nuts (optional)

Directions:

1. Mix together sugar and evaporated milk in saucepan; place over medium heat.
2. Bring to a boil, and stir constantly until mixture reaches soft-ball stage (235 degrees F.).
3. Remove from heat and stir in almond flavoring, apples, and raisins; add nuts if desired and stir well.
4. Allow mixture to cool, then press into bottom of 13 x 9 x 2-inch, parchment paper-lined, glass baking dish; refrigerate until firm.
5. Remove from refrigerator, loosen sides with sharp knife, and turn out onto surface sprinkled with confectioners' sugar.
6. Cut into 1-inch squares with knife dipped in hot water; coat all sides with confectioners' sugar.
7. Leave to air dry until firm enough to wrap; store in airtight container.

Yields: 2½ dozen.

Pacific Northwest Apple Confections

This candy is very tasty, soft, and chewy. It makes a great homemade gift.

Ingredients:

2 Tbs. unflavored gelatin
½ c. cold water
5 apples, washed, unpeeled, cut into small pieces
¼ tsp. salt
2 c. sugar
1 Tbs. cornstarch
¾ c. walnuts, coarsely chopped
1 tsp. grated lemon peel
1 Tbs. lemon juice
   confectioners' sugar

Directions:

1. Soften gelatin in cold water; set aside.
2. Place prepared apples and salt into 2-quart heavy saucepan; cook until tender in just enough water to avoid scorching.
3. Remove from heat, cool to warm, and place in blender to purée.
4. Measure 2 cups of pulp back into saucepan; cook until thickened, stirring often.
5. Mix sugar and cornstarch together, and add to apple pulp; cook again over low heat, stirring constantly, until mixture is thick.
6. Add gelatin, then stir until gelatin dissolves and mixture again thickens.
7. Remove from heat; stir in walnuts, lemon peel, and juice.
8. Spoon into 12 x 9-inch glass dish that has been rinsed with cold water.
9. Let stand 24 hours.

10. Cut into rectangles, making about 30 to 40.
11. Roll in confectioners' sugar, and place on wire rack until outside is dry.
12. Store in covered container.

Yields: 30 to 40 candies.

Apple-Flavored Divinity

This is a wonderful, easy-to-make treat that is enjoyable for all. The delicious taste of apples is apparent with each bite.

Ingredients:

2   c. sugar
½   c. apple juice
1   pinch salt
1   pt. marshmallow cream
½   c. nuts
1   tsp. vanilla extract

Directions:

1. Combine sugar, juice, and salt in medium saucepan; boil until it forms hard ball in cold water (280 degrees F. on candy thermometer).
2. Place marshmallow cream in mixing bowl; gradually beat in hot syrup.
3. Continue beating until slightly stiff and will hold peaks.
4. Gently fold in nuts and vanilla.
5. Immediately drop by spoonfuls onto wax paper.
6. Let sit to dry, then store in airtight container.

Apple-Peanut Butter Fudge

This rich fudge is easy to make. It is so tasty, you may need to make a double batch.

Ingredients:

6   oz. semisweet chocolate pieces
½   jar marshmallow cream
½   c. peanut butter
1   tsp. vanilla extract
2   c. sugar
⅔   c. apple juice
    chopped peanuts (optional)

Directions:

1. In medium bowl mix semisweet chocolate pieces, marshmallow cream, peanut butter, and vanilla; set aside.
2. In buttered, heavy 2-quart saucepan, mix sugar and apple juice.
3. Cook and stir until sugar dissolves and mixture boils.
4. Cook to soft-ball stage or until candy thermometer registers 240 degrees F., stirring frequently.
5. Remove from heat; quickly add marshmallow mixture and stir until just blended.
6. Pour into buttered 9-inch square baking pan.
7. Top fudge with chopped peanuts1 if desired.
8. Cool and cut into squares.

Yields: 3 dozen 1½-inch pieces.

Coconut Apple Balls

This is a delicious candy that is almost like a cookie. Your family and friends will love the wonderful texture and flavors.

Ingredients:

8   oz. dried apples, chopped
3   eggs
½   c. sugar
¾   c. chopped walnuts
7½ oz. vanilla wafers, crushed
2   c. flaked coconut, divided

Directions:

1. Sprinkle small amount of water over chopped apples, and let stand in sealed container overnight.
2. Combine eggs and sugar; add soaked apples.
3. In nonstick skillet cook apple mixture over low heat for 10 minutes, stirring constantly.
4. Stir in nuts, vanilla wafer crumbs, and ½ of the coconut.
5. Shape mixture into small balls; roll balls in remaining coconut.
6. This candy tastes best after aging for a few days, so store in an airtight container.

Did You Know?....

Did you know that Newton Pippin apples were the first apples exported from America? In 1768 some were sent to Benjamin Franklin in London.

The Ultimate Caramel Apple

Both children and adults will love these homemade caramel apples. Decorate the apples lavishly for an extra-special dessert or edible holiday gift.

Ingredients:

   1 c. water
   1 c. sugar
   ½ c. heavy cream
   6 Red Delicious or Golden Delicious apples, whole
   3 oz. white chocolate
   3 oz. semisweet chocolate, finely chopped
   ¼ c. natural pistachios, coarsely chopped
      Styrofoam, 2 in. thick and 10 in. square
      ice cream sticks or small wooden dowels
      cinnamon or other small candies
      gold leaf (optional)

Directions:

1. Combine water and sugar in heavy saucepan; cook over low heat, stirring gently until sugar is completely dissolved.
2. Increase heat to medium, and cook without stirring until mixture is dark amber color.
3. Remove from heat and carefully stir in heavy cream; use caution as mixture will bubble up and spatter a bit then subside.
4. Set aside to cool and thicken.
5. Cover Styrofoam with wax paper to catch caramel drippings.
6. Insert sticks into bottom center of apples.
7. Dip top half of each apple into cooled caramel.
8. Insert bottom of sticks into Styrofoam, allowing apples to stand upright so caramel runs down sides of each apple.
9. Refrigerate to harden.

10. Meanwhile, melt white chocolate in top of double boiler above gently simmering water; stir until smooth.
11. Transfer melted chocolate to pastry bag fitted with small (#1) writing tip.
12. Remove apples from refrigerator and quickly drizzle thin, random strips of white chocolate over each caramel apple.
13. Repeat melting and drizzling with semi-sweet chocolate.
14. Decorate each apple with pistachios, cinnamon candies, and a few small pieces of gold leaf if desired.
15. Refrigerate until ready to serve.
16. For gift, place decorated apples in Styrofoam square, place square on cellophane, bring cellophane up over apples, and gather with ribbon.

Apple Nut Bark

Here is a delicious and simple candy that the kids can make or at least help make.

Ingredients:

    1 lb. white confectioners' coating (almond bark)
    1 c. dried apples, chopped
    1 c. walnuts or pecans, chopped coarse

Directions:

1. Line large cookie sheet with parchment paper.
2. Place white confectioners' coating (almond bark) in double boiler over medium heat; stir until melted.
3. Add apples and nuts; spread mixture out on lined sheet, and smooth evenly.
4. Cool, then break into 1½-inch pieces.
5. Store in airtight container.

Yields: 2 dozen pieces.

Old-Fashioned Candied Apple Slices

This recipe is an interesting twist on the normal candied apple. These slices are much easier to eat and bring back memories of old-fashioned candy stores.

Ingredients:

6   med. apples, cored, peeled
2   c. sugar
½   c. water
    sugar for coating

Directions:

1. Cut apples into ½-inch-thick rings.
2. In saucepan melt sugar in water; leave on simmer.
3. Drop a few apple slices at a time into syrup.
4. Simmer just until apples are translucent.
5. Drain on plate; spread out in single layer, and dry a few hours in preheated oven at 200 degrees F. until dried and leathery.
6. Let stand overnight, then roll in sugar until slices will hold no more sugar.
7. Place on serving dish when ready to serve. If transporting candied apple slices, pack in box lined with wax paper and between layers.

Did You Know? . . . .

Did you know that the world's largest apple peel was created by Kathy Wafler Madison on October 16, 1976, in Rochester, NY? It was 172 feet, 4 inches long. (She was 16 years old at the time and grew up to be a sales manager for an apple tree nursery.)

Apple Delights Cookbook

A Collection of Apple Recipes
Cookbook Delights Series

Cookies

Table of Contents

Page

Did You Know? . . .

Did you know that apples ripen six to ten times faster at room temperature than they do if refrigerated?

Apple Almond Squares

These easy-to-make bars are an excellent combination of apples and almonds. They are great for desserts, snacks, and sack lunches.

Ingredients:

½ c. butter, softened
1   c. sugar
3   eggs
2   c. graham cracker crumbs
½ c. all-purpose flour
2   tsp. baking powder
½ tsp. ground allspice
2   tsp. ground cinnamon
1   c. milk
2   c. tart apple, peeled, finely chopped
1   c. blanched almonds, chopped
    confectioners' sugar to taste

Directions:

1. Preheat oven to 350 degrees F.
2. Beat butter and sugar until creamy; add eggs one at a time, beating well after each addition.
3. Blend together crumbs, flour, baking powder, allspice, and cinnamon; stir into creamed mixture alternately with milk.
4. Fold in apples and almonds.
5. Spread batter in well-greased and floured 13 x 9 x 2-inch baking pan.
6. Bake for 35 minutes or until wooden pick inserted in center comes out clean.
7. Dust with confectioners' sugar just before serving.

Yields: 24 servings.

Apple Butter Cookies

This is a soft, moist cookie that is pleasingly rich with the taste of apples and molasses.

Ingredients:

- 1   c. apple butter (recipe page 230)
- ¼   c. butter, softened
- 3   Tbs. molasses
- ¾   c. light brown sugar, packed
- 2   egg whites
- 1½ c. all-purpose flour
- ¼   tsp. baking soda
- ¼   tsp. baking powder
- 1   tsp. ground cinnamon
- ½   tsp. ground allspice
- ¾   c. raisins

Directions:

1. Preheat oven to 350 degrees F.
2. Cream together apple butter, butter, molasses, and brown sugar.
3. Beat in egg whites, blending well.
4. Sift together flour, soda, baking powder, cinnamon, and allspice.
5. Using wooden spoon, mix dry ingredients with wet ingredients until well combined.
6. Stir in raisins.
7. Drop by rounded tablespoonfuls onto greased cookie sheet.
8. Bake for 20 minutes or until springy to the touch.
9. Remove from oven and cool on wire rack.

Yields: About 2 dozen.

Apple Chip Cookies

Completely scrumptious and delightful, these cookies are sure to become a favorite treat!

Ingredients for cookies:

- ¼ c. butter, softened
- 1 c. brown sugar, packed
- ½ c. half-and-half
- 1 egg
- ½ tsp. baking soda
- ¼ tsp. salt
- ½ tsp. ground nutmeg
- 2 c. all-purpose flour
- 1 c. apples, pared, chopped
- ½ c. butterscotch chips
- 1 c. pecans, chopped

Ingredients for glaze:

- 4 Tbs. butter, melted
- 1 tsp. ground cinnamon
- 4 Tbs. half-and-half
- 2 c. confectioners' sugar

Directions for cookies:

1. Preheat oven to 350 degrees F.
2. Cream butter and sugar.
3. Beat in half-and-half, egg, soda, salt, nutmeg, and flour; stir in apples, chips, and nuts.
4. Drop by teaspoonfuls onto greased cookie sheet.
5. Bake for 12 to 15 minutes, being careful not to overbake; cool on wire racks.

Directions for glaze:

1. Combine ingredients, blending until smooth.
2. Spread over cooled cookies.
3. Let air dry before storing in airtight containers.

Yields: 12 servings.

Apple Cranberry Nut Bars

These bars make a great snack that is packed with the goodness of oats, nuts, and fruit.

Ingredients:

- 1   c. all-purpose flour
- 1   c. quick oats
- ⅔   c. brown sugar, packed
- 2   tsp. baking soda
- ½   tsp. salt
- ½   tsp. ground cinnamon
- ⅔   c. buttermilk
- 3   Tbs. vegetable oil
- 2   lg. egg whites
- 1   apple, cored, chopped
- ½   c. dried cranberries
- ¼   c. chopped nuts
- 2   c. flaked coconut (optional)

Directions:

1. Preheat oven to 375 degrees F.
2. In large mixing bowl combine flour, oats, brown sugar, baking soda, salt, and cinnamon; stir to blend.
3. Add buttermilk, oil, and egg whites; beat just until blended.
4. Stir in apple, cranberries, and nuts.
5. If desired spread coconut in bottom of lightly greased, 9-inch square baking pan, then spread batter evenly over coconut; if not using coconut, just spread batter evenly in pan.
6. Bake for 20 to 25 minutes or until wooden pick inserted in center comes out clean.
7. Remove from oven, cool, and cut into bars.

Yields: 10 bars.

Apple Oat Sesame Cookies

Here is a wholesome, chewy cookie to serve at snack time or even for a quick breakfast on the run.

Ingredients:

- ¾ c. all-purpose flour
- ¾ c. whole-wheat flour
- ½ c. quick-cooking oats
- ¼ c. sesame seeds
- ¼ c. sugar
- 1 tsp. ground cinnamon
- 1 tsp. baking powder
- ½ tsp. baking soda
- ½ tsp. ground nutmeg
- ¼ tsp. salt
- 1½ c. finely chopped apples
- ½ c. honey
- ½ c. vegetable oil
- ⅓ c. milk
- 1 lg. egg
- ¾ c. raisins

Directions:

1. Preheat oven to 375 degrees F.
2. In large bowl mix both flours, oats, sesame seeds, sugar, cinnamon, baking powder, baking soda, nutmeg, and salt; stir in apples to coat.
3. In small bowl beat together honey, oil, milk, and egg; add to oat mixture and stir until blended well.
4. Fold in raisins.
5. Drop by tablespoonfuls onto greased cookie sheets.
6. Bake 10 to 12 minutes or until lightly browned.
7. Transfer cookies to wire rack and cool.

Yields: About 24 cookies.

Apple Raisin Bars

For those of you who love raisins, you will enjoy this moist apple-raisin combination in delicious bars.

Ingredients for bars:

- 1   c. all-purpose flour
- ⅔ c. sugar
- 1   tsp. soda
- ½ tsp. ground cinnamon
- ⅛ tsp. cloves
- ¼ tsp. ground nutmeg
- ¼ c. butter, softened
- 1   egg
- ¾ c. raisins
- 1   c. applesauce (recipe page 169)

Ingredients for frosting:

- 3   Tbs. butter
- 2   Tbs. milk
- 2¼ c. confectioners' sugar
- 1   tsp. vanilla extract

Directions for bars:

1. Preheat oven to 350 degrees F.
2. Sift together flour, sugar, soda, and spices.
3. Add butter, egg, raisins, and applesauce; beat 2 minutes.
4. Spread in greased 13 x 9 x 2-inch baking pan.
5. Bake 25 to 30 minutes or until center springs back to touch.
6. Remove from oven, and place on wire rack to cool.

Directions for frosting:

1. Melt butter in pan until browned.
2. Stir in milk, confectioners' sugar, and vanilla, beating until smooth. (May add small amount more of milk if needed.)
3. Frost cooled bars, and cut into 24 pieces to serve.

Yields: 24 servings.

Apple Tart Cookies

These cookies are made in the shape of small tarts and have an interesting combination of ingredients you are sure to enjoy.

Ingredients:

- 1½ c. butter, room temperature
- ⅓ c. peanut butter
- 1½ c. brown sugar, packed
- 1½ c. sugar
- 4 eggs
- 2 tsp. almond extract
- 2 c. all-purpose flour
- ½ c. whole-wheat flour
- 4½ c. quick-cooking oatmeal
- ½ tsp. salt
- 1 tsp. baking powder
- 1 c. raisins
- 1 c. shredded coconut
- 1 c. pecans, chopped
- 1 pkg. soft dried apples, chopped

Directions:

1. Mix peanut butter and butter, then add sugars and cream well.
2. Crack eggs into separate bowl, add almond extract, and whip slightly; add to creamed mixture.
3. In separate bowl mix together flours, oatmeal, salt, and baking powder.
4. Mix together dry and wet ingredients until well blended.
5. Mix together raisins, coconut, nuts, and apples; fold into batter. (Dough should be stiff.)
6. Chill mixture for 1 hour.
7. Preheat oven to 350 degrees F.
8. Shape cookies using a ¼ measuring cup, packing cookie mixture in cup.

9. Drop out of cup onto greased cookie sheet, 2 inches apart.
10. Bake for 18 to 20 minutes or until light brown on tops.
11. Remove from oven, let stand 5 minutes, then transfer to wire rack to cool.

Yields: About 44 cookies.

Apple Nut Bars

These are chewy, tasty apple nut bars that will make your mouth water for more.

Ingredients:

2   egg whites
⅔   c. sugar
½   tsp. vanilla extract
½   c. all-purpose flour
1   tsp. baking powder
2   c. apples, peeled, cored, chopped
½   c. pecans, chopped

Directions:

1. Preheat oven to 350 degrees F.
2. In medium bowl whisk egg whites, sugar, and vanilla for about 2 minutes.
3. Add flour and baking powder; whisk for 1 minute.
4. Fold in apples and pecans.
5. Spread batter into greased 8-inch square baking pan coated with nonstick cooking spray.
6. Bake 25 to 30 minutes or until bars are firm when lightly pressed with finger.
7. Remove from oven; let stand 10 minutes on wire rack before cutting into squares to serve.

Yields: 1 dozen.

Brandied Apple Bars

This makes a delicious bar that is so easy to pack up for a summer picnic or potluck party, where they will hit the spot for sure!

Ingredients:

½   c. butter, softened
¼   c. sugar
1⅓ c. all-purpose flour, divided
2   eggs
1   c. brown sugar, firmly packed
⅓   c. brandy
½   tsp. baking powder
¼   tsp. salt
½   c. walnuts, chopped
3   lg. fresh apples, peeled, cored, chopped fine

Directions:

1. Preheat oven to 350 degrees F.
2. In large mixing bowl cream together butter and sugar until smooth; mix in 1 cup flour, blending well.
3. Spread crust into bottom of greased 9 x 9-inch baking pan.
4. Bake for 15 minutes, until firm.
5. In separate bowl beat eggs and brown sugar together until thick and pale.
6. Add brandy, blending in completely.
7. Combine remaining ⅓ cup flour, baking powder, and salt; stir into egg mixture.
8. Mix in walnuts and apples; spread over hot crust.
9. Bake for 30 minutes or until filling is set.
10. Remove from oven, and place on wire rack to cool completely before cutting into squares.
11. Store up to 4 weeks in airtight container.

Yields: 36 bars.

Caramel Apple Bars

Indulge yourself with these bars that are sweet and buttery with a gooey, crunchy middle.

Ingredients:

- 1¼ c. all-purpose flour, divided
- ¼ c. brown sugar, firmly packed
- ½ c. butter, softened
- ½ c. sugar
- 2 lg. eggs, beaten
- 1 tsp. vanilla extract
- 2 apples, cored, chopped
- 1 c. caramel candies, each cut in quarters
- ½ c. chopped walnuts or pecans

Directions:

1. Preheat oven to 350 degrees F.
2. In medium bowl combine 1 cup flour and brown sugar.
3. Cut in butter until mixture resembles coarse crumbs; reserve ½ cup for topping.
4. Transfer remaining mixture to lightly greased 9-inch square pan, and press into bottom of pan.
5. Bake for 10 minutes.
6. In same mixing bowl combine sugar, eggs, vanilla, and remaining ¼ cup flour; fold in apples, caramels, and nuts.
7. Spread mixture over bottom crust, and sprinkle reserved crumb mixture over top.
8. Return to oven, and bake 30 to 35 minutes or until golden; remove and cool slightly on wire rack.
9. Cut into rectangular bars of desired size.

Yields: 16 bars.

Golden Apple Oatmeal Bars

These apple bars are special with oatmeal topping. They could quickly become a favorite for everyone.

Ingredients for bars:

1   c. old-fashioned oats
1¼ c. all-purpose flour, divided
½   c. brown sugar, packed
½   tsp. baking powder
1   c. butter, softened
1   egg, beaten
4   Golden Delicious apples, pared, cored, sliced
     into 16ths
½   c. sugar
¼   tsp. ground nutmeg

Ingredients for topping:

⅓   c. rolled oats
⅓   c. all-purpose flour
⅓   c. sugar
¼   c. butter, softened

Directions for bars:

1. Preheat oven to 350 degrees F.
2. Combine oats, 1 cup flour, brown sugar, and baking powder, blending well.
3. Cut in butter until crumbly.
4. Stir in beaten egg.
5. Spread mixture into 15 x 10 x 1-inch pan.
6. Gently toss apples with sugar, remaining ¼ cup flour, and nutmeg.
7. Arrange on crust; sprinkle with topping.

Directions for topping:

1. Combine rolled oats, flour, and sugar.
2. Cut in butter until crumbly.
3. Sprinkle crumb topping over top of apples.
4. Bake for 30 to 35 minutes or until apples are tender.
5. Remove from oven and cool on wire rack before cutting into bars or squares.

Yields: 40 to 48 bars.

No-Bake Apple Cookies

Our children enjoy helping to make these no-bake cookies that are full of grated apples and so healthy.

Ingredients:

½   c. butter
2   c. sugar
2   Tbs. all-purpose flour
1   c. grated apple
3¼ c. old-fashioned oats
1   c. nuts, chopped
2   tsp. vanilla extract
    cinnamon and sugar
    confectioners' sugar
    finely ground nuts

Directions:

1. Melt butter in saucepan; add sugar, flour, and apple.
2. Bring to a boil and boil 1 minute.
3. Remove from heat; add oats, nuts, and vanilla, blending well.
4. Drop by heaping teaspoonfuls onto wax paper.
5. When cool, roll in nuts, cinnamon and sugar, or confectioners' sugar.

Yields: About 6 dozen.

Sour Cream Apple Squares

The sour cream adds to the flavor of these apple bars that are extremely tasty.

Ingredients:

2½ c. apples, peeled, cored, finely chopped
3   Tbs. lemon juice, fresh
2   c. all-purpose flour
2   c. brown sugar, packed
½   c. butter, softened
1   c. pecans or walnuts, chopped
1½ tsp. ground cinnamon
1   tsp. baking soda
1   c. sour cream
2   tsp. vanilla extract
1   egg

Directions:

1. Preheat oven to 350 degrees F.
2. Sprinkle chopped apples with lemon juice; set aside.
3. Combine flour, sugar, and butter; mix until crumbly.
4. Add nuts and mix.
5. Press 2¾ cup of this mixture into greased and floured 13 x 9 x 2-inch pan.
6. To remaining crumb mixture add cinnamon, baking soda, sour cream, vanilla, and egg; blend well using hand mixer.
7. Fold in apples; spoon mixture evenly over crust.
8. Bake for 30 to 35 minutes or until wooden pick inserted in center comes out clean
9. Cool in pan on wire rack before cutting.

Yields: 12 to 16 servings.

Apple Delights Cookbook

A Collection of Apple Recipes
Cookbook Delights Series

Desserts

Table of Contents

Page

Did You Know? . . .

Did you know that cider apples are generally too tart and acerbic to eat fresh? But they give cider a rich flavor that dessert apples cannot.

Apple Blanc Mange

This great desert is made with applesauce. It is delicious when chilled.

Ingredients:

- 2 c. milk
- 2 Tbs. sugar
- ¼ tsp. salt
- 1 lemon rind
- 2½ Tbs. cornstarch
- 1 c. applesauce (recipe page 169)

Directions:

1. Heat milk, sugar, salt, and lemon rind to scalding.
2. Add cornstarch dissolved in a little cold milk; cook 10 minutes.
3. Remove lemon rind and add mixture to applesauce, stirring well.
4. Place in mold and chill.
5. Serve with cream.

Yields: 5 servings.

Apple Ice

In Italy this refreshing, naturally-flavored ice is called "granita." It is often served after a rich meal or in the middle of a hot day. This ice makes a great dessert.

Ingredients:

- 6 c. Granny Smith apples, peeled, sliced
- 1 c. water
- ¾ c. sugar
- ½ tsp. finely grated lemon zest

Directions:

1. In large saucepan simmer apples, water, and sugar until apples are tender, about 20 minutes.
2. In food processor or blender, purée mixture until smooth; stir in lemon zest.
3. Transfer mixture to 8- or 9-inch metal pan; freeze until almost solid.
4. Return to food processor or blender, and purée until chunks break up and mixture is fluffy.
5. Refreeze until firm.

Apple Cream Soufflé

These delicious cold soufflés make a refreshing summer treat to enjoy with your family.

Ingredients:

½ c. butter, softened
¼ c. sugar
3 eggs, slightly beaten
1 c. cream
2 c. applesauce (recipe page 169)
½ tsp. ground cinnamon

Directions:

1. Preheat oven to 350 degrees F.
2. Cream together butter and sugar.
3. Add eggs, cream, applesauce, and cinnamon.
4. Pour mixture into individual buttered cups or ramekins.
5. Bake for 30 minutes.
6. Remove from oven and cool; refrigerate until ready to serve.
7. Serve cold, and garnish with apple slices if desired.

Yields: 6 servings.

Apple Cheese Crisp

Cheddar cheese is always a nice combination with apples. This recipe makes a flavorful apple crisp with the unique addition of melted cheese on top.

Ingredients:

6   med. apples, peeled, cored, sliced
1   tsp. ground cinnamon
1   tsp. lemon juice
¾   c. all-purpose flour
1   c. rolled oats
¾   c. brown sugar, firmly packed
½   c. butter, softened
¾   c. cheddar cheese, shredded

Directions:

1. Preheat oven to 375 degrees F.
2. Place apples in ungreased 2-quart casserole dish.
3. Sprinkle with cinnamon and lemon juice.
4. In medium bowl combine flour, rolled oats, and brown sugar.
5. Using pastry blender or fork, cut in butter until crumbly.
6. Sprinkle crumb mixture evenly over apples.
7. Bake for 25 to 35 minutes or until apples are tender.
8. Remove from oven and top with cheese; bake an additional 2 to 3 minutes or until cheese melts.
9. Cool to lukewarm and serve.

Yields: 8 servings.

Did You Know? . . . .

Did you know that it takes about 36 apples to make one gallon of apple cider?

Apple, Cranberry, and Pear Crisp

This variation of the traditional apple crisp uses pears for half of the apples with cranberries and toasted hazelnuts adding even more flavor to this delicious dessert.

Ingredients:

2   fresh apples, peeled, cored, cubed
2   fresh pears, peeled, cored, cubed
½   c. dried cranberries
½   c. plus 1 Tbs. all-purpose flour, divided
2   Tbs. honey
1½ Tbs. lemon juice
½   c. brown sugar, firmly packed
½   c. quick-cooking oats
¼   c. toasted hazelnuts, ground
½   c. butter, cut into pieces

Directions:

1. Preheat oven to 375 degrees F.
2. Lightly grease 8-inch baking dish.
3. Mix apples, pears, cranberries, 1 tablespoon flour, honey, and lemon juice in prepared dish.
4. In small bowl mix ½ cup flour, brown sugar, oats, nuts, and butter to consistency of coarse crumbs.
5. Sprinkle crumb mixture loosely over fruit in baking dish.
6. Bake for 45 minutes or until brown and crisp on top.
7. Remove from oven, and cool in pan on wire rack before serving.

Yields: 12 servings.

Apple Danish Cheesecake

This is a dessert that is light and elegant enough to serve as part of your brunch get-together with friends.

Ingredients for crust:

> 1 c. all-purpose flour
> ½ c. ground almonds
> ¼ c. sugar, divided
> ½ c. butter, chilled
> ¼ tsp. almond extract

Ingredients for filling:

> 8 oz. cream cheese, softened
> ¼ c. sugar
> ¼ tsp. cream of tartar
> 1 egg

Ingredients for topping:

> ⅓ c. brown sugar, firmly packed
> 1 Tbs. all-purpose flour
> 1 tsp. ground cinnamon
> 4 c. thinly sliced apples
> ⅓ c. blanched slivered almonds

Directions for crust:

1. In small bowl combine flour, ground almonds, and sugar; cut in butter and almond extract until crumbly.
2. Shape dough into ball; gently press dough against bottom and up sides of 9-inch springform or cake pan.
3. Refrigerate for 30 minutes.

Directions for filling:

1. Preheat oven to 350 degrees F.
2. In medium bowl, beat cream cheese, sugar, and cream of tartar until smooth.
3. Add egg; beat on low just until combined.
4. Pour into unbaked crust.

Directions for topping and assembly:

1. In medium bowl combine brown sugar, flour, and cinnamon; add apples and stir until coated.
2. Spoon over filling; sprinkle top with slivered almonds.
3. Bake 40 to 45 minutes or until golden brown.
4. Remove from oven, and cool on wire rack for 10 minutes; carefully run knife around edge of pan to loosen, and cool 1 hour longer.
5. Refrigerate overnight; remove from pan to serve.

Yields: 8 servings.

Sweetened Whipped Cream

There is nothing as rich and delicious as sweetened whipped cream.

Ingredients:

1 c. heavy cream
¼ c. sugar
1 tsp. vanilla extract

Directions:

1. Whip cream until almost stiff.
2. Add sugar and vanilla; beat until cream holds peaks.
3. Spread over top of cooled pie or dollop on bread pudding, gingerbread, cobblers, or other desserts.

Apple Huckleberry Crisp

This crisp is a flavorful blend of huckleberries and apples. It is delicious served warm with whipped cream or with ice cream.

Ingredients for filling:

5 med. Granny Smith apples, peeled, cored, sliced
1 Tbs. lemon juice
½ tsp. ground cinnamon
1 c. sugar
½ c. frozen huckleberries

Ingredients for topping:

1¼ c. rolled oats
⅓ c. unbleached, all-purpose flour
¼ c. brown sugar, firmly packed
4 tsp. canola oil
½ tsp. ground cinnamon
1 tsp. orange juice

Directions for filling:

1. Preheat oven to 375 degrees F.
2. Lightly oil 9½ x 11-inch baking dish.
3. Mix apples with lemon juice, cinnamon, and sugar.
4. Press into baking dish; sprinkle frozen berries on top.

Directions for topping:

1. Mix topping ingredients together, and sprinkle over filling.
2. Bake for 30 minutes, until crumbs are lightly browned.
3. Test apples with fork for tenderness.

Apple Indian Pudding

This dessert recipe has been passed through generations of our family, and your family is sure to enjoy it as well.

Ingredients:

- 3   c. milk
- ½   c. cornmeal
- 1½ tsp. ground cinnamon
- 1½ c. brown sugar
- 2½ c. milk, cold
- 3   Tbs. butter
- 4   c. sweet apples, cored, cut in eighths

Directions:

1. Preheat oven to 300 degrees F.
2. In saucepan over medium heat, scald 3 cups milk; sift in cornmeal, stirring rapidly, and cook 5 minutes.
3. Remove from heat; add cinnamon, sugar, cold milk, butter, and apples.
4. Pour mixture into large, deep covered casserole dish.
5. Bake for 4 hours or until wooden pick inserted in center comes out clean.
6. Remove from oven, and cool in dish before serving.

Yields: 8 to 12 servings.

Did You Know? . . . .

Did you know that the apple is the best-known example of a pome? Some other examples of plants that produce fruit classified as a pome are cotoneaster, hawthorn, pear, quince, rowan, and whitebeam.

Apple Pudding

This is a very moist apple pudding recipe. It is good served warm or cold.

Ingredients:

1	c. all-purpose flour
1	tsp. baking powder
1	c. plus 3 Tbs. sugar, divided
2	eggs, well beaten
6	lg. apples, cored, sliced
1½	tsp. ground cinnamon
1	tsp. ground nutmeg
3	Tbs. butter
¼	c. water

Directions:

1. Preheat oven to 350 degrees F.
2. Sift together flour and baking powder.
3. Add 1 cup sugar to beaten eggs, blending well, then combine with flour mixture.
4. Place apples in greased, deep baking dish; cover with flour and egg mixture.
5. Combine remaining 3 tablespoons sugar, cinnamon, and nutmeg; sprinkle over flour mixture.
6. Dot with butter and sprinkle with the water.
7. Bake for 40 minutes.
8. Remove from oven and cool to lukewarm to serve.

Yields: 8 to 10 servings.

Did You Know? . . . .

Did you know that more than 7,500 varieties of apples are grown worldwide?

Apple Walnut Cobbler

Here is another tasty cobbler to take to a potluck. The walnuts add a distinctly different flavor. This cobbler is also good served cold for a breakfast treat.

Ingredients:

8   c. tart apples, peeled, cored, thinly sliced
1   c. brown sugar, firmly packed
1½ tsp. ground cinnamon
1½ c. walnuts, coarsely chopped, divided
2   eggs, beaten
¾   c. milk
⅓   c. butter, melted
2   c. all-purpose flour
2   c. sugar
2   tsp. baking soda
    Sweetened Whipped Cream (recipe page 155)

Directions:

1. Preheat oven to 325 degrees F.
2. Place apples in bottom of greased 13 x 9 x 2-inch baking dish.
3. Mix together brown sugar, cinnamon, and 1 cup walnuts; sprinkle over apples.
4. In large bowl combine egg, milk, and butter.
5. In another bowl sift together flour, sugar, and baking soda; add to egg mixture all at once and blend until smooth.
6. Pour over apples; sprinkle with remaining walnuts.
7. Bake about 50 minutes or until done.
8. Serve warm with whipped cream and a shake of cinnamon on top.

Yields: 24 servings.

Bread Pudding

This old-fashioned family recipe is a favorite of my husband.

Ingredients:

3   c. applesauce (recipe page 169)
1   tsp. lemon juice
5   slices whole-wheat raisin bread
3   Tbs. butter
¼   c. marmalade
1½ tsp. ground cinnamon
2   Tbs. sugar

Directions:

1. Preheat oven to 350 degrees F.
2. Combine applesauce and lemon juice; place half of mixture in small casserole dish.
3. Spread bread sides with butter and marmalade.
4. Cut 4 slices into cubes; cut remaining slice in 4 triangles.
5. Place cubes on applesauce in casserole.
6. Combine cinnamon and sugar; sprinkle half over cubes and top with remaining applesauce.
7. Arrange bread triangles in pattern on top casserole; sprinkle with remaining cinnamon and sugar.
8. Bake for 30 minutes.

Yields: 6 servings.

Did You Know? . . . .

Did you know that the top apple producing states include Washington, New York, Michigan, Pennsylvania, California, and Virginia?

Deep Apple Pudding with Sauce

This tasty apple pudding is especially flavorful with the warm sauce.

Ingredients for pudding:

½   c. brown sugar, firmly packed
5   apples, peeled, cored, sliced
⅔   c. sugar
1   egg
½   c. milk
1¾ c. all-purpose flour
3   tsp. baking powder

Ingredients for sauce:

3   Tbs. butter
3   Tbs. all-purpose flour
½   c. brown sugar, firmly packed
1   c. water
½   tsp. vanilla extract

Directions for pudding:

1. Preheat oven to 350 degrees F.
2. Spread brown sugar in greased 13 x 9 x 2-inch pan.
3. Place apples over brown sugar.
4. Beat together sugar, egg, and milk.
5. Stir in flour and baking powder; pour over apples.
6. Bake for 30 minutes or just until apples are cooked.
7. Remove from oven, and place on wire rack to cool while making sauce.

Directions for sauce:

1. Melt butter in saucepan over medium heat.
2. Add flour and brown sugar.
3. Gradually add water and stir continually until thickened.
4. Remove from heat and add vanilla.
5. Pour sauce over top of warm pudding before serving.

Yields: 12 to 14 servings.

Special Apple Pudding

This is an easy-to-make dessert that your children will enjoy. Try different molds for special occasions.

Ingredients:

    6 med. apples, peeled, cored, thinly sliced
    1 c. butter
    1 c. sugar

Directions:

1. Preheat oven to 300 degrees F.
2. Place layer of apple slices in greased, deep glass baking dish; sprinkle liberally with sugar, and add another layer of apple slices.
3. Repeat until all apples and sugar are used.
4. Top layer should be of sugar, dotted with butter.
5. Cover and bake for 2 hours.
6. Remove from oven and cool on wire rack.
7. Place in refrigerator to chill; turn out onto serving dish if desired.
8. When cold, pudding will turn out like a jelly mold and is ready to serve.

Yields: 6 to 8 servings.

Did You Know? . . . .

Did you know that in 2005 the average U.S. consumer ate 46.1 pounds of fresh apples and processed apple products—down from 50.6 pounds in 2004?

Swedish Apple Dessert

This is an easy Swedish dessert, made with your favorite apples.

Ingredients:

6 c. apples, peeled, cored, sliced
2 Tbs. sugar
1 tsp. ground cinnamon
1 egg, beaten well
1 c. all-purpose flour
¾ c. melted butter
1 c. brown sugar, firmly packed
¼ c. pecans or walnuts

Directions:

1. Preheat oven to 350 degrees F.
2. Butter 9-inch square baking pan.
3. Place apples in pan; mix sugar and cinnamon together, and sprinkle over top.
4. Combine beaten egg, flour, melted butter, brown sugar, and nuts; pour over apples.
5. Bake for 45 minutes or until apples are soft when knife is inserted.
6. Remove from oven, and place on wire rack to cool before cutting into squares to serve.

Yields: 10 to 12 servings.

Did You Know? . . . .

Did you know that Apple Day, an annual celebration in England, was held for the first time on October 21, 1990, in Covent Garden, London?

Apple Bake Dessert

This is a simple dessert to make when you are in a hurry. Even though it is quick and easy, it will still impress your guests.

Ingredients:

- 1 egg
- ¾ c. sugar
- ½ c. all-purpose flour
- 1½ tsp. baking powder
- ½ tsp. ground cinnamon
- ½ tsp. ground nutmeg
- 1½ c. apples, chopped
  Sweetened Whipped Cream (recipe page 155) or ice cream

Directions:

1. Preheat oven to 350 degrees F.
2. Cream egg and sugar until light.
3. Mix together flour, baking powder, cinnamon, and nutmeg.
4. Fold in apples.
5. Spread in greased 9-inch pie pan.
6. Bake for 30 minutes or until apples are soft when wooden pick is inserted in middle.
7. Remove from oven; cool on wire rack.
8. Exceptionally delicious served warm with whipped cream or ice cream.

Apple Delights Cookbook

A Collection of Apple Recipes
Cookbook Delights Series

Dressings, Sauces, and Condiments

Table of Contents

Page

Apple and Onion Condiment

This is both an old and unusual condiment to serve with meats, pasta, or even hamburgers.

Ingredients:

½ c. sugar
½ c. distilled white vinegar
3 tart apples, peeled, cored, julienned
⅔ c. chopped onion
½ c. chopped dill pickle

Directions:

1. In small bowl combine sugar and vinegar.
2. In medium bowl mix together apples, onion, and pickle; toss with vinegar mixture.
3. Refrigerate until thoroughly chilled.

Apple Basil Dressing

This dressing has only one teaspoon of fat. Being a little unusual in texture, it is recommended for a coleslaw- type salad.

Ingredients:

4 Tbs. rice vinegar
4 Tbs. fresh basil, minced
2 Tbs. lemon juice
1 Tbs. gingerroot, minced
1 c. unsweetened applesauce
1 Tbs. brown sugar
1 tsp. chili sauce
1 tsp. toasted sesame oil
   salt and pepper to taste

Directions:

1. Combine vinegar, basil, lemon juice, and gingerroot until well blended.
2. Add applesauce, brown sugar, chili sauce, and sesame oil; blend well.
3. Salt and pepper to taste.
4. Chill until ready to serve.

Apple Cranberry Salad Dressing

This is a delicious dressing over greens or just fruits. The whole family will enjoy it.

Ingredients:

1   fresh apple, unpeeled, cored, chopped fine
½ c. whole-berry cranberry sauce
¼ c. apple wine vinegar
1   c. mayonnaise
⅛ tsp. ground nutmeg
2   Tbs. sugar
¼ c. light olive oil

Directions:

1. Place chopped apple, cranberry sauce, and vinegar in medium bowl; let marinate 1 hour.
2. Place mixture in blender, and combine with mayonnaise and nutmeg; whisk several times.
3. Add sugar and olive oil; blend until smooth.
4. Add small amount of additional vinegar if too thick for desired consistency.
5. May be kept in refrigerator, covered, for up to 1 week.

Yields: 2½ cups dressing.

Apple Maple Topping

Try this simple topping on pancakes, waffles, or ice cream.

Ingredients:

¾ c. applesauce (recipe page 169)
¼ c. maple syrup

Directions:

1. Heat ingredients in pan over low heat until hot.

Yields: 1 cup.

Apple Avocado Salsa

Try this salsa with beef, pork, or chicken.

Ingredients:

2 apples, unpeeled, cored, diced
½ ripe avocado, peeled, diced
1 Tbs. diced green onion, including top
1 tsp. chopped fresh cilantro leaves
1 tsp. sugar
1 tsp. fresh lime juice
½ tsp. minced jalapeño pepper
¼ tsp. minced garlic
1 dash pepper

Directions:

1. Mix all ingredients together thoroughly.

Yields: 2½ cups.

Applesauce

Our children love the tastier homemade applesauce and eat a lot of it. The different spices make this recipe delicious and unique.

Ingredients:

- 3 lb. apples, peeled, cored, cubed
- 2 Tbs. lemon juice
- ¾ c. apple cider
- 5 Tbs. butter
- 3 cinnamon sticks
- 2 tsp. ground nutmeg
- 4 Tbs. sugar

Directions:

1. Place apples in bowl and add lemon juice.
2. In large stock pot combine cider and butter, mixing together well.
3. Allow to come to slow boil over medium-low heat.
4. Add apples and stir continuously.
5. Increase heat to medium; add spices and sugar and bring to a boil.
6. Reduce heat and simmer for 20 to 30 minutes, stirring to avoid scorching or solidifying the apples.
7. Remove from heat and remove cinnamon sticks; whisk to make smooth.
8. Cool or serve warm; add a shake of cinnamon or nutmeg over the top of each serving dish if desired.

Did You Know? . . . .

Did you know that apples are grown in every state in the continental United States, but they are grown commercially in 36 states?

Apple, Raisin, and Nut Chutney

This is one of those delicious chutneys that is hard to find.
It goes well with hot meals or just snacks and appetizers.

Ingredients:

12 cloves garlic
1   piece gingerroot (4-in. length), chopped
2½ c. cider vinegar, divided
4½ c. brown sugar, firmly packed
1   c. chopped onion
8   fresh apples, peeled, cored, cubed in 1-in. pieces
1   c. raisins
1   c. walnuts, coarsely chopped
1   Tbs. cayenne pepper
1   Tbs. paprika
1   Tbs. dry mustard
1½ tsp. salt

Directions:

1. Purée garlic and ginger with 1 cup vinegar in blender; transfer to 6-quart nonreactive saucepan.
2. Mix in brown sugar, onion, and remainder of vinegar; boil until sugar dissolves.
3. Reduce heat until thickened; add remaining ingredients and cook until mixture resembles thick jam, stirring occasionally, about 1 hour.
4. If sealed in regular containers and not boiled in jars, chutney will keep for 6 months refrigerated.
5. Serve with any meats or main dishes or as an appetizer side dish.

Apple Salad Dressing

This is another dressing that can be used for green or fruit salads. It can also be used as a glaze over meats.

Ingredients:

- 1   med. apple, peeled, cored, chopped fine
- 2   Tbs. fresh lemon juice
- 1   egg
- 4   Tbs. cornstarch
- ½ c. sugar
- ½ c. pecans, crushed well
- 1   c. crushed pineapple, drained
- ½ c. currants or raisins, chopped fine
- ½ c. celery, chopped fine
-     yellow food coloring
-     mayonnaise

Directions:

1. Combine apple with lemon juice and set aside.
2. Combine egg, cornstarch, sugar, and yellow food coloring; cook until thickened.
3. Cool, then add desired amount of mayonnaise to make a thick creamy dressing.
4. Add apple mixture, nuts, crushed pineapple, currants or raisins, and celery; blend well.
5. Use pineapple juice to thin dressing if necessary.

Did You Know? . . . .

Did you know that apples account for 50 percent of the world's deciduous fruit tree production?

Red Onion and Cider Vinaigrette

This vinaigrette is excellent over Romaine lettuce topped with chopped apples and toasted pecans. Make sure to use a good grade of vinegar for the best flavor.

Ingredients:

1¼ c. vegetable oil
⅓   c. apple cider vinegar
3   Tbs. frozen apple juice concentrate, thawed
2   Tbs. minced red onion
1¾ tsp. salt
½   tsp. ground nutmeg
½   tsp. ground ginger
¼   tsp. ground black pepper

Directions:

1. Whisk all ingredients together in small bowl.
2. Can be made 1 day ahead; refrigerate.
3. Whisk before using.

Apple Banana Sauce

This simple combination of apples and bananas served warm over ice cream is a real treat.

Ingredients:

1   c. water
5   sm. red apples, peeled, cored, quartered
1   tsp. ground nutmeg
1½ tsp. ground cinnamon
1   lg. banana, chopped

Directions:

1. Bring water to a boil in saucepan.
2. Add apples, spices, and banana; reduce heat, and simmer 5 minutes or until apples become mushy.
3. Remove from heat, and mash ingredients together until well mixed but chunky.
4. Serve warm over vanilla ice cream, or chill 1 hour and serve plain.

Apple and Poppy Seed Dressing

This is a flavorful autumn salad dressing.

Ingredients:

1 sm. fresh apple, peeled, cored, chopped fine
½ c. plus 2 Tbs. fresh lemon juice, divided
½ c. sugar
2 tsp. diced onion
1 tsp. Dijon-style prepared mustard
½ tsp. salt
⅔ c. olive oil
1 Tbs. poppy seeds

Directions:

1. Combine apples and 2 tablespoons lemon juice in small bowl; set aside.
2. In blender or food processor, combine sugar, remaining ½ cup lemon juice, onion, mustard, and salt; process until well blended.
3. With machine still running, add oil in slow, steady stream until mixture is thick and smooth.
4. Add apple mixture and poppy seeds; process just a few seconds more to mix.
5. Chill until ready to serve.

Asian Ginger Apple Dressing

This is one of those elegant dressings that you will enjoy serving for company or a special dinner.

Ingredients:

1	sm. fresh apple, peeled, cored, chopped fine
2	Tbs. fresh lemon juice
1	tsp. lemon zest
3	cloves garlic, minced
2	Tbs. minced fresh gingerroot
¾	c. olive oil
⅓	c. rice vinegar
½	c. soy sauce
¼	c. water
3	Tbs. honey

Directions:

1. Combine chopped apple with lemon juice and lemon zest; set aside.
2. In large glass jar or shaker, combine garlic, ginger, olive oil, rice vinegar, soy sauce, and water.
3. Cover jar with tight-fitting lid; shake well.
4. Remove lid and add apple mixture and honey; shake just enough to dissolve honey.
5. Place in refrigerator to chill; shake again before serving.
6. Store, covered, in refrigerator.

Did You Know? . . . .

Did you know that in 2005, apples trailed only oranges and grapes in the number of acres committed to fruit production?

Melon Apple Chutney

This recipe makes more chutney than you will need for the ham and cornbread rounds appetizer. Use the leftovers as a condiment for cheese and crackers or for roasted meats. You can substitute mangos for the melon in this recipe.

Ingredients:

- 1   piece cinnamon stick (1½-in. length)
- 2   whole cloves
- 5   whole allspice
- ¾   c. cantaloupe or honeydew, cut into ¼-in. dice, or a combination of both
- 1   Granny Smith apple, peeled, cut into ¼-in. dice
- ½   c. sugar
- ¼   c. plus 2 Tbs. distilled white vinegar
- 3   Tbs. dried currants
- 2   Tbs. minced, peeled fresh gingerroot
- 1   pinch salt

Directions:

1. Wrap cinnamon stick, cloves, and allspice in cheesecloth, and tie with string to form bag.
2. Crush spices gently in bag with rolling pin or bottom of heavy skillet.
3. Bring melon, apple, sugar, vinegar, currants, ginger, cheesecloth bag, and pinch of salt to a boil in 1- to 1½-quart heavy saucepan.
4. Reduce heat and simmer uncovered, stirring occasionally, until syrup is thick and most of liquid is evaporated, 30 to 35 minutes.
5. Discard cheesecloth bag and cool chutney. (Syrup will continue to thicken as it cools.)
6. Chutney can be made 2 days ahead and chilled, covered; bring to room temperature before using.

Yields: 1 cup.

Ranch Spicy Apple Dip or Dressing

This is a versatile and easily-made dressing that is delicious with almost anything, so do not just stop at salads, try it with your main dishes, meats, and appetizers.

Ingredients:

> 1 c. prepared ranch dressing
> 1 c. grated or chopped tart apples
> 1 Tbs. horseradish
> 1 tsp. lemon juice
> ½ tsp. pumpkin or apple pie spice

Directions:

> 1. Combine ranch dressing, chopped apples, and horseradish in small bowl; blend well.
> 2. Stir in lemon juice and spice; cover and chill at least 1 hour.
> 3. When ready to serve, spoon into serving bowl.

Yields: 2 cups.

Apple Slaw Dressing

This is a light dressing that the whole family will enjoy. It is nice to serve for company as well.

Ingredients:

> ½ c. sugar
> 1   tsp. dry mustard
> 1   tsp. salt
> 4½ Tbs. apple cider vinegar, divided
> 2   tsp. grated onion
> 1   c. light olive oil
> 1   Tbs. celery seed

Directions:

1. With electric mixer combine sugar, mustard, and salt.
2. Blend in 2 tablespoons cider vinegar and grated onion.
3. Gradually beat in olive oil; beat until thick and light.
4. Slowly beat in remaining vinegar; stir in celery seed.
5. Pour into shaker jar or jar with lid, and shake vigorously to blend well.
6. Store covered in refrigerator; shake well before using.

Apple Soy Marinade

This makes a delicious marinade for beef brisket or a juicy roast.

Ingredients:

2½ c. apple juice
½ c. soy sauce
¼ c. vegetable oil
3 bay leaves
2 cloves garlic, minced
1 lg. onion, chopped
½ tsp. ground ginger
¼ tsp. freshly ground black pepper

Directions:

1. Combine all ingredients.
2. Add meat and chill 12 to 24 hours before cooking.

Yields: Enough for 4- to 5-pound roast or brisket.

Tequila, Apple, and Dried Cranberry Compote

Make this compote a day ahead so the flavors can meld. Warm the leftovers, and serve over vanilla ice cream or on French toast.

Ingredients:

3 lb. Granny Smith apples (about 8 med.), peeled, cored, cut into ½-in. pieces
2¼ c. apple cider
1¾ c. dried cranberries
¾ c. tequila
½ c. sugar
1 cinnamon stick
¾ tsp. freshly ground black pepper

Directions:

1. Combine all ingredients in large pan.
2. Set pan over medium heat, and bring mixture to simmer.
3. Cook until apples are tender and cranberries are plump, stirring occasionally, about 20 minutes.
4. Cool to room temperature; cover and refrigerate until compote is well chilled, about 2 hours.
5. Compote can be prepared up to 1 day ahead. Keep refrigerated.

***Did You Know?* . . . .**

Did you know that the Fuji apple is the unrivaled best-selling apple in Japan?

Apple Delights Cookbook

A Collection of Apple Recipes
Cookbook Delights Series

Jams, Jellies, and Syrups

Table of Contents

Page

Did You Know? . . . .

*Did you know that the apple blossom has five petals?
Apple blossoms typically form in a cluster of five, Red
Delicious apples usually have five bumps on the base of the
apple, and there are five seed cavities in the fruit.*

A Basic Guide for Canning Jams, Jellies, and Syrups

1. Wash jars in hot, soapy water inside and out with brush or soft cloth.
2. Run your finger around rim of each jar, discarding any with cracks or chips.
3. Rinse well in clean, clear, hot water, using tongs to avoid burns to hands or fingers.
4. Place upside down on clean cloth to drain well.
5. Place lids in boiling water for 2 minutes to sterilize and keep hot until placing on rim of jar.
6. Immediately prior to filling each jar, immerse in very hot water with tongs to heat jar (avoids breakage of jar with hot liquid).
7. Fill jar to within 1 inch of top of rim or to level recommended in recipe.
8. Wipe rim with clean damp cloth to remove any particles of food, and check again for any chips or cracks.
9. With tongs, place lid from hot bath directly onto rim of jar.
10. Using gloves, cloth, or holders, tighten lid firmly onto jar with ring or use single formed lid in place of ring to cover inner lid. Do not tighten down too hard as it may impede sealing.
11. Place on protected surface to cool, taking care to not disturb lid and ring. A slight indentation of lid will be apparent when sealed.
12. Leave overnight until thoroughly cooled.
13. When cooled, wipe jars with damp cloth, then label and date each.
14. Store upright on shelf in cool, dark place.

Apple Pie Jam

With this jam you can have the flavor of apple pie to spread on your toast, bagels, or biscuits.

Ingredients:

4½ c. sugar
1   c. light brown sugar, firmly packed
1   lb. tart green apples, such as Granny Smith
1   c. water
⅓   c. lemon juice
1   tsp. ground cinnamon
¼   tsp. ground nutmeg
1   box powdered pectin (1¾ oz.)

Directions:

1. Wash 5 or 6 pint jars, and fill with hot water until needed; prepare lids as manufacturer directs.
2. Measure sugars into medium bowl and set aside.
3. Peel, core, and finely chop enough apples to measure 2 cups.
4. Place in large saucepan with water, lemon juice, cinnamon, and nutmeg; stir in pectin.
5. Place pan over high heat and stir until it comes to a full boil; boil hard for 1 minute, stirring constantly.
6. Remove from heat and immediately stir in sugars.
7. Return to full rolling boil and boil hard for 1 minute more, stirring constantly.
8. Remove from heat; skim foam from surface, and stir jam for about 5 minutes to prevent fruit from floating.
9. Ladle hot jam into jars, leaving ¼-inch headspace.
10. Wipe jar rims with clean, damp cloth; attach lids.
11. Following canning directions on page 180, process in water-bath canner for 10 minutes (15 minutes at 1,000 to 6,000 feet; 20 minutes above 6,000 feet).

Yields: 5 to 6 pints.

Apple and Raspberry Jelly

This combination of apples and raspberries makes a jelly that is great on toast or English muffins.

Ingredients:

- 3 lb. raspberries, rinsed
- 3 lb. apples, washed, cut in quarters
  sugar, as per directions below

Directions:

1. In nonreactive pot cover raspberries with water, and cook until soft; cool to room temperature.
2. Drain through jelly bag, removing seeds and pulp; save juice.
3. Repeat procedure with apples; save juice.
4. Combine raspberry and apple juices in equal proportions.
5. Add ⅔ cup sugar for each cup juice.
6. Boil rapidly until jelly begins to sheet from spoon.
7. Process following canning directions on page 180.

Apple Cider Jelly

This is a great-tasting jelly made from just one ingredient! The flavor is dependent on the quality and flavor of the apple cider. It is delicious on toast or muffins or anything you choose.

Ingredients:

- 2 qt. apple cider

Directions:

1. Heat cider in heavy saucepan over moderate heat, and bring to a simmer; cook for 45 to 60 minutes to jelling point, 220 degrees F.
2. Remove from heat and cool.
3. Store chilled in refrigerator for up to 6 weeks.
4. Serve slightly chilled or at room temperature.
5. Or, process following canning directions on page 180.

Apple Marmalade

This is a delicious marmalade made without spices to enjoy the pure fruit flavor of apples. If you like the taste of cinnamon or other spices, just add a couple of teaspoons of the ones you prefer to the cooking process, and adjust to taste after simmering for approximately 20 minutes with each addition.

Ingredients:

6   lb. sugar
1   qt. cider
12 lb. apples, peeled, cored, finely chopped
     ground cinnamon or nutmeg (optional)

Directions:

1. Place all ingredients into large nonreactive kettle.
2. Cook very gently until fruit is soft.
3. Place in glass jars.
4. Process following canning directions on page 180.

Apple Date Jam

You will find this a delectable, delicious, and nutritious jam for the whole family. Watch them go after it!

Ingredients:

- 2   c. chopped apples
- 2   c. chopped dates
- ¾   c. pineapple juice
- 1   pkg. powdered fruit pectin (1¾ oz.)
- 2   c. sugar

Directions:

1. Place apples, dates, pineapple juice, and pectin in nonreactive deep cooking pot.
2. Bring to full rolling boil; remove from heat and stir in sugar.
3. Return to heat; boil hard, uncovered, for 1 minute, stirring constantly with long-handled spoon.
4. Remove from heat; quickly skim off foam with metal spoon.
5. Pour into sterilized jars, and process following canning directions on page 180.

Yields: 2½ pints.

Candy Apple Jelly

Use this pretty pink jelly to spice up your toast or muffins.

Ingredients:

- 4   c. apple juice
- ½   c. red hot candies
- 1   pkg. powdered fruit pectin (1¾ oz.)
- 4½ c. sugar

Directions:

1. Combine juice, candy, and pectin in large pot.
2. Bring to full boil over high heat, stirring constantly.
3. Stir in sugar; return to a full boil; boil for 2 minutes, stirring constantly.
4. Remove from heat; skim off foam and unmelted candy.
5. Pour into hot jars, leaving ¼-inch headspace.
6. Process following canning directions on page 180.

Yields: 3 pints.

Apple Pepper Jelly

This is a sweet jelly that goes perfectly with your favorite meat.

Ingredients:

2   c. water
6   oz. frozen apple juice, thawed
1   pkg. powdered fruit pectin (1¾ oz.)
3¾ c. sugar
⅛   tsp. red food coloring (optional)
    crushed red pepper to taste

Directions:

1. Stir water, apple juice concentrate, and pectin in 3-quart saucepan until pectin is dissolved.
2. Heat to boiling, stirring constantly.
3. Add sugar and red pepper, then heat to a rolling boil, stirring constantly.
4. Remove from heat and strain.
5. Add red food color if using.
6. Immediately pour into hot sterilized jars or glasses or freezer containers.
7. Cover tightly and cool.
8. Refrigerate no longer than 4 weeks, or freeze no longer than 2 months. Serve with meat.

Yields: 4 half-pints.

Apple Jelly

Preserving jelly is a great idea. It is so nice to have it available throughout the winter months.

Ingredients:

> 4 c. apple juice (about 3 lb. apples and 3 c. water)
> 2 Tbs. lemon juice (optional)
> 3 c. sugar

Directions:

1. Select about ¼ slightly under ripe apples and ¾ fully ripe apples.
2. Sort, wash, and remove stems and blossom ends; do not peel or core.
3. Cut apples into small chunks.
4. Add water, cover, and bring to a boil over high heat.
5. Reduce heat, and simmer about 20 to 25 minutes or until apples are soft; cool to room temperature.
6. Drain apples through jelly bag.
7. Measure apple juice into saucepan to equal 4 cups, adding water if necessary to equal 4 cups.
8. Add lemon juice and sugar; stir to dissolve sugar.
9. Boil over high heat, stirring constantly; cook until jelly sheets from metal spoon.
10. Remove from heat and skim off foam quickly.
11. Pour into sterilized jars and seal, following canning directions on page 180.

Did You Know? . . . .

Did you know that applejack, known also as "Jersey Lightning," was used at one time during the colonial period to pay road construction crews?

Apple Pear Jam

Fresh apples and pears combined together make a great jam that you are not likely to find in the store—at least, not one this delicious!

Ingredients:

> 2½ lb. ripe pears
> 2 lb. red apples, fresh or thawed frozen
> 1 pkg. powdered fruit pectin (1¾ oz.)
> 2 Tbs. lemon juice
> ¼ tsp. ground nutmeg
> 5 c. sugar

Directions:

1. Peel, core, and coarsely grind pears and apples; measure 3 cups of each fruit for a total of 6 cups.
2. In 2-quart kettle combine chopped pears, apples, pectin, lemon juice, and nutmeg.
3. Bring to full rolling boil; stir in sugar.
4. Boil hard, uncovered, for 1 minute, stirring constantly with long-handled spoon.
5. Remove from heat; quickly skim off foam with metal spoon.
6. Pour into sterilized jars and seal, following canning directions on page 180.

Yields: 6 to 7 half-pints.

Did You Know? . . . .

Did you know that in the United States, more than 60 percent of all the apples sold commercially are grown in Washington state?

Cider Syrup

This tasty syrup goes well over whole-wheat, apple, or pumpkin pancakes or waffles.

Ingredients:

- ½ c. sugar
- 1 Tbs. cornstarch
- ⅛ tsp. pumpkin pie spice
- 1 c. apple cider
- 1 Tbs. lemon juice
- 2 Tbs. butter

Directions:

1. In medium saucepan combine sugar, cornstarch, and pumpkin pie spice; stir in apple cider and lemon juice.
2. Cook, stirring constantly, until mixture thickens and boils for 1 minute.
3. Remove from heat and stir in butter.

Cinnamon Apple Syrup

What a wonderful treat, apples simmered with sugar and cinnamon! This makes a great sundae topping over ice cream or as a pancake topping at breakfast.

Ingredients:

- 2 tart apples, peeled, cored, cubed
- ½ c. sugar
- 1 Tbs. ground cinnamon
- 2 Tbs. water

Directions:

1. In saucepan combine apples, sugar, cinnamon, and water.
2. Stir to dissolve sugar, and bring to a boil.
3. Reduce heat to low, and simmer for 10 minutes or until apples are soft and syrup has thickened.
4. Serve over pancakes or ice cream.
5. If making a large amount of this recipe, you may preserve by processing following canning directions on page 180.

Crab Apple Jelly

Crab apples are always delicious, no matter the season, so enjoy your efforts in picking and making jelly with them.

Ingredients:

3 lb. crab apples
⅔ c. sugar to each cup of juice

Directions:

1. Wash crab apples; do not pare.
2. Remove stems and blossom ends, cut in halves, and remove seeds.
3. In nonreactive kettle, cover with water and cook until soft.
4. Drain through jelly bag; measure juice.
5. Return juice to pan and bring back to boiling.
6. Add ⅔ cup sugar for each cup juice; bring back to full rolling boil.
7. Boil rapidly until jelly sheets from spoon and is about 220 degrees F. on thermometer.
8. Pour into sterilized jars and seal, following canning directions on page 180.

Green Tomato Apple Jam

This is a delicious way to use up those green tomatoes that are left over in the fall. Combine them with apples and enjoy!

Ingredients:

    2 c. fresh apple purée
    2 Tbs. lemon juice
    1 tsp. lemon zest
    2 c. fresh green tomato purée
    4 c. sugar
    1 pkg. powdered pectin (1¾ oz.)
    1 pkg. fruit-flavored gelatin (3 oz.)

Directions:

1. Combine apple purée, lemon juice, and lemon zest in bowl; set aside.
2. In large saucepan over medium-high heat, combine tomato purée, apple purée mixture, and sugar; bring to a boil.
3. Reduce heat and simmer for 20 minutes, stirring occasionally.
4. Remove from heat and stir in pectin; return to heat, bring to a boil, and boil 1 minute.
5. Remove from heat and add gelatin mix; stir until completely dissolved.
6. Pour into sterilized jars and seal, following canning directions on page 180.

Did You Know? . . . .

Did you know that the value of the 2005 worldwide apple crop was about $10 billion?

Apple Mint Jelly

Mint leaves add a delightfully refreshing taste to this jelly.

Ingredients:

4   c. apple juice
1½ c. fresh mint leaves
2   Tbs. lemon juice
1   box powdered fruit pectin (1¾ oz.)
5¼ c. sugar
    green food coloring (optional)

Directions:

1. In Dutch oven combine apple juice, mint leaves, lemon juice, and pectin over medium-high heat.
2. Bring to a rolling boil.
3. Add sugar.
4. Stirring constantly, bring to a rolling boil again and boil 1 minute.
5. Remove from heat; skim off foam.
6. Strain mixture; discard mint leaves.
7. Tint jelly green if desired.
8. Pour into heat-resistant jars; top with lids.
9. Store in refrigerator.

Yields: About 3 pints.

***Did You Know?* . . . .**

Did you know that what North Americans refer to as the "candy apple" is called a "toffee apple" by the rest of the English-speaking world?

Apple, Pear, and Plum Jam

What a delightful mix of flavors in this jam!

Ingredients:

    3   lb. cooking apples, peeled, cored, sliced
    2   lb. pears, peeled, cored, sliced
    2   lb. plums, halved, stoned
    1   lemon, juice and zest
    1   piece gingerroot (1-in. length), bruised
    4½ lb. sugar

Directions:

1. Place all fruit in large, heavy-bottom pan, adding enough water to cover bottom.
2. Simmer until fruit is tender, about 45 minutes.
3. Remove pan from heat and add sugar, stirring until fully dissolved.
4. Add lemon juice, zest, and gingerroot; return to heat and boil rapidly until setting point is reached, about 15 minutes. (To test for setting, remove pan from heat, and place a drop of jam onto plate that has been chilled. Press edge of drop, and if it wrinkles slightly, setting point has been reached.)
5. When setting point has been reached, remove gingerroot, then pour into sterilized jars and seal, following canning directions on page 180.
6. When cooled, label and store.

Did You Know? . . . .

Did you know that in Arthurian legend, the mythical isle of Avalon's name is believed to mean "isle of apples"?

Apple Delights Cookbook

A Collection of Apple Recipes
Cookbook Delights Series

Main Dishes

Table of Contents

Page

Did You Know? . . . .

Did you know that the Jonathan apple was originally
called the "Rick apple"? It was renamed by Judge Buel,
President of the Albany New York Horticultural Society, after
Jonathan Hasbrouck who brought it to his attention.

Apple and Apricot Brisket

Serving brisket with this fruit-flavored gravy really brings out the flavors of the meat.

Ingredients:

- 2 Tbs. vegetable oil
- 6 lb. beef brisket
- 1 onion, chopped
- 2 cloves garlic, crushed
- 1 pkg. dry onion soup mix
- 1 c. dried apples
- 1 c. dried apricots
   water and apple juice, mixed half and half

Directions:

1. Preheat oven to 325 degrees F.
2. In large, heavy skillet heat oil over medium-high heat; brown beef on all sides. (Cut in half if too large, and brown in two stages.)
3. Place meat in large Dutch oven with lid.
4. Add onions to drippings in skillet; sauté over medium heat until onions are beginning to brown; stir in garlic, and cook for 2 or 3 more minutes.
5. Pour over brisket in Dutch oven; empty onion soup mix over browned onions and meat.
6. Arrange apples and apricots on top of soup mix.
7. Pour enough apple juice-water mixture around outside of meat (not on top) to cover sides of brisket; cover with lid.
8. Bake for 1 hour; check liquid, adding a bit more apple water around meat if it appears too dry.
9. Cover and cook another hour, then remove lid and stir apricots into gravy.
10. Leave uncovered and cook for another hour.
11. Stir gravy again; add more water if gravy is too thick.
12. Meat should be very tender; if necessary, bake for an additional ½ hour.
13. Remove from oven and lift to serving platter; cut across grain to serve.
14. Place fruit gravy in serving dish, and pass with meat.

Yields: 6 to 8 servings.

Apple and Orange Chicken

What an absolutely wonderful recipe for apple and orange chicken! Your family and guests will be delighted with this delicious dish!

Ingredients:

4 bone-in chicken breast halves, skinless
1 pkg. dry onion soup mix
1 pkg. dry cream of chicken soup mix
2 Tbs. soy sauce
2 cloves garlic, crushed
1 c. apple juice
1 c. orange juice
   salt and pepper to taste

Directions:

1. Preheat oven to 350 degrees F.
2. Place chicken pieces in lightly greased 13 x 9 x 2-inch baking/serving dish.
3. In medium bowl combine soup mixes, soy sauce, garlic, apple and orange juices, and salt and pepper; mix together and pour over chicken.
4. Cover and bake for 1 hour; remove cover and bake for another 30 minutes to brown chicken.
5. Remove from oven, and place on table in serving dish.

Yields: 4 servings.

***Did You Know?* . . . .**

Did you know that in the United States there are about 2,500 known varieties of apples grown?

Apple BBQ Sauce with Baby Back Ribs

This recipe takes a little time, but the delicious taste and wonderful aroma are well worth it.

Ingredients:

- 4 c. barbeque sauce
- 4 c. applesauce (recipe page 169)
- 4 lb. baby back pork ribs
  - salt and black pepper to taste
  - cayenne pepper to taste
  - garlic powder to taste

Directions:

1. Mix barbeque sauce and applesauce in bowl.
2. Line baking dish with doubled aluminum foil that hangs well over sides; place ribs on sheet and rub on all sides with salt, pepper, cayenne pepper, and garlic powder.
3. Pour sauce over ribs to coat; seal ribs in foil, and marinate in refrigerator at least 8 hours or overnight.
4. When ready to cook, preheat grill for high heat.
5. Place ribs in foil on grill grate, and cook 1 hour.
6. Remove ribs from foil, and place directly on grill grate.
7. Continue cooking 30 minutes, basting frequently with sauce and turning as needed, until ribs are done; remove to serving platter and enjoy!

Yields: 8 servings.

Apple Curry Turkey Pita

This is a delicious way to use turkey leftovers–very simple, quick, and flavorful. To add even more flavor, use wine in place of the lemon, if desired, and sour cream in place of the yogurt.

Ingredients:

   2 Tbs. olive oil
   1 c. sliced onion
   2 Tbs. lemon juice
   ½ lb. cooked turkey, cut into small chunks
   1 Tbs. curry powder or to taste
   1 med. apple, cored, thinly sliced
   3 pita bread rounds
   ½ c. plain yogurt

Directions:

   1. Heat oil in skillet over medium heat; stir in onion and lemon juice.
   2. Cook until onion is tender, then add turkey; season with curry powder to taste, and continue cooking until heated through.
   3. Remove from heat; stir in apple.
   4. Stuff warmed pita bread rounds with slightly cooled apple-turkey mixture.
   5. Place on serving plates, and drizzle yogurt over stuffing to serve.

Yields: 3 servings.

Apple Glazed Roast Pork

This pork is delicious and tender after marinating in the crock-pot. It will melt in your mouth.

Ingredients:

- 4 lb. pork loin roast
- 6 apples, cored, quartered
- ¼ c. apple juice
- 3 Tbs. brown sugar
- 1 tsp. ground ginger
- 6 potatoes, quartered
-    olive oil
-    salt and pepper to taste

Directions:

1. Rub roast with olive oil, salt, and pepper.
2. Brown roast under broiler to remove excess fat; drain well.
3. Place apple quarters in bottom of crock-pot.
4. Place roast on top of apples.
5. Combine apple juice, brown sugar, and ginger.
6. Spoon over top surface of roast, moistening well.
7. Cover and cook on low for 10 to 12 hours, until done, or roast in oven at 350 degrees F. until done.
8. Approximately 1 hour before done, add potatoes on top of meat.
9. If using oven, brush potatoes and apples with olive oil.
10. Remove from oven or pot, place on serving platter, slice, and spoon potatoes and apples around roast.

Did You Know? . . . .

Did you know that throughout the world, growers produce about 55 million tons of apples annually?

Apple Sage Pork Chops

My husband enjoys pork chops, and this is a nice variation to try.

Ingredients:

6	pork loin chops
1½	tsp. salt, divided
1½	tsp. dried sage, crumbled
1	Tbs. canola oil
3	Granny Smith apples or other tart variety
3	Tbs. molasses
3	Tbs. all-purpose flour
2	c. hot water
1	Tbs. vinegar
⅓	c. raisins

Directions:

1. Preheat oven to 350 degrees F.
2. Season pork chops evenly on both sides with 1 teaspoon salt and sage.
3. In large skillet heat canola oil over medium heat.
4. Brown pork chops in hot oil on both sides; transfer pork chops to shallow baking dish, reserving drippings.
5. Peel, core, and slice apples ¼ inch thick.
6. Arrange apples slices over pork chops; drizzle molasses over top.
7. Sprinkle flour over skillet drippings; cook until brown, stirring occasionally.
8. Slowly add water, stirring constantly, until smooth, then bring to a boil.
9. Stir in vinegar, ½ teaspoon salt, and raisins; pour mixture over pork chops.
10. Cover pan with foil and bake 50 to 60 minutes.

Yields: 6 servings.

Applesauce Glazed Chicken

This dish is a complement to any meal and makes a great potluck dish.

Ingredients:

    2 boneless, skinless chicken breasts
    ¼ c. orange marmalade
    1 tsp. cornstarch
    ¼ tsp. ground ginger
    ½ tsp. garlic, minced
    1 c. unsweetened applesauce
    2 Tbs. green onions, sliced, for garnish
       cooked rice (optional)

Directions:

1. Preheat oven to 400 degrees F.
2. Wash chicken and pat dry.
3. Cut each breast lengthwise into 4 pieces.
4. Place in single layer in 13 x 9 x 2-inch baking pan lined with foil.
5. In 1-quart saucepan combine marmalade, cornstarch, ginger, and garlic; mix well then add applesauce.
6. Cook over medium heat, stirring constantly, until mixture starts to boil, then spread evenly over chicken in baking pan.
7. Bake for about 20 minutes or until chicken is tender and juices run clear.
8. Remove from oven, and place on serving platter; garnish with green onions.
9. Slice and serve hot over rice if desired.

Yields: 4 servings.

Apple Stir-Fried Pork

*We do not normally think of garlic and apples together,
but they make a great combination in this flavorful stir-fry.*

Ingredients:

- 2 lb. pork steak, deboned, cut into ⅛-inch strips
- 2 Tbs. light soy sauce
- 2 Tbs. dry sherry
- ¼ tsp. freshly grated ginger
- 3 Tbs. peanut oil
- 4 cloves garlic, peeled, sliced paper thin
- 1 lg. yellow onion, sliced
- 3 Golden Delicious apples, cored, sliced
- 1 Tbs. sesame oil
- ¼ tsp. freshly ground black pepper
- 4 green onions, chopped, for garnish

Directions:

1. Cut pork steak as instructed, and marinate for 15 minutes in soy, sherry, and ginger.
2. Heat wok or large frying pan; add oil and garlic.
3. Drain marinade from meat; sauté meat over very high heat until done to your liking, about 6 minutes.
4. Remove meat from pan; add onion slices and sauté until tender.
5. Add apple slices; sauté just until apples begin to brown.
6. Return meat to pan; add sesame oil and pepper, and toss.
7. Top with green onions as garnish; serve immediately.

Yields: 6 servings.

Chicken Apple Curry

Our family loves this recipe that has a Thai influence and an interesting combination of apples and curry.

Ingredients:

- 2 Tbs. vegetable oil
- 8 shallots, thinly sliced, for garnish
- 1 lb. chicken breasts, skinless, boneless
- 2 Tbs. red curry paste
- 1 Tbs. curry powder
- ½ c. red apples, peeled, cubed
- ½ c. green apples, peeled, cubed
- ½ c. coconut milk
- ¼ c. puréed tomato
- 2 Tbs. fish sauce
- 1 Tbs. palm sugar
- 2 med. tomatoes, cut into wedges
- 1 bunch cilantro, chopped, for garnish

Directions:

1. Heat vegetable oil in medium skillet over low heat.
2. Add shallots, and stir-fry until brown and tender; drain, reserving oil, and set aside.
3. Coat chicken with curry paste and powder, then place in skillet; add water to cover and bring to boil.
4. Reduce heat, cover skillet, and simmer until chicken is no longer pink and juice runs clear.
5. Stir in apples, coconut milk, tomato purée, fish sauce, palm sugar, and ½ the tomato wedges.
6. Cook and stir over low heat until mixture is creamy.
7. Mix in remaining tomatoes and continue cooking until tender; garnish with cilantro and fried shallots.

Glazed Apple Meatloaf

The applesauce inside and the glaze over the top add flavor and moistness to this meatloaf. Even the children are bound to like it!

Ingredients for meatloaf:

- 1 med. onion, finely chopped
- 2 c. soft bread crumbs
- 1 c. applesauce (recipe page 169)
- 1 egg, beaten
- ⅛ tsp. pepper
- 1 lb. ground beef
- 1 lb. ground pork

Ingredients for glaze:

- 1 c. applesauce (recipe page 169)
- 2 Tbs. apple cider vinegar
- 1 Tbs. Dijon mustard
- 2 Tbs. brown sugar

Directions for meatloaf:

1. Preheat oven to 350 degrees F.
2. Cook onion in microwave 2 to 3 minutes until tender.
3. Combine onion, bread crumbs, applesauce, egg, and pepper in large bowl; mix well.
4. Stir in beef and pork, and mix gently just until combined.
5. Shape mixture into loaf and place in 1-quart baking dish; bake for 1½ hours.

Directions for glaze:

1. Combine applesauce, vinegar, mustard, and brown sugar in small saucepan.
2. Heat and stir until well blended.
3. After meatloaf has been in oven for ½ hour, spoon some of apple glaze over and continue baking.
4. Baste with glaze every 20 minutes.
5. Let meatloaf sit for 15 minutes before serving.

Yields: 10 servings.

Hot Apple and Gouda Quesadillas

These quesadillas are wonderful, sweet, salty, and barbequed for a different pace to your meal. For variation you can add barbequed chicken or chopped jalapeño peppers. Serve warm with sour cream, salsa, guacamole, or all three!

Ingredients:

8 flour tortillas (8-in.)
2 Tbs. olive oil
2 Tbs. Dijon mustard
2 green onions, chopped
2 red apples, unpeeled, cored, thinly sliced
2 c. shredded Gouda cheese

Directions:

1. Brush oil onto one side of a tortilla, and place on plate oil side down.
2. Spread about ½ tablespoon of mustard on top side; top with green onion, apple slices, and about ½ cup shredded cheese.
3. Place second tortilla on top, and brush top with olive oil.
4. Repeat with remaining tortillas and ingredients, stacking quesadillas on plate.
5. Preheat grilling surface at high heat, brush with oil, and place quesadillas carefully on grill.
6. Grill for about 3 minutes or until bottom is crisp; flip and grill on other side until crisp.
7. Remove from grill to serving plates, and cut into quarters; serve warm.

Yields: 4 servings.

Pork Chops with Apple Cider Sauce

These seasoned pork loin chops, baked with apple cider and finished with sherry, make even the pickiest eaters in your family say, "Wow!"

Ingredients:

- 3 Tbs. olive oil
- 4 pork loin chops
- ½ tsp. poultry seasoning
- 3 Tbs. Worcestershire sauce
- 1 can frozen apple cider concentrate (8 oz.)
- ¼ c. dry sherry
  - seasoning salt to taste
  - black pepper to taste
  - garlic powder to taste

Directions:

1. Preheat oven to 375 degrees F.
2. Heat olive oil in large oven-safe frying pan over medium-high heat.
3. Sprinkle chops with salt, pepper, garlic powder, and poultry seasoning; place in hot oil and brown on both sides.
4. Drizzle Worcestershire sauce over chops, and pour in apple cider concentrate.
5. Bake for 25 minutes; remove chops to a plate, and return frying pan to stove over medium-high heat.
6. Stir sherry into pan, and boil until sauce thickens, stirring frequently.
7. Serve sauce over chops or in small bowl for guests to use if desired.

Yields: 4 servings.

Pork Chops with Apple Rings and Raisin Sauce

This dish makes an attractive presentation with different colors of apple skin, raisins, and apricots served with a tasty sauce.

Ingredients:

- 2 lg. apples (1green, 1 red), cored
- 3 Tbs. butter
- 4 boneless, lean, center-cut pork chops, ¾ inch thick
- ½ tsp. salt
- ½ tsp. pepper
- ½ tsp. celery salt
- ½ tsp. sage
- ½ c. dry white wine
- 3 Tbs. dried apricots
- 3 Tbs. golden raisins
- 2 Tbs. brown sugar, firmly packed

Directions:

1. Slice apples into rings about ½ inch thick.
2. In large, deep skillet melt butter to sizzling; add apple rings, and sauté lightly on both sides to crisp-tender; remove and set aside.
3. Add pork chops, and brown well on both sides in pan juices; sprinkle with seasonings.
4. Cover skillet, and cook over low heat for 15 minutes, turning once.
5. Add apples on top of chops, and sprinkle with apricots, raisins, and brown sugar; cook 10 minutes longer.
6. Serve while hot.

Pork Tenderloin with Apple Cream Sauce

This is elegant, easy-to-make tenderloin, and the cream sauce is excellent. Salad on the side makes a delicious light dinner.

Ingredients:

- 1 tsp. oil
- 8 pork loin medallions or pork chops
- 1 c. whipping cream
- ½ c. apple juice
- 1 med. apple, cored, chopped
- ½ c. celery, sliced thin
- ¼ tsp. thyme
  - salt and pepper to taste
  - French bread, pasta, or rice

Directions:

1. Salt and pepper pork to taste; brown both sides in oil in hot skillet.
2. Stir in whipping cream, apple juice, chopped apple, celery, and thyme.
3. Reduce heat to low; salt and pepper to taste.
4. Cover and simmer for 30 or more minutes until meat is tender, stirring occasionally.
5. Sauce can be thickened to taste with small amount of cornstarch mixed with water and added to sauce.
6. Serve while hot over pasta, rice, or French bread.

Yields: 8 servings.

Did You Know?....

Did you know that Apfelwein (German for apple wine) is the German form of cider, produced from apples?

Pork with Apples and Sauerkraut

My relatives emigrated from Slovakian countries and always brought their own pork and sauerkraut recipes.

Ingredients:

1 lb. red potatoes, unpeeled, cut in 1-in. pieces
2 lb. sauerkraut, drained, lightly rinsed
1 green apple, unpeeled, cored, coarsely chopped
¼ c. onions, chopped
1½ lb. lean, boneless, country-style pork ribs
½ lb. kielbasa or Polish sausage
¾ c. apple juice
3 Tbs. brown sugar, firmly packed
1 tsp. caraway seed
1 tsp. ground mustard
½ tsp. whole allspice

Directions:

1. Place potatoes in 4-quart crockery slow cooker.
2. In large bowl combine sauerkraut, apple, and onions; spoon half of mixture over potatoes.
3. Cut sausage into 1½-inch chunks.
4. Brown and drain all meat separately for extra flavor, then place on top of ingredients in cooker.
5. Spoon remaining sauerkraut mixture over meat.
6. Combine apple juice, brown sugar, and remaining seasonings; pour over sauerkraut mixture.
7. Cover and cook on low for 8 hours or until meat is done and vegetables tender.
8. Place on serving platter and surround with vegetables.

Apple Delights Cookbook

A Collection of Apple Recipes
Cookbook Delights Series

Pies

Table of Contents

Page

Did You Know? . . .

Did you know that the five most popular apples in the United States are Red Delicious, Golden Delicious, Gala, Fuji, and Granny Smith?

A Basic Recipe for Pie Crust

This is a very good recipe for a delicious, flaky crust.

Ingredients for single crust:

 1½ c. sifted all-purpose flour
 ½   tsp. salt
 ½   c. shortening
 4-5 Tbs. ice water

Ingredients for double crust:

 2   c. sifted all-purpose flour
 1   tsp. salt
 ⅔   c. shortening
 5-7 Tbs. ice water

Directions for single crust:

1. In large bowl stir together flour and salt.
2. Cut in shortening with pastry blender or mix with fingertips until pieces are size of coarse crumbs.
3. Sprinkle 2 tablespoons ice water over flour mixture, tossing with fork.
4. Add just enough remaining water 1 tablespoon at a time to moisten dough, tossing so dough holds together.
5. Roll pastry into 11-inch circle, and wrap in plastic wrap; refrigerate for 1 hour.
6. Preheat oven to 425 degrees F.
7. Remove plastic wrap from pastry, and fit pastry into a 9-inch pie plate.
8. Fold edge under, then crimp between thumb and forefinger to make fluted crust.
9. For filled pie with an instant or cooked filling (cream-filled, custard-filled, etc.), prick crust all over with fork then bake 15 to 20 minutes until done.
10. If preparing pie with uncooked filling (such as pumpkin), do not prick crust; pour filling into unbaked pastry shell, then bake as directed.

Directions for double crust:

1. Turn desired filling into pastry-lined pie plate; trim overhanging edge of pastry ½ inch from rim of plate.
2. Cut slits with knife in top crust for steam vents.
3. Place over filling; trim overhanging edge of pastry 1 inch from rim of plate.
4. Fold and roll top edge under lower edge, pressing on rim to seal; flute.
5. Cover fluted edge with 2- to 3-inch-wide strip of aluminum foil to prevent excessive browning.
6. Remove foil during last 15 minutes of baking.

Yields: 1 pie crust (9-inch single or double).

A Basic Cookie or Graham Cracker Crust

This is a great crust for use with cream pies or for an unbaked pie. Use your favorite flavor of cookie to complement your filling or use graham crackers.

Ingredients:

2 c. cookie or graham cracker crumbs, finely crushed
⅓ c. sugar
½ c. butter, melted

Directions:

1. Combine crumbs, sugar, and butter.
2. Press mixture firmly against bottom and up sides of 9-inch pie plate.
3. Baking is not necessary, but if preferred crust may be baked at 400 degrees F. for 10 minutes.

Yields: 1 pie crust (9-inch).

Apple and Tart Cherry Pie

In this pie the flavors of cardamom, apples, dried cherries, and cherry preserves contrast beautifully. Remember to cover the crust with foil 15 minutes into baking to avoid having the crust get too brown.

Ingredients:

¾   c. sugar
4½   Tbs. cornstarch
1   tsp. ground cinnamon
⅛   tsp. ground cloves
⅛   tsp. ground cardamom
3-3¼ lb. Granny Smith or Pippin apples (about 6 lg.), peeled, quartered, cored, sliced crosswise
¾   c. dried tart cherries
¼   c. cherry preserves
1   egg, beaten to blend, for glaze
      pastry for double-crust pie (recipe page 210)

Directions:

1. Preheat oven to 400 degrees F.; position rack in lowest third of oven.
2. Prepare pastry; divide into 2 sections.
3. In large bowl stir together sugar, cornstarch, cinnamon, cloves, and cardamom.
4. Mix in apples, dried cherries, and preserves.
5. Roll out 1 section of pastry dough on lightly floured surface to 13-inch round.
6. Transfer dough to 9-inch-diameter glass pie dish.
7. Brush inside and top edge of crust with glaze.
8. Spoon filling into crust.
9. Roll out second section of dough on floured surface to 13-inch round.
10. Cut out small hole from center.
11. Arrange dough over filling; seal top crust to bottom crust at edge.
12. Trim double overhang to ¾ inch; fold under and crimp edge.
13. Brush crust (except edge) with glaze.
14. Place pie on baking sheet.

15. Bake until apples are tender, about 1 hour 15 minutes. (Cover crust with foil if browning too quickly.)
16. Cool on rack.
17. Can be made 1 day ahead; store at room temperature.

Yields: 8 servings.

Apple Custard Pie with Streusel Topping

This delicious apple pie has a smooth and creamy custard filling that will delight all who have a serving to enjoy.

Ingredients:

    1   unbaked 9-inch pastry shell (recipe page 210)
    4   c. apples, peeled, cored, sliced
    2   eggs
    1   can sweetened condensed milk (14 oz.)
    ¼   c. butter, melted
    1   tsp. ground cinnamon
    ¼   tsp. ground nutmeg
    4   Tbs. nuts, chopped
    3   Tbs. light brown sugar, firmly packed

Directions:

1. Preheat oven to 425 degrees F.
2. Arrange apple slices in prepared pastry shell.
3. In medium bowl beat eggs; stir in condensed milk, butter, cinnamon, and nutmeg, blending well.
4. Pour over apple slices.
5. In small bowl combine nuts and brown sugar; sprinkle over pie.
6. Place in bottom third of oven; bake 10 minutes.
7. Reduce oven temperature to 375 degrees F., and continue baking 35 to 40 minutes or until golden brown.
8. Remove from oven, and place on wire rack to cool before slicing to serve.

Apple Pie with Honey

This apple pie uses honey instead of sugar and is very tasty. Choose your favorite type of honey for the best flavor.

Ingredients:

- 11 oz. honey
- 2 Tbs. cornstarch
- ¼ tsp. ground nutmeg
- 1 tsp. ground cinnamon
- 4 lg. cooking apples, peeled, cored, sliced
- 2 Tbs. butter
  pastry for double-crust pie (recipe page 210)
  vanilla ice cream (optional)

Directions:

1. Preheat oven to 400 degrees F.
2. Combine honey, cornstarch, and spices.
3. Add sliced apples and stir until coated.
4. Spoon into unbaked pie shell, and dot top of apples with butter.
5. Place top crust over pie; turn edge under bottom edge, and flute to seal.
6. Cut vents into top shell; place pie on cookie sheet.
7. Bake for 15 minutes, then reduce heat to 375 degrees F.; bake another 30 minutes or until knife inserted through slits comes out clean.
8. Remove from oven, and cool on wire rack before slicing to serve.
9. Excellent with vanilla ice cream while warm.

Yields: 8 servings.

Fried Apple Pies

These unique fried pies make a tasty dessert, especially when served warm.

Ingredients:

        5 c. dried apples
        4 c. all-purpose flour, sifted
        2 tsp. baking powder
        6 Tbs. butter
        2 eggs, beaten
        1 c. milk
        1 tsp. ground nutmeg
        2 tsp. ground cinnamon
        2 Tbs. sugar
           oil for deep-frying

Directions:

1. Cover dried apples with water; cover and simmer for 30 to 40 minutes, then drain and let cool.
2. Sift together flour and baking powder; cut in butter.
3. Add eggs and milk; mix to form soft dough.
4. Roll dough out thin, and cut into 6 circles about 5 inches in diameter.
5. Combine nutmeg, cinnamon, and sugar.
6. Divide apples into 6 equal amounts, and place in center of half of each circle; sprinkle each one evenly with cinnamon-sugar mixture, then fold other half over top.
7. Wet edges with a little milk, and seal with fork.
8. Fry at about 370 degrees F. in deep fryer until golden brown; remove and drain on paper towels.

Yields: 6 servings.

Apple Raisin Pie

This apple pie has the great addition of raisins. It is a unique pie and is very tasty.

Ingredients:

¼ c. light brown sugar, firmly packed
¼ c. sugar
1 Tbs. all-purpose flour
1 Tbs. grated lemon zest
1 tsp. ground cinnamon
¼ tsp. ground nutmeg
8 med. apples, peeled, cored, sliced thin
1 c. raisins
1 lg. egg, beaten
1 tsp. sugar
pastry for double-crust pie (recipe page 210)

Directions:

1. Preheat oven to 450 degrees F.
2. Spray 9-inch, deep-dish pie plate with vegetable cooking spray, and line with half of prepared crust.
3. In large bowl combine brown sugar, sugar, flour, lemon zest, cinnamon, and nutmeg; blend well.
4. Add apples and raisins to sugar mixture; stir to coat.
5. Spoon into prepared pie plate.
6. Place top crust over filling, trim and seal edges, then cut slits in top for steam vents.
7. To glaze, lightly brush pie crust with beaten egg; sprinkle with sugar.
8. Bake about 35 to 40 minutes, until pie crust is golden brown.
9. Remove from oven, and place on wire rack to cool.

Caramel Apple Pecan Pie

This recipe makes an interesting change from ordinary apple pie. The apples go well with caramel and pecans.

Ingredients:

4   tart apples, peeled, cored, thinly sliced
¾   c. pecans, chopped
¼   c. sugar
¼   lb. caramels, coarsely chopped
2   Tbs. all-purpose flour
⅓   c. milk
    pastry for double-crust pie (recipe page 210)
    milk and sugar for top

Directions:

1. Preheat oven to 375 degrees F.
2. Line bottom of 9-inch pie plate with half of pastry.
3. In large bowl toss together apples, pecans, sugar, caramels, flour, and milk.
4. Spoon mixture into pie shell; top with remaining rolled out pastry.
5. Fold edge of top pastry under bottom layer edge; pinch together and flute edge.
6. Cut several slits in top for steam to escape.
7. Brush top with milk and sprinkle with sugar.
8. Bake until crust is golden brown, about 45 minutes.
9. Remove from oven, and cool to lukewarm on wire rack before slicing to serve.

Yields: 8 servings.

Double-Crusted Cheddar Apple Pie

In this recipe, you get the cheese in the crust.

Ingredients for crust:

2⅔ c. all-purpose flour
½ tsp. salt
¾ c. cold unsalted butter, cubed
4 Tbs. cold shortening
4 oz. sharp cheddar cheese, grated fine, chilled well
2 egg yolks beaten lightly with ⅓ c. cold water
milk

Ingredients for filling:

3 lb. McIntosh apples (about 8)
¾ c. sugar
2 Tbs. all-purpose flour
1 tsp. ground cinnamon
¼ tsp. freshly grated nutmeg
¼ tsp. salt
1 Tbs. fresh lemon juice
2 Tbs. cold unsalted butter, cut into bits

Directions for crust:

1. In food processor combine flour and salt.
2. Add butter and shortening; pulse until it resembles very coarse meal.
3. Add cheddar, and pulse until it again resembles coarse meal.
4. Transfer mixture to bowl.
5. Add yolk mixture, tossing with fork until it forms dough.
6. Add more cold water 1 tablespoon at a time if necessary.

7. Form dough into ball, flatten into disc, and dust with flour.
8. Wrap dough in wax paper, and chill for at least 1 hour or overnight.
9. Roll out half the dough ⅛ inch thick on lightly floured surface.
10. Fit into 9-inch glass pie plate, and trim edge, leaving ¾-inch overhang.
11. Chill shell and remaining dough while making filling.

Directions for filling:

1. Preheat oven to 450 degrees F.
2. Peel, core, and cut apples into eighths.
3. In large bowl toss together apples, sugar, flour, cinnamon, nutmeg, salt, and lemon juice until mixture is combined well.
4. Transfer filling to shell and dot with butter.
5. Roll out remaining dough into 13- to 14-inch round on lightly floured surface; drape over filling and trim, leaving 1-inch overhang.
6. Fold overhang under bottom crust, pressing edge to seal, and crimp edge decoratively.
7. Brush crust lightly with milk, and cut slits with sharp knife to form steam vents.
8. Bake on large baking sheet in middle of oven for 10 minutes.
9. Reduce temperature to 350 degrees F., and bake for 20 to 25 minutes more or until crust is golden and apples are tender.

Yields: 8 servings.

Did You Know? . . . .

Did you know that Calvados is an apple brandy from the French region of Lower Normandy?

No-Sugar Apple Pie

This pie makes a delicious dessert for diabetics or for someone watching their weight. It contains no artificial sweeteners!

Ingredients:

- 3 Tbs. cornstarch
- 1 Tbs. ground cinnamon
- 1 can unsweetened apple juice concentrate (12 oz.)
- 6 c. sliced green apples
- pastry for double-crust pie (recipe page 210)

Directions:

1. Preheat oven to 350 degrees F.
2. In small bowl whisk together cornstarch, cinnamon, and ⅓ cup thawed apple juice concentrate; set aside.
3. In large saucepan simmer apples with remaining apple juice concentrate until apples are crisp tender, about 10 minutes.
4. Stir in cornstarch mixture, and continue to simmer until thickened; remove from heat.
5. Spoon apple mixture into pastry-lined, 9-inch pie plate.
6. Cover with top crust, seal and flute edges, and cut steam vents in top.
7. Bake for 45 minutes or until crust is golden brown.
8. Remove from oven, and cool slightly before slicing to serve warm.
9. May be chilled in refrigerator after cooling, if pie is preferred cold.

Yields: 8 servings.

Traditional Apple Pie

This is a traditional apple pie recipe. It is even more delicious served with ice cream or a slice of cheddar cheese melted over each slice.

Ingredients:

  6 apples, peeled, cored, thinly sliced
  2 Tbs. all-purpose flour
  1 c. sugar
  1 tsp. ground cinnamon
  ½ c. butter
     pastry for double-crust pie (recipe page 210)

Directions:

  1. Preheat oven to 325 degrees F.
  2. Line 9-inch pie plate with half of crust.
  3. Place apples in bottom crust, mounding in center to about ⅔ full.
  4. Combine flour, cinnamon, and sugar; sprinkle over apples.
  5. Place dots of butter evenly over apples.
  6. Place top crust over apples and seal edges.
  7. Cut slits in top crust for steam vents.
  8. Bake for 1 to 1½ hours or until crust is light brown and apples test soft when knife is inserted.
  9. Remove from oven, and cool on wire rack before serving.

Yields: 8 servings.

***Did You Know?* . . . .**

Did you know that one of George Washington's hobbies was pruning his apple trees?

Warm Apple Buttermilk Custard Pie

This is a sweet custard pie with a streusel topping.

Ingredients for apple filling:

¼ c. butter
2   tart apples, peeled, cored, sliced
½ c. sugar
½ tsp. ground cinnamon
    pastry for single-crust pie (recipe page 210)

Ingredients for buttermilk custard:

¼ c. butter, softened
1⅓ c. sugar
4   eggs
1   tsp. vanilla extract
2   Tbs. all-purpose flour
¾ c. buttermilk

Ingredients for streusel topping:

¼ c. sugar
¼ c. brown sugar, firmly packed
½ c. all-purpose flour
¼ tsp. ground cinnamon
3   Tbs. butter

Directions for apple filling:

1. Preheat oven to 300 degrees F.
2. Melt butter in skillet over medium heat; add apples, sugar, and cinnamon.
3. Cook 3 to 5 minutes, until tender; set aside.

Directions for buttermilk custard:

1. In large mixing bowl combine butter and sugar; beat until creamy.
2. Add eggs one at a time, beating until yellow disappears.
3. Mix in vanilla then flour.
4. Combine thoroughly then pour in buttermilk, beating until smooth.
5. Fit pastry into 9-inch pie plate, and prick with fork.
6. Spoon apple mixture into crust, then pour buttermilk custard over it.
7. Bake for 30 minutes.

Directions for streusel topping:

1. While pie is baking, combine sugars, flour, and cinnamon in small bowl.
2. Cut in butter until mixture is crumbly.
3. Remove pie from oven after 30 minutes, and sprinkle streusel topping over custard.
4. Return to oven, and bake for an additional 40 to 50 minutes, until knife inserted in center comes out clean.
5. Let stand 1 hour before serving.

Yields: 8 servings.

Did You Know? . . . .

Did you know that washing or peeling an apple before eating it may reduce pesticide intake, but peeling will also reduce the intake of the beneficial nutrients?

French Apple Pie

This French apple pie is easy to make and is very delicious.
It is great served warm with ice cream or whipped cream.

Ingredients:

1   c. graham cracker crumbs
½   c. all-purpose flour
1   c. sugar
1½ tsp. ground cinnamon
½   tsp. ground nutmeg
¼   tsp. ground ginger
8   med. cooking apples, peeled, cored, sliced
8   Tbs. butter, melted
    pastry for single-crust pie (recipe page 210)

Directions:

1. Preheat oven to 350 degrees F.
2. Combine cracker crumbs, flour, sugar, and spices
   until well blended; reserve ½ cup.
3. Line 9-inch deep-dish pie plate with pastry; sprinkle
   1 tablespoon crumb mixture over bottom.
4. Add layer of apple slices followed by layer of dry
   mixture; continue alternating layers until apples are
   mounded in middle of pie shell.
5. Top with reserved crumb mixture.
6. Drizzle melted butter over top of apple mixture.
7. Bake for approximately 1 hour or until knife test
   comes out clean.
8. Remove from oven, and cool on wire rack before
   slicing to serve.

Yields: 8 servings.

Apple Delights Cookbook

A Collection of Apple Recipes
Cookbook Delights Series

Preserving

Table of Contents

Did You Know? . . . .

Did you know that when a bottle of vinegar is opened, mother of vinegar may develop? It is considered harmless and can be removed by filtering.

A Basic Guide for Canning, Dehydrating, and Freezing

1. Place empty jars in hot, soapy water. Wash well inside and out with brush or soft cloth.
2. Run your finger around rim of each jar, discarding any that are chipped or cracked.
3. Rinse in clean, clear, very hot water, being careful to use tongs to avoid burning skin or fingers.
4. Place upside down on towel or fabric to drain well.
5. Place lids in boiling water bath for 2 minutes to sterilize and keep hot until ready to place on jar rims.
6. Immediately prior to filling jars with hot food, immerse in hot bath for 1 minute to heat jars. Heating jars avoids breakage.
7. If filling with room-temperature food, you need not immerse immediately prior to filling.
8. Fill jars with food to within ½ inch of neck of jars.
9. When ladling liquid over food, fill jars to 1 inch from top rim in each jar. This leaves air allowance for sealing purposes.
10. Wipe rims of jars with damp, clean cloth to remove any particles of food and again check for chips or cracks.
11. Using tongs, place lids from hot bath directly onto jars.
12. Place rings over lids, and using cloth, gloves, or holders, tighten down firmly while hanging onto jars.
13. Do not tighten down too hard as air may become trapped in jars and prevent them from sealing.
14. For fruits, tomatoes, and pickled vegetables, place each jar into water bath canning kettle so water covers jars by at least 1 inch.
15. For vegetables, process them in a pressure canner according to manufacturer's directions.
16. Follow time recommended for food being canned.
17. Do not mix jars of food in same canning kettle as times may vary for each kind of food.

18. At end of time recommended for canning, gently lift each jar out of bath with tongs, and place on protected surface.
19. Turn lids gently to be sure they are firmly tight.
20. Place filled, ringed jars on cloth to cool gradually.
21. Do not disturb rings, lids, or jars until sealed.
22. Lids will show slight indentation when sealed.
23. When cool, wipe jars with damp cloth then label and date each jar.
24. Leave overnight until thoroughly cooled.
25. Jars may then be stored upright on shelves.

Dehydrating

1. Always begin with fresh, good quality food that is clean and inspected for damage.
2. Pretreatment is not necessary, but food that is blanched will keep its color and flavor better. Use the same blanching times as you would for freezing. Fruit, especially, responds well to pretreatment.
3. Doing some research on pretreatments may help you decide what procedure you would like to use.
4. You can marinate, salt, sweeten, or spice foods before you dehydrate them.
5. Jerky is meat that has been marinated and/or flavored by rubbing spices into it; avoid oil or grease of any kind as it will turn rancid as the food dries.
6. Vegetables and fruit can be treated the same way.
7. Slice or dice food thin and uniform so that it will dehydrate evenly. Uneven thicknesses may cause food to spoil because it did not dry as thoroughly as other parts.
8. Space food on dehydrator tray so that air can move around each piece.
9. Try not to let any piece touch another.
10. Fill your trays with all the same type of food as different foods take different amounts of time to dry.

11. You can, of course, dry different types of food at the same time, but you will have to remember to watch and remove the food that dehydrates more quickly. You can mix different foods in the same dehydrator batch, but do not mix strong vegetables like onions and garlic as other foods will absorb their taste while they are dehydrating.

12. The smaller the pieces, the faster a food will dehydrate. Thin leaves of spinach, celery, etc., will dry fastest. Remove them from the stalks before drying them or they will be overdone, losing flavor and quality. In very warm areas, they might even scorch. If they do, they will taste just like burned food when you rehydrate them.

13. Dense food like carrots will feel very hard when they are ready. Others will be crispy. Usually, a food that is high in fructose (sugar) will be leathery when it is finished dehydrating.

14. Remember that food smells when it is in the process of drying, so outdoors or in the garage is an excellent place to dry a big batch of those onions!

15. Always test each batch to make sure it is "done."

16. You can pasteurize finished food by putting it in a slow oven (150 degrees F.) for a few minutes.

17. Let the food cool before storing.

18. Store in airtight containers to guard against moisture. Jars saved from other food work well as long as they have lids that will keep moisture out.

19. Zip-closure food storage bags work well.

20. Jars of dehydrated carrots, celery, beets, etc., may look cheerful on your countertop, but the colors and flavors will fade. Dehydrated food keeps its color and flavor best if stored in a dark, cool place.

21. Dehydrating food takes time, so do not rush it. When you are all done, you will have a dried food stash to be proud of!

Freezing

1. Wash all containers and lids in hot, soapy water using soft cloth.
2. Rinse well in clear, clean, hot water.
3. Cool and drain well.
4. Place food into container to within 1 inch of rim. This allows for expansion of food during freezing.
5. Wipe rim of container with clean damp cloth, checking for chips or breaks.
6. Be certain cover fits the container snugly to avoid leaks. Burp air from container.
7. If food is hot when placing in container, cool prior to placing in freezer.
8. Label and date each container.
9. Store upright in freezer until frozen solid.

Apple Juice

Preserving apple juice not only makes the juice tastier but is also very handy.

Ingredients:

  fresh apples, unpeeled, quartered
  water

Directions:

1. Place apples in large nonreactive pan.
2. Add enough water to cover 2 inches over top of apples; cook on low heat until apples are tender.
3. Remove from heat and completely cool overnight.
4. Without mixing, carefully pour off clear liquid through colander; discard pulp.
5. Strain clear liquid through paper coffee filter or in strainer lined with cheesecloth.
6. Return liquid to stove and heat quickly, stirring occasionally, until juice begins to boil.
7. Process according to directions for canning found on page 226.

Apple Butter

This apple butter is one of our family favorites and is really delicious on whole-grain or oatmeal toast.

Ingredients:

- 7 lb. apples, stems removed, quartered
- 1½ c. apple cider
- 2½ c. sugar
- 2½ tsp. ground cinnamon
- 1 tsp. ground allspice
- ½ tsp. ground cloves

Directions:

1. Place apples in large nonreactive kettle; cover with water and bring to boil.
2. Reduce heat, and simmer until apples are tender.
3. Drain and cool.
4. Purée through food mill or sieve into 3-quart saucepan.
5. Discard seeds and skins; reserve juice and pulp.
6. Add cider, sugar, and spices to apple pulp; cook over low heat, stirring occasionally, until thickened, about 1½ hours.
7. Pour into sterilized jars and seal, following directions for canning jams and jellies on page 180.

Did You Know? . . . .

Did you know that two-thirds of the fiber and a lot of antioxidants are found in the peel of an apple?

Apple Butter Made Easy in Crock-Pot

This delicious apple butter is easy to make, and your family will love the fragrance while it is cooking. To make things easy, you can simply freeze what is left to have on hand in a hurry. This apple butter is great on warm toast with butter.

Ingredients:

6   lb. apples, peeled, finely chopped
2   c. brown sugar, firmly packed
1½ c. sugar
3   tsp. ground cinnamon
¼   tsp. ground cloves
¼   tsp. ground nutmeg

Directions:

1. Place apples in slow cooker.
2. Add sugars and spices, mixing well.
3. Cover and cook on high for 1 hour, then reduce heat to low.
4. Cover and cook 9 to 11 hours or until mixture is thick and dark brown, stirring occasionally.
5. Uncover and cook an additional hour.
6. If smoother apple butter is desired, may purée in blender or food mill after cooling to lukewarm.
7. Follow directions for freezing foods found on page 229, or pour hot apple butter into sterilized jars and seal, following directions for canning jams and jellies on page 180.

Apple Leather

My children love fruit leather, and this variation is delicious.

Ingredients:

3-5   lb. apples
¼-½ c. sugar (optional)
⅛   c. lemon juice (optional)
1   tsp. ground cinnamon
1   tsp. ground nutmeg

Directions:

1. Peel, core, and slice apples.
2. Cook uncovered in heavy, 3-quart saucepan over low heat.
3. If apples become dry, add a little water to prevent scorching.
4. Cook until apples are brown and look like apple butter.
5. Add sugar if apples are not sweet enough, and add lemon juice if apples are not tart enough.
6. Add spices; mix completely and let cook a little longer to allow flavors to blend.
7. When apple mix clings to upturned spoon, it is ready.
8. Cool in uncovered pot.
9. Preheat oven to 125 degrees F.
10. Spread mix evenly and thinly on 2 wax paper-lined cookie sheets.
11. Let dry in warm oven overnight or on counter, uncovered, for 2 to 3 days.
12. Check apple leather for dryness. When it can be touched with your finger and it is not sticky, it is dry enough; it should be flexible, not brittle.
13. Cut into ½-inch strips.
14. Wrap in wax paper or plastic wrap; eat like a fruit roll.
15. Store in tightly sealed containers; leather can also be frozen and will keep well for months.

Apple Pie Preserves

Preserves are a little more like jams with a slightly thicker consistency than apple butter and also retain small pieces of the apple rather than just smooth pulp.

Ingredients:

1½ c. water
4 Tbs. fresh lemon juice
1½ lb. firm, tart apples, peeled, cored, cubed
3½ c. sugar
6 Tbs. apple brandy
¼ tsp. ground cinnamon
¼ tsp. ground ginger
⅛ tsp. ground nutmeg

Directions:

1. Combine water and lemon juice in heavy, medium nonreactive saucepan; add apples and toss to coat with liquid.
2. Cover pan and bring to a boil, then reduce heat and simmer mixture for 3 minutes.
3. Mix sugar, brandy, and spices into apple mixture.
4. Bring to a boil over medium heat, stirring until sugar dissolves; reduce heat and simmer about 45 minutes, stirring occasionally.
5. Ladle into clean jars, cover, and refrigerate for up to 3 months, or seal, following directions for canning found on page 226.

Did You Know? . . . .

Did you know that apples rank as the chief fruit crop in Canada with production of about 500,000 tons yearly?

Apple Pumpkin Butter

This unusual combination makes a tasty fruit butter with an autumn mix of fragrant apples and pumpkin. This is a delicious butter served on biscuits, bread, corn muffins, or hot cereal.

Ingredients:

1¾ c. pumpkin (15-oz. can)
1¾ c. apples, peeled, cored, grated
1½ c. apple juice
½ c. brown sugar, packed firmly
¾ tsp. pumpkin pie spice

Directions:

1. Combine pumpkin, apples, and juice in deep, heavy, nonreactive saucepan.
2. Bring to a boil, reduce heat to low, and add brown sugar and spice, stirring well.
3. Cook for 1½ hours, stirring occasionally.
4. Follow directions for freezing foods found on page 229, or follow directions for canning jams and jellies found on page 180.

Yields: 3 cups.

Freezer Apples

This is an economical way to preserve those extra apples in the fall to have on hand during the winter and spring months.

Ingredients:

1 can frozen lemon juice (6 oz.)
2 c. sugar
   apples, peeled, cored, sliced

Directions:

1. In large bowl dilute lemon juice according to directions on can.
2. Add sugar and stir until dissolved. (Amount of sugar needed depends upon natural sweetness of apples.)
3. Place apple slices into bowl of prepared juice to prevent discoloration of fruit; use amount of apple slices desired up to quantity of juice available.
4. Drain and process, following directions for freezing found on page 229.

No-Cook Apple Raspberry Jam

There is nothing like the flavorful combination of apples and raspberries. This hearty, no-cook jam is tasty and delicious on warm toast with butter.

Ingredients:

3 c. fully ripe raspberries
1 c. apples, peeled, cored, finely ground
2 Tbs. fresh lemon juice
4 c. sugar
1 pouch liquid fruit pectin

Directions:

1. Thoroughly crush berries using potato masher; sieve half of pulp to remove some seeds, if desired.
2. Measure 1½ cups prepared berries; pour into large bowl.
3. Add lemon juice to apples; let stand 10 minutes.
4. Add sugar and liquid fruit pectin to bowl; stir for 3 minutes (a few sugar crystals will remain).
5. Follow directions for freezing foods found on page 229.

Yields: 4½ cups.

Peach Apple Salsa

Here is a wonderful and delicious salsa to make ahead and have on hand.

Ingredients:

- 6 c. chopped Roma tomatoes (3 lb.)
- 2½ c. diced yellow onions
- 2 c. chopped green bell peppers
- 10 c. chopped hard, unripe peaches (about 9 med.)
- 2 c. chopped Granny Smith apples
- 4 Tbs. mixed pickling spice
- 1 Tbs. canning salt
- 2 tsp. crushed red pepper flakes
- 3¾ c. light brown sugar (1¼ lb.), packed
- 2¼ c. cider vinegar (5 percent)

Directions:

1. Place pickling spice on clean, double-layered, 6-inch-square piece of 100-percent cheesecloth.
2. Bring corners together and tie with clean string. (Or use muslin spice bag.)
3. Wash and peel tomatoes (place washed tomatoes in boiling water for 1 minute, then immediately place in cold water and slip off skins); chop into ½-inch pieces.
4. Peel, wash, and seed bell peppers; chop into ¼-inch pieces.
5. Combine chopped tomatoes, onion, and pepper in 8- or 10-quart Dutch oven or saucepot.
6. Wash, peel, and pit peaches; cut into halves and soak 10 minutes in ascorbic acid solution.
7. Quickly chop peaches and apples into ½-inch cubes to prevent browning.
8. Add chopped peaches and apples to saucepot with vegetables.
9. Add pickling spice bag to saucepot.
10. Stir in salt, red pepper flakes, brown sugar, and vinegar; bring to boiling, stirring gently to mix ingredients.

11. Reduce heat and simmer 30 minutes, stirring occasionally.
12. Remove spice bag from pan and discard.
13. With slotted spoon, transfer salsa solids into hot, clean pint jars, leaving 1¼-inch headspace.
14. Cover with cooking liquid, leaving ½-inch headspace.
15. Follow canning instructions found on page 226.
16. Process in boiling water bath canner.
17. At altitudes from 0 to 1,000 feet, process 15 minutes; at 1,001 to 6,000 feet, process 20 minutes; above 6,000 feet, process 25 minutes.

Yields: About 7 pints.

Apple and Peach Conserve

Peach blends nicely with the apples in this delicious conserve.

Ingredients:

    2 c. tart apples, unpeeled, chopped small
    2 c. peaches, chopped small
    2 lemons, juice of
    3 c. sugar

Directions:

1. Combine apples and peaches with lemon juice and sugar.
2. Cook slowly until apples are transparent, about 20 minutes.
3. Pour into sterilized glasses and seal following canning directions found on page 226.

Yields: 7 jars (6-ounces each).

Spiced Crab Apples

Spiced crab apples are quite delicious, and preserving them especially for winter use is very handy.

Ingredients:

6   lb. crab apples
4½ c. apple cider vinegar with 5-percent acidity
4   c. water
7   c. sugar
5   tsp. whole cloves
5   sticks cinnamon
7   cubes fresh gingerroot

Directions:

1. Remove blossom petals and wash apples, but leave stems attached.
2. Puncture skin of each apple 4 times with ice pick or toothpick.
3. Mix vinegar, water, and sugar; bring to a boil.
4. Add spices tied in spice bag or cheesecloth.
5. Using blancher basket or sieve, immerse ⅓ of the apples at a time in boiling vinegar-syrup solution for 2 minutes.
6. Place cooked apples and spice bag in clean 1- or 2-gallon crock, and add hot syrup.
7. Cover and let stand overnight.
8. Remove spice bag; drain syrup into large saucepan, and reheat to boiling.
9. Process following canning directions found on page 226.

Did You Know? . . . .

Did you know that one of the oldest varieties of apple in existence is the Lady or Api?

Tomato Apple Conserve

This conserve is delicious with the combination of fruits and nuts. Use it just as you would jams and preserves or as a complement to meats at your meals.

Ingredients:

  2 lemons, thinly sliced, seeded
  6 lb. ripe tomatoes
  3 lb. tart apples, peeled, cored, cut into chunks
  5 c. sugar
  1 c. seedless raisins
  ½ tsp. salt
  ¼ c. chopped candied or preserved ginger
  1 c. roughly chopped walnuts

Directions:

  1. Place lemon slices in small nonreactive saucepan, and cover with cold water; bring to a boil and simmer until very tender.
  2. Drain off 1 cup of liquid, and place with rind in large kettle.
  3. Wash and peel tomatoes (place washed tomatoes in boiling water for 1 minute, then immediately place in cold water and slip off skins).
  4. Cut in large pieces, and add to kettle along with apple chunks.
  5. Add sugar, raisins, and salt; cook and stir over moderate heat until sugar dissolves.
  6. Simmer, stirring often, until mixture thickens and fruit is translucent; stir in ginger and walnuts.
  7. Process following canning directions found on page 226.

Yields: 8 half-pints.

Dried Apples

These make great portable snacks and are also healthy while still being delicious. Children love them, and they are also great Easter basket fillers in place of candy.

Ingredients:

3-5 sm. Red Delicious apples, cored, unpeeled
3   Tbs. lemon juice
2   c. water
¼   tsp. salt

Directions:

1. Preheat oven to 200 degrees F.
2. Cut apples into ⅛-inch-thick slices of any size to keep thickness even for adequate drying.
3. Combine lemon juice and water; pour mixture over apples.
4. Stir so all sides of slices are well coated; drain on paper towels.
5. Lightly sprinkle salt on both sides of apple slices.
6. Place on wire racks that sit on cookie sheets or baking pans to catch drips as they dry.
7. Bake for 4 to 6 hours or until evenly dried, with door ajar to let moisture escape.
8. Let slices cool; if not dried thoroughly, return slices to oven until apple slices are pliable but not crisp.
9. When completely cooled, store in zip-closure food storage bag or an airtight jar until ready to use.

Did You Know? . . . .

Did you know that a bushel of apples weighs about 42 pounds and will yield 20 to 24 quarts of applesauce?

Apple Delights Cookbook

A Collection of Apple Recipes
Cookbook Delights Series

Salads

Table of Contents

Page

Did You Know? . . . .

Did you know that in 2005 the People's Republic of China was the largest producer of apples worldwide, producing 40 percent of the total? The United States was second with 7.5 percent.

Appetizer Salad with Apples and Crab

This refreshing combination of crab and apples makes a colorful appetizer salad.

Ingredients:

3 Red Delicious apples, cored, diced
⅓ c. French vinaigrette-style dressing
8 oz. Alaska Snow crab, frozen or canned
½ c. cucumber, diced
⅔ c. celery, diced
⅓ c. mayonnaise
2 tsp. lemon juice
¾ tsp. dried dill weed
  salad greens

Directions:

1. In large bowl toss unpeeled, diced apples with French dressing.
2. Drain and chop crab into medium-size chunks; toss crab, cucumber, and celery with apples.
3. In separate bowl blend mayonnaise, lemon juice, and dill weed.
4. Cover both containers, and refrigerate until ready to serve.
5. When ready to serve, mix dressing with crab/apple mixture, and spoon onto salad plates lined with greens.

Yields: 6 to 8 servings.

Did You Know? . . . .

Did you know that a peck of apples weighs 10.5 pounds?

Apple and Fennel Salad

This salad is a very "woodsy" combination of apples, fennel, and juniper berries. Try this blend of flavors for an unusual treat.

Ingredients:

- 1½ fennel bulbs
- 1½ Granny Smith apples, cored, thinly sliced
- ½ c. pecans, toasted, chopped
- 3 Tbs. lemon juice
- 3 Tbs. olive oil
- ⅛ tsp. salt
- ¼ tsp. pepper
- ½ c. Parmesan cheese, freshly grated
- 12 juniper berries, finely chopped (optional)
  fresh fennel fronds for garnish

Directions:

1. Trim base from fennel bulbs; cut bulbs in half, and thinly slice, reserving fennel fronds for garnish.
2. Stir together fennel, apple, pecans, lemon juice, oil, and seasonings.
3. Stir in cheese and, if desired, juniper berries.
4. Cover; refrigerate and chill until ready to serve.
5. Garnish with fennel fronds for appearance and taste if desired.

Yields: 6 servings.

Did You Know? . . . .

Did you know that Louis Pasteur showed in 1864 that vinegar results from a natural fermentation process?

Apple and Green Chili Salad

Here is a delicious salad that presents a refreshing blend of flavors and textures.

Ingredients:

- 2 med. apples (1 red, 1 green), cored, chopped
- 3 stalks celery, chopped
- ⅔ c. walnuts, toasted, chopped
- 1 sm. can diced green chilies
- ⅓ c. prepared ranch-style salad dressing
- ¼ c. mayonnaise
- lettuce leaves

Directions:

1. Toss together apples, celery, nuts, and chilies.
2. Blend together salad dressing and mayonnaise in medium bowl.
3. Pour dressing over apple mixture; cover and refrigerate for at least 1 hour or until ready to serve.
4. Serve on individual plates on top of shredded lettuce leaves.

Yields: 8 servings.

***Did You Know?* . . . .**

Did you know that apple cider vinegar will reduce inflammation, bruising, and swelling in about a third of the time that ice will take?

Smoked Turkey and Apple Salad

The apples topping this tasty salad are fried just before serving.

Ingredients for vinaigrette:

- 2 Tbs. cider vinegar
- 6 Tbs. olive oil
- 1 Tbs. Dijon mustard
  salt and pepper to taste

Ingredients for salad:

- 1 bunch watercress
- 1 carrot, peeled, julienned
- 16 cherry tomatoes
- 10 oz. smoked turkey, coarsely chopped
- 2 c. vegetable oil
- 4 apples, peeled, cored, quartered

Directions for vinaigrette:

1. Whisk together vinegar, olive oil, and mustard; add salt and pepper.
2. Refrigerate until needed.

Directions for salad:

1. Arrange watercress, carrot, tomatoes, and turkey on salad plates.
2. Heat vegetable oil in heavy, 1-quart skillet.
3. When hot, fry apples until golden brown.
4. Remove from oil and place on paper towels to drain.
5. Arrange apples on plates and top all with vinaigrette.

Yields: 4 servings.

Apple and Potato Salad

Apples are a tart addition to the simple potatoes in this salad. The garnish with colorful beets and hard-boiled eggs makes this salad special.

Ingredients:

- 1 lb. tart green apples, cored, diced
- 1 lb. potatoes, cooked, peeled, diced
- ¼ c. olive oil
- ¼ c. white wine vinegar
- 2 beets, cooked, skins slipped, sliced, for garnish
- 2 hard-boiled eggs, sliced, for garnish
  salt and pepper to taste

Directions:

1. Combine apples and potatoes in bowl.
2. Whisk together oil, vinegar, salt, and pepper until well blended.
3. Pour over apples and potatoes, toss gently but thoroughly, and chill until ready to serve.
4. When ready to serve, place on individual serving dishes, and garnish with slices of beets and egg.

Yields: 4 to 6 servings.

***Did You Know?* . . . .**

Did you know that the Granny Smith apple, an Australian native, was discovered in 1868 as a chance seedling by "Granny" Anne Smith of Ryde, New South Wales?

Apple Cider Gelatin Salad

This makes a unique gelatin salad with the addition of dates and walnuts.

Ingredients:

- 1 pkg. lemon gelatin (3 oz.)
- 2 c. hot cider
- 3 Tbs. lemon juice
- 1⅓ c. red apples, chopped
- ¾ c. walnuts, broken
- ½ c. pitted dates, sliced
- 1 Tbs. grated lemon rind (optional)
  lettuce leaves

Directions:

1. Dissolve gelatin in hot cider.
2. Add lemon juice and chill until partially set.
3. Fold in apples, walnuts, dates, and lemon rind.
4. Turn into 1-quart mold.
5. Cover and refrigerate until firm.
6. When ready to serve, remove from refrigerator, and dip mold up to rim briefly in very warm water.
7. Place serving plate over top and invert onto plate.
8. Cut into wedges, and serve on top of lettuce leaves.

Yields: 6 servings.

Did You Know? . . . .

Did you know that Irish folklore claims that if an apple is peeled into one continuous ribbon and thrown behind a woman's shoulder, it will land in the shape of her future husband's initials?

Apple Coleslaw

Apples add extra flavor to this coleslaw and produce an interesting taste.

Ingredients:

    1   c. mayonnaise
    1   Tbs. honey
    3   c. green cabbage, shredded
    2   c. red cabbage, shredded
    1½ c. apples, chopped
        salt and pepper to taste

Directions:

1. Blend together mayonnaise and honey in small bowl.
2. Toss together cabbages and apples; salt and pepper to taste.
3. Pour dressing over apple mixture, refrigerate, and chill until ready to serve.

Yields: 6 servings.

Stuffed Apple Salad

The trick with this simple salad is to artistically design the apples to look like a beautiful flower.

Ingredients:

    4   ripe red apples
    2   Tbs. mayonnaise
    3   Tbs. lemon juice, divided
    3   Tbs. nuts of choice, chopped
    ¼   tsp. salt
        lettuce leaves

Directions:

1. With teaspoon gently hollow out apples, leaving thinnest shell possible.
2. Cut ½-inch petals halfway down shell.
3. Stir half of lemon juice into ice water; add apples and let stand so "petals" will curl back.
4. Chop apple pieces and marinate with remainder of lemon juice and salt; mix with mayonnaise.
5. Add nuts just before serving.
6. Fill inverted shells and serve on lettuce leaf.

Yields: 4 servings.

Red Apple Salad

This apple-raisin salad recipe also includes maraschino cherries and peanuts, a variation from the usual walnuts.

Ingredients:

5   lg. red apples, peeled, cored, diced
¾   c. raisins
2   oz. maraschino cherries, chopped
1   sm. pkg. dry-roasted peanuts, chopped fine
1   lg. banana, diced
    mayonnaise

Directions:

1. Combine apples, raisins, cherries, and peanuts; mix with enough mayonnaise to make a creamy mixture.
2. Pour a little cherry juice in with mixture; stir again.
3. Fold in bananas and stir lightly.
4. Cover and place in refrigerator to enhance flavor; chill up to 1 hour until ready to serve.

Yields: 4 to 6 servings.

Apple, Mango, and Radish Salad

The unique combination of fruits and vegetables in this salad is very tasty.

Ingredients:

    2   med. apples, peeled, cored, thinly sliced
    15 radishes, thinly sliced
    2   celery stalks, thinly sliced
    1   sm. ripe mango, peeled, cut into chunks
    ½   c. dairy sour cream
    2   tsp. creamed horseradish
    1   Tbs. fresh dill, chopped
        salt and freshly ground black pepper to taste
        dill for garnish (optional)

Directions:

1. Combine prepared apples, radishes, celery, and mango in large serving bowl.
2. In small bowl whisk together sour cream, horseradish, and dill.
3. Pour dressing over vegetables and fruit, tossing gently until all ingredients are well coated.
4. Adjust seasoning as desired.
5. Chill until ready to serve, then garnish with dill sprigs.

Yields: 4 servings.

Did You Know? . . . .

Did you know that apple colors range from various shades of red to green and yellow, and their flavor varies from tart to sweet?

Apple Peanut Salad with Tuna

This is a refreshing, cool salad with a tempting combination of apples, tuna, and peanuts.

Ingredients:

    1   med. apple, cored, sliced thin
    1   tsp. lemon juice
    2   stalks celery, thinly sliced
    1   can tuna (3½ oz.), drained
    ½   c. peanut halves
    4   Tbs. mayonnaise or salad dressing
    2   Tbs. apple juice
        lettuce leaves

Directions:

1. Place lettuce leaves onto 2 individual serving plates.
2. Sprinkle lemon juice over apples, and arrange on one side of each plate; add celery to other side of each plate.
3. Place tuna in center; sprinkle peanuts over top of tuna on each plate.
4. In small bowl stir together mayonnaise and enough apple juice to make thin salad dressing.
5. Place in refrigerator to chill, and when ready to serve, drizzle dressing over each salad.

Yields: 2 servings.

Did You Know? . . . .

Did you know that a Granny Smith Festival is held each year at Eastwood, New South Wales, a suburb of Sydney, where the variety was first grown?

Apple Pineapple Salad

This is a tasty combination of fruits with whipped cream, making a delicious light meal when served with a roll and drink on the side.

Ingredients:

1 Tbs. all-purpose flour
½ c. sugar
2 Tbs. instant tapioca
2 Tbs. cider vinegar
1 can crushed pineapple (8 oz.), reserve juice
4 apples, cored, chopped
2 c. unsalted peanuts
1 c. whipped cream, sweetened to taste

Directions:

1. In medium saucepan stir together flour, sugar, tapioca, vinegar, and reserved pineapple juice.
2. Cook over medium heat, stirring constantly, until thickened.
3. Remove from heat; cover and chill in refrigerator.
4. In large bowl combine crushed pineapple, apples, peanuts, and chilled tapioca mixture.
5. Fold in whipped cream, and chill for at least 1 hour before serving.

Yields: 12 servings.

Did You Know? . . . .

Did you know that candy apple red, referring to the coating on candy apples, inspired Joe Bailon to create the automobile paint of that color?

Apple Salad and Tofu Honey Dressing

Try this healthy combination for an appealing and quite delicious salad.

Ingredients for dressing:

> 1   c. plain yogurt
> ½   c. tofu
> 2   Tbs. honey
> 1½ tsp. ground cinnamon

Ingredients for salad:

> 5   med. Red Delicious apples, cored, sliced
> ⅓   c. fresh lemon juice
> 4   stalks celery, diced
> 1   sm. can pineapple tidbits, unsweetened, drained
>   mint sprigs for garnish

Directions for dressing:

1. Combine yogurt, tofu, honey, and cinnamon in food processor; blend until smooth.
2. Cover and chill.

Directions for salad:

1. Toss sliced apples in lemon juice.
2. At serving time, combine apples with celery and pineapple.
3. Just before serving, combine apple mixture with dressing and toss gently.
4. Garnish with mint sprigs.

Yields: 8 servings.

Apple Spice Chicken Salad

This is another refreshing salad with a distinctive combination of fresh chicken, apples, and nutmeg. It would be great for your next lunch or dinner party!

Ingredients:

2½ c. cooked chicken, diced
2   c. celery, chopped
2½ c. apples, cored, chopped
⅓ c. raisins
2   Tbs. mayonnaise
2   Tbs. plain yogurt
¼ tsp. ground nutmeg
½ tsp. ground cinnamon
¼ tsp. salt
⅛ tsp. ground black pepper

Directions:

1. Combine chicken, celery, apples, and raisins in large bowl.
2. In small bowl blend together mayonnaise, yogurt, nutmeg, and cinnamon.
3. Fold into chicken mixture; season with salt and pepper.
4. Cover and place in refrigerator to chill until ready to serve.

Yields: 6 to 8 servings.

Did You Know? . . . .

Did you know that apples are eaten with honey at the Jewish New Year of Rosh Hashanah to symbolize a sweet new year?

Classic Waldorf Salad with Cabbage

The slaw dressing and cabbage give this old classic salad a new and tangy taste that is absolutely delicious!

Ingredients for dressing:

>   1 c. mayonnaise or salad dressing
>   ¼ c. vinegar or lemon juice
>   1 tsp. celery seed
>   2 tsp. sugar
>   1 tsp. salt
>   ¼ tsp. pepper

Ingredients for salad:

>   6 c. green cabbage, coarsely shredded
>   1 lg. apple, cored, cut into bite-size chunks
>   ½ c. raisins
>   ¼ c. walnuts, chopped

Directions for dressing:

>   1. Combine dressing ingredients thoroughly.

Directions for salad:

>   1. Toss together cabbage, apple chunks, and raisins.
>   2. Add dressing and toss gently to coat well.
>   3. Cover and chill to blend flavors.
>   4. Before serving, garnish with chopped walnuts and more apple chunks dipped in lemon juice to prevent browning.

Yields: 12 servings.

Greens with Apples and Bacon

Steamed greens are the base for this attractive, simple salad.

Ingredients:

1 bunch watercress
1 bunch dandelion greens
1 sm. red onion, sliced thin
1 apple, peeled, cored, sliced thin
6 oz. bacon, cooked crisp, crumbled
1 lemon

Directions:

1. In 2-quart saucepan bring 2 cups water to a boil; place strainer over pan but not in water.
2. Toss watercress and dandelion greens together in strainer; cover and steam for 2 to 3 minutes, checking frequently. (Do not overcook.)
3. When greens are just wilted, place on 4 plates.
4. Arrange onion slices on greens, and top with apple slices and crumbled bacon.
5. Squeeze lemon juice over each salad.

Yields: 4 servings.

Did You Know? . . . .

Did you know that applejack is a strong alcoholic beverage produced from apples, originating from the American colonial period? It is made by concentrating hard cider.

Apple Delights Cookbook

A Collection of Apple Recipe
Cookbook Delights Series

Side Dishes

Table of Content

Did You Know? . . . .

Did you know that the largest U.S. apple crop on record (277.3 million cartons) was harvested in 1998?

Apple Cheddar Pie with
Sweet Potato Crust

In this delicious and attractive apple pie, the sweet potato crust is quite unique and very flavorful.

Ingredients for crust:

- 1   c. sweet potato, cooked, mashed
- 1   egg, lightly beaten
- ¼ c. butter, melted
- 2   Tbs. fresh orange juice
- 1   c. all-purpose flour
- 1   tsp. baking powder

Ingredients for filling:

- 2½ apples, peeled, cored, grated
- ¾ c. sweet wine
- 1¾ c. cheddar cheese, grated
- 3   eggs
- 1¾ c. cream
- 1   pinch ground nutmeg

Directions for crust:

1. In bowl combine cooked potato, egg, butter, and orange juice, blending well.
2. Stir in flour and baking powder; mix just until mixture forms a clinging ball.
3. Press dough onto bottom and sides of large, buttered pie plate; set aside.

Directions for filling:

1. Marinate apples in wine for 2 hours; drain well.
2. Preheat oven to 350 degrees F.
3. Sprinkle apples and cheese over bottom of crust.
4. Beat eggs and cream together; add nutmeg.

5. Pour over apples and cheese in crust; bake for 45 minutes.
6. Remove from oven, and let stand in pie plate for 15 minutes before cutting to serve.

Yields: 8 to 10 servings.

Caramelized Roasted Vegetables with Apple Juice

These caramelized roasted vegetables made with white wine syrup are oh-so-good!

Ingredients:

3   c. apple juice
1   c. dry white wine
3   Tbs. butter
1¼ lb. turnips
1¼ lb. parsnips
1¼ lb. carrots
1¼ lb. sweet potatoes
1¼ lb. rutabagas
    salt and pepper to taste

Directions:

1. Boil apple juice and wine in large saucepan until reduced to ¾ cup, about 30 minutes; whisk in butter.
2. Preheat oven to 425 degrees F.
3. Peel and cut vegetables into ½-inch pieces; divide between 2 roasting pans.
4. Pour apple juice mixture over vegetables; sprinkle with salt and pepper, then toss to coat.
5. Roast until vegetables are tender and golden; stirring occasionally, about 40 minutes.

Yields: 8 servings.

Apple Onion Turkey Roll

This tasty turkey roll can be served to company as an appetizer or to your family as a main or side dish.

Ingredients:

- 1 lb. ground turkey
- 2 c. diced apples
- 2 c. bread crumbs
- 1 sm. onion, diced
- ½ tsp. sage
- ½ tsp. poultry seasoning
  cheddar cheese, grated

Directions:

1. Preheat oven to 350 degrees F.
2. On wax paper, roll out turkey into rectangle ½ inch thick.
3. Combine apples, bread crumbs, onion, sage, and poultry seasoning; mix well and spread over meat.
4. Start from long edge, and roll as for jellyroll using wax paper as a guide.
5. Place in lightly buttered 13 x 9 x 2-inch baking dish.
6. Bake for 45 minutes.
7. Remove from oven and sprinkle cheese over top; return to oven until cheese is melted.
8. Turn oven off, and let roll sit 15 minutes with door open before removing to slice and arrange on serving platter.

Yields: 4 main dish servings; 6 side dish servings.

Did You Know? . . . .

Did you know that one apple has 5 grams of fiber?

Apple Pecan Sage Stuffing

For a special family meal, stuff roasted chicken and bake. Another delicious way to serve is to stuff extra-thick pork chops or brown thinner pork chops and layer between.

Ingredients:

½ lb. bacon, chopped
1   c. butter
1   c. onion, finely diced
1   c. carrot, finely diced
1   c. celery, finely diced
4   lg. apples, unpeeled, cored, finely diced
1   tsp. thyme
2   bay leaves
1   c. fresh sage, chopped
2   Tbs. fresh parsley, chopped
¼   tsp. ground cinnamon
1   c. apple juice
1   c. chicken stock
8   c. coarse bread crumbs
1¼ c. pecans, crushed
    salt and pepper to taste

Directions:

1. Cook bacon until crisp; drain off grease.
2. In same pan with bacon, sauté onion, carrots, and celery in added butter for 6 to 8 minutes.
3. Add apples, thyme, bay leaves, sage, parsley, and cinnamon.
4. Cook for another 5 minutes; add apple juice and chicken stock.
5. Bring to a boil, remove from heat, and place mixture in large mixing bowl.
6. Add bread crumbs and pecans.
7. Mix well and season to taste with salt and pepper.
8. May be used to stuff your choice of meat, or place in a covered, buttered baking dish and bake in oven preheated to 350 degrees F. for 30 minutes to serve separately.

Avocado Halves with Apples and Crab

This is a delicious side to a main meal, or just serve as a snack and still enjoy the unusual combination.

Ingredients for vinaigrette:

- 2 tsp. sugar
- ½ tsp. dry mustard
- 1 clove garlic, crushed
- 3 Tbs. white wine vinegar or lemon juice
- 9 Tbs. olive oil
- 3 Tbs. heavy cream (optional)

Ingredients for avocado halves:

- 2 avocados
- 8 oz. crab meat
- 1 sm. apple, cored, diced

Directions for vinaigrette:

1. Place sugar, mustard, garlic, vinegar, and oil into screw-top jar; shake vigorously.
2. Shake well each time before serving.
3. For creamy vinaigrette, add 3 tablespoons heavy cream to vinaigrette; use this portion immediately as it will not keep.

Directions for avocado halves:

1. Halve avocados and remove stones.
2. Mix crab meat with vinaigrette and apple; fill avocados with this mixture.
3. Cover, refrigerate, and chill for several hours until quite firm.
4. Cut avocados into quarters lengthwise after chilling, and place on serving dish.
5. Return to refrigerator until ready to serve.
6. Serve as side dish with the main meal or as a snack.

Baked Apples with Sweet Potato Stuffing

These baked apples are stuffed with a sweet potato, pineapple, and pecan filling and topped with marshmallows to make them quite a yummy combination!

Ingredients:

- 6 baking apples, peeled
- ½ c. cinnamon red hot candies
- 1 c. water
- 1 can sweet potatoes (29 oz.), drained
- ⅓ c. brown sugar, firmly packed
- ½ c. crushed pineapple, drained
- ¼ c. chopped pecans
- 6 lg. marshmallows

Directions:

1. In large pot over medium heat, combine candies and water; stir until candies are dissolved.
2. Add slightly hollowed out apples, and baste frequently until apples become crisp-tender.
3. Remove from heat; lift out of liquid to drain and allow cooling.
4. Preheat oven to 350 degrees F.
5. Oil 4-quart, round casserole dish with cooking spray.
6. Mix together sweet potatoes, brown sugar, pineapple, and pecans; stuff cooled apples with mixture, and mound remaining mixture on top of apples.
7. Place in prepared casserole dish, and bake for 20 minutes; remove from oven.
8. Place 1 marshmallow on each apple; return to oven, and cook until marshmallows are golden brown.

Yields: 6 servings.

Fresh Fruit Cocktail with Sauce

This very tasty fruit cocktail is great as a side dish with a main meal, just as a snack, or even a delicious dessert.

Ingredients for fruit:

2   c. apple juice
1   Tbs. lemon juice
½ tsp. orange zest
2   cinnamon sticks (3-in. lengths)
2   Red Delicious apples, cored, diced
1½ c. fresh pineapple, diced
1   orange, peeled, sectioned, halved
½ c. seedless grapes, halved

Ingredients for sauce:

1   c. dairy sour cream
¼ c. apricot preserves
2   Tbs. dry white wine
¼ c. grated coconut
½ c. macadamia nuts, chopped

Directions for fruit:

1. In medium nonreactive saucepan, combine apple juice, lemon juice, orange zest, and cinnamon sticks.
2. Heat to boiling and simmer, uncovered, for 10 minutes; remove from heat and cool to room temperature.
3. In large serving bowl, combine apples, pineapple, orange, and grapes.
4. Remove cinnamon sticks, and pour apple juice mixture over fruit.
5. Refrigerate to blend flavors and chill before serving; drain juice mixture before adding sauce.

Directions for sauce:

1. Combine sour cream, apricot preserves, and wine; blend well.
2. Add coconut and chopped nuts, stirring well.
3. Pour over fruit combination and chill before serving.

Yields: 4 servings.

Sauerkraut with Apple and Caraway

Those who love plain sauerkraut will enjoy it even more with the addition of the sweet and tart flavors of apples and brown sugar.

Ingredients:

2 cans or jars sauerkraut (1 lb. each), rinsed, drained well
2 Granny Smith apples, peeled, chopped
¾ c. dry white wine
1 c. chicken broth
3 Tbs. brown sugar, firmly packed, or to taste
¾ tsp. caraway seeds

Directions:

1. In large, heavy saucepan combine sauerkraut, apples, wine, broth, brown sugar, and caraway seeds.
2. Simmer, covered, stirring occasionally, for 1 hour.
3. Sauerkraut may be made 1 day in advance, kept covered and chilled, and reheated before serving.

Yields: 8 servings.

Spicy Apple Side Dish

This is a tangy, sweet, and delicious way to serve fresh apples instead of cooked for a side dish.

Ingredients:

⅓ c. balsamic vinegar
¼ c. brown sugar, firmly packed
¼ tsp. coarsely ground black pepper
5 Granny Smith apples, peeled, cored, diced

Directions:

1. In large bowl mix together balsamic vinegar, brown sugar, and black pepper.
2. Taste, and adjust sugar and vinegar to your personal preference.
3. Add apples and stir to coat.
4. Cover, and refrigerate for 1 hour to marinate flavors before serving.

Yields: 5 servings.

Apple, Raisin, and Apricot Chutney

This chutney is very flavorful and a nice addition to your dinner table. It is quite delicious served with meats.

Ingredients:

1 c. dried apricots
1 c. hot water
3 lg. garlic cloves, peeled, chopped
1 sm. piece fresh gingerroot, peeled, chopped
¼ c. cider vinegar
½ c. sugar
¼ c. raisins
1 lg. apple, cored, diced
 dash of cayenne
 salt to taste

Directions:

1. Place dried apricots in bowl with hot water, and let soak 4 hours.
2. Peel and chop ginger and garlic; blend with vinegar.
3. Put apricots with their soaking water and ginger-garlic mixture into large nonreactive saucepan.
4. Add sugar, cayenne, and salt; bring to a boil, and simmer gently for 8 minutes, stirring occasionally to prevent burning.
5. Add raisins, and continue cooking until chutney thickens and begins to turn shiny.
6. Remove from heat and stir in diced apple.
7. Cool, then cover and refrigerate until ready to serve.

Delicious Apple Spice Dressing

This recipe is especially delicious with this unique combination of spices that gives added flavor.

Ingredients:

2   apples, peeled, cored, grated
¼   tsp. ground nutmeg
¼   tsp. ground cinnamon
¼   c. sugar
¼   c. butter, melted
3   c. seasoned dressing cubes, dry
2   c. water or more as needed

Directions:

1. Combine apples, spices, sugar, and butter in large bowl; stir in dry dressing.
2. Add 2 cups water, mix, and continue to add until dressing becomes consistency desired.
3. Stuff meat, and cook according to directions for that particular meat.
4. Or place in casserole dish, and cooked separately in oven at 350 degrees F. for 1 hour.

Vegetarian Stuffing

For those in your family who are vegetarians, this is a wonderful and delicious stuffing. Multi-grain, nut, and sourdough breads all work great in this recipe.

Ingredients:

- 1   loaf day-old bread (1 lb.)
- 1   can condensed cream of mushroom soup (10 oz.)
- 1   can vegetable broth (10 oz.)
- ¼   c. water
- 1   tsp. poultry seasoning
- ½   c. wild rice, cooked
- ¼   c. dried cranberries
- ½   c. chopped mushrooms
- ¼   c. chopped walnuts
- ¼   c. cubed apples
-     salt to taste
-     ground black pepper to taste

Directions:

1. Preheat oven to 350 degrees F.
2. Mix together bread, mushroom soup, broth, water, poultry seasoning, and salt and pepper to taste.
3. Add rice, cranberries, mushrooms, walnuts, and apples, mixing well. (Mixture will be somewhat sticky to touch.)
4. Shape into loaf; wrap in oil-sprayed foil.
5. Bake for about an hour.
6. Remove from oven, let cool slightly, then slice like meatloaf to serve.

Yorkshire Apple Pudding

This Yorkshire pudding is a real treat with the addition of apple in the recipe. It dresses up any meat in a delicious way.

Ingredients:

- 4 eggs
- 2 c. milk
- 2 c. sifted all-purpose flour
- 1 tsp. salt
- 1 med. apple, cored, diced
  meat drippings

Directions:

1. Preheat oven to 400 degrees F.
2. Beat eggs with milk.
3. Sift together flour and salt; stir into egg mixture and beat until well blended.
4. Fold in diced apples, stirring just until mixed.
5. Discard most of fat from pan in which meat was roasted; reserve drippings.
6. Heat 11 x 7-inch baking pan or ring mold, and pour into it ¼ cup of meat drippings.
7. Pour in pudding mixture and bake for 10 minutes.
8. Reduce oven temperature to 350 degrees F., and bake 15 to 20 minutes longer or until puffy and delicately browned.
9. Remove from oven, cut into squares, and serve immediately with roasted meat.

Yields: 10 to 12 servings.

Butternut Squash with Apple and Onion Au Gratin

This is a delicious dish to serve with the holiday meals. It can be made vegetarian by leaving out the bacon and substituting the chicken stock with vegetable broth.

Ingredients:

- ¼ c. all-purpose flour
- 1 tsp. salt
- 1 pinch ground cinnamon
- 1 med. butternut squash, peeled, seeded, sliced
- 4 med. apples, peeled, cored, sliced
- ½ sweet onion, thinly sliced
- 1 c. chicken stock
- 1 c. shredded sharp cheddar cheese
- 3 slices bacon, cooked, crumbled
- cooking spray

Directions:

1. Preheat oven to 350 degrees F.
2. Place flour, salt, and cinnamon in large plastic bag.
3. Add squash, apples, and onions; shake until lightly dusted.
4. Spray 13 x 9 x 2-inch glass baking dish with cooking spray; layer ½ of squash, apples, and sweet onion.
5. Pour ½ cup chicken stock over, then sprinkle with ½ of cheese.
6. Layer with remaining squash, apple, and onions; pour remaining chicken stock over top, cover with foil, and bake for 40 minutes.
7. Remove from oven, and sprinkle with bacon crumbles and remaining cheese.
8. Return, uncovered, to oven; bake for another 5 minutes to melt cheese.
9. Remove from oven, and let stand for 5 minutes before serving.

Yields: 10 servings.

Maple-Apple Baked Beans

Baked beans, always a tasty side dish, are made even better with the addition of apples.

Ingredients:

4   c. dried navy beans
10 c. water
1   lb. sliced bacon, quartered
1   lg. onion, chopped
2   tsp. salt
1   tsp. ground mustard
1   c. maple syrup
3   med. tart apples, peeled, sliced
½   c. butter, softened
1   c. brown or maple sugar, firmly packed

Directions:

1. Place beans in soup kettle or Dutch oven; add water to cover by 2 inches.
2. Bring to a boil; boil for 2 minutes.
3. Remove from heat; cover and let stand for 1 hour.
4. Drain and rinse beans; discard liquid.
5. Return beans to pan; add 10 cups water.
6. Bring to a boil.
7. Reduce heat; cover and simmer for 30 minutes.
8. Preheat oven to 350 degrees F.
9. Drain beans, reserving ½ cup liquid.
10. Line bottom of 4-quart baking dish with bacon.
11. In bowl combine beans, onion, salt, and mustard.
12. Spoon over bacon; pour syrup over top.
13. Cover and bake for 3 hours, gently stirring occasionally and adding reserved bean liquid if needed.
14. Arrange sliced apples over top.
15. In small mixing bowl cream butter and brown sugar; spread over apples.
16. Cover, and bake 1 hour longer or until beans are tender.

Yields: 12 servings.

Celery Root and Apple Purée

This soft, creamy purée goes better with pork than applesauce. Celery root has a smoother, more subtle flavor than celery without the fibrous texture.

Ingredients:

  5 lb. celery root (celeriac)
  4 Gala, Empire, or McIntosh apples (1½ lb.)
  ¼ c. unsalted butter
  2 tsp. salt
  1 c. heavy cream
  ½ tsp. white pepper
  ½ tsp. freshly grated nutmeg
     celery leaves for garnish

Directions:

  1. Peel celery root with sharp knife, then cut into 1-inch cubes.
  2. Peel and core apples, then cut into 1-inch pieces.
  3. Melt butter in 6- to 8-quart heavy pan over medium-low heat.
  4. Add celery root, apples, and salt, stirring to coat with butter.
  5. Cover with tight-fitting lid and cook (without adding liquid), stirring occasionally, until celery root is tender, 50 minutes to 1 hour.
  6. Purée mixture in batches in food processor until smooth, about 2 minutes per batch.
  7. Return purée to pot and stir in cream, white pepper, and nutmeg.
  8. Reheat, covered, over medium heat, stirring occasionally, until hot, about 5 minutes.
  9. Purée can be made 1 day ahead and cooled completely, uncovered, then chilled, covered.
  10. Reheat, covered, over low heat, stirring occasionally, until hot, about 15 minutes.

Yields: 10 to 12 servings.

Apple Delights Cookbook

A Collection of Apple Recipes
Cookbook Delights Series

Soups

Table of Contents

Did You Know? . . . .

Did you know that America's longest-lived apple tree was reportedly planted in 1647 by Peter Stuyvesant in his Manhattan orchard and was still bearing fruit when a derailed train struck it in 1866?

Apple and Butternut Squash Soup

Autumn gardens yield lots of apples and squash. This recipe offers a tasty combination of both.

Ingredients:

4 Tbs. unsalted butter
2 lg. onions, chopped
2 Tbs. curry powder
1 tsp. chili powder
1 lg. butternut squash, peeled, seeded, chopped
3 firm apples, peeled, cored, diced
5 c. chicken stock
½ c. whipping cream
  fresh parsley or cilantro, chopped, for garnish
  salt to taste
  freshly ground black pepper

Directions:

1. In heavy skillet melt butter over medium heat.
2. Add onions and sauté until translucent; add curry and chili powders, and cook for 5 minutes.
3. Transfer mixture to soup kettle; add squash, apples, and half of stock, and bring to a boil.
4. Reduce heat; season with salt and pepper.
5. Simmer 45 minutes to 1 hour or until squash is tender, stirring occasionally to prevent sticking.
6. Remove from heat, strain soup, and reserve liquid.
7. Place pulp in food processor, and pulse until puréed; return purée to reserved liquid.
8. Add cream and remaining chicken stock, and simmer until hot.
9. Ladle into bowls, and sprinkle with chopped parsley or cilantro.

Yields: 6 to 8 servings.

Apple and Potato Chowder

Our family always enjoys this interesting variation of chowder.

Ingredients:

- ¾ lb. bacon, diced in ¼-inch pieces
- 1½ c. onion, finely chopped
- 1½ lb. potatoes, diced in ½-inch pieces
- 1½ lb. tart apples, peeled, cored, cut in ½-inch pieces
- 8 c. chicken broth
- ½ tsp. pepper
- 2 c. light cream or half-and-half
- ½ c. sliced green onions

Directions:

1. Fry bacon over medium heat until browned and crispy; remove bacon bits from fat and drain on paper towel, reserving for garnish.
2. Cook onion for 2 minutes, scraping up browned bits from bottom with wooden spoon.
3. Place onion in 3-quart kettle; add potatoes and cook 5 minutes.
4. Add apples and chicken broth to kettle, and bring to boiling.
5. Season to taste with pepper.
6. Lower heat; simmer 25 minutes or until potatoes and apples are very soft.
7. Stir several times with whisk to purée some of apples and potatoes but still leaving soup chunky; remove from heat and add cream.
8. Ladle chowder into soup bowls; sprinkle with bacon and green onions for garnish.
9. Serve while hot.

Yields: 6 to 8 servings.

Apple Autumn Harvest Soup

This soup boasts butternut squash and apples paired with nutmeg, ginger, and toasted pecans for a lightly spiced soup to go with a meal. It can also be meal by itself with crusty bread, salad, and a beverage.

Ingredients:

- 3 Tbs. butter
- 1 c. chopped onion
- 1 butternut squash, peeled, seeded, cut into chunks
- 1 med. Golden Delicious apple, cored, cut into chunks
- ½ c. chopped pecans, toasted
- 1 Tbs. brandy (optional)
- 1 can chicken or vegetable broth (14 oz.)
- 1 tsp. ground ginger
- ½ tsp. ground nutmeg
- ¾ c. whipping cream
-    sour cream

Directions:

1. Melt butter over medium heat in large saucepan; add onion, and sauté about 3 minutes or until slightly softened.
2. Add squash, apple, pecans, and brandy; cook over medium heat, stirring occasionally, for 1 minute.
3. Stir in broth, ginger, and nutmeg; bring to a boil, then reduce heat.
4. Cover and simmer, stirring occasionally, about 25 minutes or until squash and apple are tender; remove from heat and cool slightly.
5. Working in batches, blend squash mixture in blender or food processor until smooth.
6. Return squash mixture to saucepan; stir in whipping cream, blending well.

7. When ready to serve, heat through, but do not boil.
8. Top each serving with dollop of sour cream if desired.

Yields: 6 servings.

Creamed Apple Soup

This is one of those delicious, cold soups that is wonderful to serve on a hot summer afternoon.

Ingredients:

4 lg. apples, peeled, pared, diced
¼ c. sugar
3 c. hot water
4 Tbs. all-purpose flour
½ c. heavy cream

Directions:

1. Combine apples, sugar, and water; cook until tender.
2. Remove 1 cup broth; thicken with flour and mix back into soup.
3. Simmer until soup begins to thicken; remove from heat and cool.
4. Cover and chill if desired; add cream after removing from refrigerator and just before serving.
5. If serving at room temperature, add cream and serve.

Yields: 4 to 6 servings.

Apple Cheese Soup

This is a very hearty soup with the great combination of ham, bacon, apples, and cheese. We have two vegetarians in our family and this soup can be made without the ham and bacon. Substitute canned vegetable broth for chicken broth for the vegetarian version.

Ingredients:

1	Tbs. white peppercorns
3	sprigs fresh thyme
2	bay leaves
¼	c. peanut oil
1	c. ham scraps and/or 1 ham bone
1	stalk celery, diced
2	cloves garlic, minced
2	onions, diced
8	tart Granny Smith apples, peeled, cored, quartered
1	c. white port
6	c. chicken broth
4	slices bacon, apple or hickory smoked
4	Tbs. unsalted butter, softened
¼	c. all-purpose flour
1½	lb. sharp cheddar cheese, grated
1	sm. Red Delicious apple for garnish
1	sm. Granny Smith apple for garnish
1	lemon, juiced
	salt and pepper to taste
	cilantro, chopped, for garnish

Directions:

1. Tie peppercorns, thyme, and bay leaves together in cheesecloth; set aside.
2. In large saucepan heat oil over medium-high heat.
3. Add ham scraps, celery, garlic, and onions; sauté about 4 minutes or until onions are translucent.
4. Reduce heat to medium and add apple quarters.
5. Cover and cook, stirring frequently, for about 10 minutes or until apples soften.

6. Add port and simmer for 5 minutes more.
7. Add chicken broth, spice bag, and ham bone if using.
8. Reduce heat to low and simmer, partially covered, for about 20 minutes to blend flavors.
9. Remove spice bag and discard.
10. Note: Soup may be made a day or two in advance up to this point; cool and refrigerate.
11. Cut bacon into l-inch diced pieces, and fry over medium heat until browned and crisp; drain on paper towels.
12. In small bowl knead softened butter and flour together until smooth to make 'beurre manié.'
13. Whisk mixture into soup to thicken it; cook for 5 minutes longer, stirring frequently.
14. Remove from heat; add grated cheese to soup, stirring constantly until it is melted. Do not simmer over direct heat after adding cheese.
15. Strain soup through fine sieve into top of double boiler set over gently boiling water to keep soup hot; do not press too hard on solids.
16. Season with remaining lemon juice and salt and pepper to taste.
17. Leaving skin on, cut green and red apples into ⅛-inch diced pieces to use for garnish–about 2 tablespoons of each color.
18. Put diced apples in small glass or ceramic bowl, and sprinkle with 1 tablespoon lemon juice.
19. When ready to serve, ladle soup into bowls or tureens, and sprinkle apple and bacon over top for garnish; serve warm.
20. Note: If made ahead, when reheating soup, add beurre manié, then the cheese and seasonings. Do not prepare the apple and bacon garnish until a few hours before serving.
21. This soup can be completed up to 2 hours before serving, but keep it warm in top half of double boiler set over hot water. Do not simmer over direct heat after cheese has been added or soup will separate.

Yields: 6 servings.

Apple Cider Soup with Cinnamon Dumplings

Our family loves dumplings, so this soup is always a treat.

Ingredients for soup:

1	c. onions, chopped
1	c. carrots, diced
2	cloves garlic
6	apples, peeled, cored, diced
8	tsp. butter
6	Tbs. all-purpose flour
2	qt. apple cider
2	lemons, juiced
½	tsp. ground nutmeg
1½	tsp. ground cinnamon
¾	tsp. white pepper

Ingredients for dumplings:

6	Tbs. butter, softened
4	lg. eggs, beaten
6	Tbs. all-purpose flour
2	Tbs. onion, minced
½	tsp. ground cinnamon

Directions for soup:

1. In saucepan sauté onions, carrots, garlic, and apples in butter until soft; add flour and stir well.
2. Add cider slowly, stirring to blend; cover and simmer for 20 minutes.
3. Cool to lukewarm, then purée in blender; add lemon juice and seasonings to taste.
4. Return mixture to pan and bring to a simmer.

Directions for dumplings:

1. Beat butter until soft; add beaten eggs.
2. Blend in flour, onion, and cinnamon just until moistened.
3. Drop 1 tablespoon at a time into simmering liquid, using all of batter.
4. Cover pan, and let simmer gently for about 7 minutes.
5. Remove from heat, ladle into bowls, and garnish with cinnamon sticks if desired.

Yields: 10 to 12 servings.

Cheese and Apple Soup

This is a thick, hearty, and cheesy soup that is really delicious served on a cold, wintry day. Add some crusty, fresh-baked bread to make a meal!

Ingredients:

⅓ c. butter
⅓ c. all-purpose flour
½ tsp. salt
2½ c. milk
4 c. Gouda cheese or cheddar, shredded
1 c. apple juice

Directions:

1. Melt butter in saucepan over low heat.
2. Blend in flour and salt; cook for 2 minutes.
3. Gradually add milk, stirring constantly until thickened; add cheese, stirring until melted.
4. Add juice; heat thoroughly, stirring occasionally.
5. Remove from heat and ladle into bowls to serve.

Yields: 4 servings.

Broccoli Apple Soup

Here is a wonderfully delicious combination for a soup that will satisfy even the most picky eaters!

Ingredients for soup:

2½ c. broccoli flowerets
1 c. broccoli stems, cut in 1-in. pieces
3 Tbs. butter
1 sm. onion, peeled, chopped
1 med. apple, peeled, cored, chopped
4 c. chicken broth
½ tsp. coriander
   salt to taste

Ingredients for crème fraîche:

½ c. whipping cream
½ c. sour cream

Directions for soup:

1. Prepare broccoli flowerets and stems; steam flowerets separately until crisp-tender; reserve ½ cup for garnish.
2. Heat butter in heavy saucepan; sauté onion and apple for 2 minutes or until heated through.
3. Add broccoli stems and chicken broth; heat to boiling.
4. Reduce heat to low, add flowerets, and simmer 10 minutes or until broccoli is cooked through.
5. Remove from heat, cool to warm, then place mixture into blender container or food processor fitted with steel blade; process until puréed.
6. Add coriander and salt to taste; heat to serving temperature.
7. Garnish soup with reserved broccoli flowerets.
8. Serve with crème fraîche to spoon over individual servings at the table.

Directions for crème fraîche:

1. Whip cream until stiff.
2. Fold in sour cream.
3. Serve in small bowl at table for garnish.

Yields: 4 servings.

Apple, Squash, and Walnut Soup

This is a rich, hearty autumn soup with an interesting blend of flavors.

Ingredients:

2   c. winter squash, cooked, puréed
2   Tbs. unsalted butter
1   c. unsweetened applesauce
1   c. light cream
1½ c. chicken stock
¼   c. walnuts, toasted, ground
2   tsp. dried chervil, crumbled
½   tsp. ground mace
¾   c. toasted walnut pieces for garnish
     salt and white pepper to taste

Directions:

1. Combine squash, butter, applesauce, cream, and chicken stock in large saucepan; stir to blend well.
2. Add ground walnuts, chervil, and mace.
3. Cook over medium heat until warmed through, about 6 to 8 minutes; salt and pepper to taste.
4. Remove from heat and ladle into soup bowls; add a few toasted pieces of walnut as garnish.

Yields: 6 servings.

Chilled Curried Apple Soup

This is a delicious soup served cold, and it is a real treat on a hot summer day for lunch.

Ingredients:

1   lb. dessert apples, cored, chopped
2   Tbs. lemon juice
2   Tbs. butter
½   onion, finely chopped
1   Tbs. curry powder
2   c. vegetable stock
½   cinnamon stick
½   c. plus 2 Tbs. milk
6   Tbs. regular cream
    watercress for garnish

Directions:

1. Sprinkle chopped apples with lemon juice to prevent discoloration.
2. Melt butter in medium saucepan, and add apples and onion; cover and cook gently until soft, stirring occasionally.
3. Add curry powder, and cook over medium heat for 2 to 3 minutes, stirring continually; add stock and cinnamon stick.
4. Bring to a boil, then reduce heat and simmer for 10 minutes; remove and discard cinnamon stick.
5. Cool to lukewarm; pass soup through sieve, or blend in food processor until smooth.
6. Stir in milk and cream; cover and refrigerate until ready to serve.
7. Garnish with watercress.

Yields: 4 servings.

Delicious Apple Soup

This recipe is an interesting combination of apples and a touch of white wine to add flavor.

Ingredients:

- 4   apples, peeled, cored, chopped
- 5   c. water
- ½   Tbs. lemon peel, grated
- 1   cinnamon stick (2-in. length)
- ¼   c. maple syrup
- 1   Tbs. arrowroot
- 1   Tbs. lemon juice
- ¼   c. white wine
- ½   c. sour cream

Directions:

1. Simmer apples, water, lemon peel, cinnamon, and maple syrup until apples are tender, about 20 minutes; remove and discard cinnamon stick.
2. Remove from heat and cool slightly; purée in blender, then return to saucepan.
3. Remove about 1 cup of liquid; combine with arrowroot.
4. When thickened, return mixture to soup.
5. Stir in lemon juice and wine; heat through.
6. Ladle into bowls, and serve each topped with a spoonful of sour cream.

Yields: 8 to 10 servings.

Did You Know? . . . .

Did you know that some apple trees can grow to over 40 feet tall and live for over a hundred years?

Fall Apple Onion Soup

Apple cider and brandy make this onion soup a cozy dish for those chilly fall afternoons. Add some crusty bread for a delicious lunch.

Ingredients:

½   c. butter, divided
4   lg. onions, thinly sliced
2   lg. Granny Smith apples, peeled, cored, chopped
2   Tbs. brandy (optional)
4   c. chicken broth
1½ c. apple cider
1   Tbs. ground cinnamon
1   Tbs. sugar
2   Tbs. olive oil
½   c. shredded Gouda cheese
6   slices French bread, sliced 1 inch thick

Directions:

1. Set slow cooker to low heat, and put in half of the butter to melt.
2. Add onions and apples; cover and cook on low heat for 6 to 8 hours, until both are soft.
3. Add brandy, chicken broth, and apple cider; set slow cooker to high heat, and cook for 1 to 2 hours, until mixture is simmering.
4. Mix together cinnamon, sugar, olive oil, and remaining butter; spread onto one side of each slice of bread.
5. Place bread with cinnamon side up on a baking sheet, and broil in preheated oven until toasted, about 3 minutes.
6. Remove from oven, and flip slices over so cinnamon is on bottom; sprinkle Gouda cheese on top, and return to broiler until cheese is melted.
7. Ladle soup into serving bowls; cut toast into points, and place cheese side up for garnish.

Yields: 6 to 8 servings.

Pumpkin Apple Soup

This recipe is very unique and can be served inside of hollowed out pumpkins for a fall treat.

Ingredients:

8 small pumpkins (1 for each serving), washed
1 can solid-pack pumpkin (28 oz.)
1 can chicken broth (28 oz.)
1 c. applesauce (recipe page 169)
¼ c. honey or maple syrup
1 c. cream or as desired
   salt and pepper to taste
   ground cinnamon to taste
   chopped parsley
   crushed sugared nuts

Directions:

1. Cut top off each pumpkin, then scoop out seeds and excess strings.
2. Use as is for soup, or rub with oil, and bake until crisp-tender to retain firmness.
3. Bake at 325 degrees F. about 25 minutes for mini pumpkins and about 35 to 40 minutes for larger.
4. Combine canned pumpkin, chicken broth, and applesauce; heat through.
5. Add sweetener; salt and pepper to taste.
6. When ready to serve, stir in cream; ladle soup into pumpkin bowls.
7. Garnish as desired with cinnamon, parsley, and sugared nuts.

Yields: 8 servings.

Savory Apple Cream Soup

This is a tasty blend of flavors that adults and children alike seem to enjoy. This soup is even better after flavors have time to blend.

Ingredients:

5   slices bacon, diced
1   lg. onion, diced
2   cloves garlic, minced
½   head cabbage, shredded
1   red apple, cored, chopped
3   Tbs. all-purpose flour
2   sm. cans chicken broth
⅛   tsp. black pepper
⅛   tsp. ground nutmeg
¼   tsp. ground cinnamon
½   c. heavy cream
2   egg yolks
2   tsp. Dijon mustard

Directions:

1. Sauté bacon, then remove and leave 2 tablespoons of fat in pan; reserve bacon.
2. Sauté onions and garlic, then add cabbage and apple and sauté.
3. Stir in flour and cook for 3 minutes.
4. Add chicken broth, pepper, nutmeg, and cinnamon; stir well then add reserved bacon.
5. Bring to a boil; turn heat down and simmer, stirring occasionally, for about 25 minutes.
6. When ready to serve, blend cream with egg yolks and some hot soup.
7. Pour egg mixture back into pot, add mustard, and stir; serve while hot.

Yields: 4 servings.

Apple Delights Cookbook

A Collection of Apple Recipes
Cookbook Delights Series

Wines and Spirits

Table of Contents

Page

About Cooking with Alcohol

Some recipes in this cookbook contain, among other ingredients, liquors. It is for the purpose of obtaining desired flavor and achieving culinary appreciation and not to be abused in any way. In cooking and baking, alcohol evaporates and only the flavor may be enjoyed. When mixed in cold, however, such as in desserts, caution must be exercised. These recipes are intended for people who may consume small amounts of alcohol in a responsible and safe manner.

I live in Washington State, and we are proud of our wine production. Washington State is rapidly gaining prestige as a premier wine producer. Do enjoy the art of wine tasting, and enjoy the completeness and uniqueness of each wine. It is an art to enjoy and savor in moderation.

If consumption of even small amounts of alcoholic ingredients presents a problem, in whatever form, please substitute coffee flavor syrups, found in coffee sections of supermarkets. For example, instead of Southern Comfort liqueur, substitute with Irish Cream or Amaretto Syrup.

Karen Jean Matsko Hood

Apple Lime Margarita

This is a refreshing drink to have with a spicy meal with or without the tequila.

Ingredients:

    2 c. apple juice
    1 c. lime cordial
    ½ c. tequila
       green food coloring (optional)
       crushed ice

Directions:

1. In large pitcher mix together juice, lime cordial, tequila , and food coloring.
2. Pour into daiquiri-style glasses filled with crushed ice, and serve.

Yields: 6 servings.

Hot Apple Wine

This combination of cider and wine makes a delicious drink to share with company.

Ingredients:

3　c. apple cider
¼ c. sugar
1　stick cinnamon (3-in. length)
6　whole cloves
¼ peel of lemon, cut into strips
1　bottle dry white wine (one-fifth)
2　Tbs. lemon juice

Directions:

1. In saucepan combine apple cider, sugar, cinnamon, cloves, and lemon peel.
2. Bring to boiling, stirring until sugar is dissolved.
3. Simmer, uncovered, for 15 minutes; strain to remove spices and peel.
4. Add wine and lemon juice; heat through but do not boil.
5. Serve in preheated mugs.

Yields: 10 servings.

Apple Brandy Brew

Since this drink is made in the crock-pot, it is handy to keep hot and serve for a party.

Ingredients:

- 1 bottle apple-flavored wine (four-fifths qt.)
- 2 c. apple cider
- 1 c. peach brandy
- 1 cinnamon stick

Directions:

1. Combine ingredients in slow cooker.
2. Cover, and heat on low for 3 to 4 hours.
3. Serve hot.

Yields: 8 servings.

Apple Sloe Gin Cocktail

Try this recipe for a refreshing cocktail at the day's end.

Ingredients:

- 3 c. apple juice
- ½ c. sugar
- 6 Tbs. frozen orange juice concentrate, thawed
- 3 Tbs. lemon juice
- ¼ c. grenadine syrup
- 5 c. lemon-lime soda
  sloe gin to taste
  fresh strawberries for garnish

Directions:

1. In 3-quart saucepan heat together apple juice and sugar, stirring occasionally, until dissolved.
2. Remove from heat, and stir in thawed orange concentrate and lemon juice.
3. Cool completely, then add grenadine syrup.
4. Place in refrigerator to chill and blend flavors.
5. When ready to serve pour into tall, chilled glasses; fill ¾ full with lemon-lime soda.
6. Add sloe gin to preference.
7. Garnish with strawberries if desired.

Yields: About 10 cups.

Apple Blossom

This is a delicious beverage to warm up with on a cold winter evening.

Ingredients:

1   oz. brandy
2   oz. apple juice
¼   oz. fresh lemon juice
1   dash vodka

Directions:

1. Shake all ingredients well with ice cubes.
2. Strain into glass.

Yields: 1 serving.

Apple and Strawberry Vodka Slush

This is a festive and delicious drink for a large party. Your guests will be delighted with it!

Ingredients:

    3 apples, cored, sliced
    1 qt. fresh strawberries, washed, hulled, quartered
    3 oranges, sliced
    4 c. sugar, divided
    1 pt. strawberry liquor
    2 qt. water, boiling
    2 cans frozen apple juice concentrate (12 oz. each)
    2 env. unsweetened strawberry drink mix
    1 bottle dark rum (one-fifth)
    1 qt. vodka
    2 qt. apple juice
    2 qt. champagne
       crushed ice

Directions:

1. Combine apples, strawberries, oranges, and 1 cup sugar with strawberry liquor; cover and chill overnight.
2. Dissolve remaining sugar in boiling water, and allow to cool completely; add apple juice concentrate, strawberry drink mix, reserved liquor mixture, rum, and vodka.
3. Place this punch base in suitable size freezer containers; place in freezer.
4. Allow base to freeze; usually takes 4 to 5 days.
5. Combine apple juice with champagne; add chopped frozen punch base, and mix well.
6. Serve in chilled tall glasses filled with crushed ice.

Apple Berry Vodka Cordial

The combination of apples and berries gives this cordial a smooth and satisfying flavor.

Ingredients:

    1   c. sweet ripe apples, cored, finely chopped
    2   c. red boysenberries or raspberries
    3   c. vodka
    1½ c. sugar
    1   c. water
    ½   tsp. glycerin (found in drugstores)

Directions:

1. Mash berries, and transfer with juice and chopped apples into 1-gallon, lidded jar; cover with vodka.
2. Seal jar, shake to mix, and set aside in cool, dark place for 6 weeks.
3. Strain contents of jar through fine sieve into 4- to 6-cup glass bowl; discard fruit.
4. Rinse sieve, and fit with damp coffee filter; strain flavored vodka back into bowl.
5. Combine sugar and water in small saucepan; bring to a boil over medium heat, stirring until sugar dissolves.
6. Reduce heat to low, and simmer for 5 minutes or until clear syrup forms.
7. Remove pan from heat and cool to room temperature.
8. Add cooled syrup and glycerin to liqueur in bowl; stir mixture gently to blend.
9. Using funnel, divide liqueur between 2 lidded decanters of equal size.
10. Cordial should be ready to drink in 2 to 3 days and has a shelf life of 2 to 3 months. Refrigerate for longer life expectancy.

Yields: About 3 cups.

Apple Strawberry Knocker

This drink is sure to be a hit at parties during the winter holidays.

Ingredients:

1½ oz. vodka
2   Tbs. apple cider
1   tsp. lemon juice
1   tsp. strawberry liqueur
    ice

Directions:

1. Combine all ingredients in shaker.
2. Cover and shake.

Yields: 1 serving.

Apple Knocker

This makes a wonderful autumn beverage to enjoy.

Ingredients:

3   cinnamon sticks
2   tsp. whole cloves
½   tsp. ground nutmeg
½   gal. apple cider
1   c. sugar
2   c. orange juice
½   c. lemon juice
1   c. brandy (any fruit flavor)

Directions:

1. Tie cinnamon, cloves, and nutmeg in cheesecloth.
2. Simmer cider and sugar with spices for about 15 minutes.
3. Remove bag of seasonings.
4. Add orange juice, lemon juice, and brandy.
5. Heat to bubbling and serve.

Yields: 12 servings.

Apple and Berry Vodka Slush

Looking for a different beverage? Try this combination of apples blended with berries.

Ingredients:

2   c. apple juice, chilled
½   c. frozen blueberries
½   c. frozen strawberries
½   c. vodka or to taste
12 ice cubes

Directions:

1. Process apple juice and berries in blender for 1 minute.
2. Add vodka, then add ice cubes 2 at a time; cover and blend until smooth.
3. Pour into chilled, tall glasses to serve.

Yields: 4 servings.

Apple Pie Liquor

This delicious drink is wonderful for the fall holidays with the spicy flavors.

Ingredients:

- 1 qt. apple juice
- 1½ Tbs. apple pie spice
- 1½ c. honey
- 3 c. grain alcohol (151 or 190 proof)

Directions:

1. Warm (do not boil) apple juice in 2-quart pan.
2. Add apple pie spice and honey; mix well.
3. Add alcohol and divide into bottles; cap and let age 1 month.
4. Serve cold or hot.

Yields: About 2 quarts.

Pitcher Punch with Assorted Liquors

What a fun punch to serve for a gathering or party. Everyone can choose their favorite!

Ingredients:

- 1 c. boiling water
- 5 lemon-flavored herbal tea bags
- 1 Tbs. sugar
- 3 c. apple juice
- 1½ c. apricot nectar
  assorted liquors and liqueurs
  ice

Directions:

1. In teapot pour boiling water over tea bags; cover and brew 5 minutes.
2. Remove tea bags and stir in sugar; cool.
3. In pitcher combine tea, juice, and nectar; chill.
4. Pour into tall glasses of ice to ⅔ full, and fill up with liquor or liqueur of choice.

Yields: 6 servings.

Apple Wine

This recipe makes a medium dry wine.

Ingredients:

1   gal. apple cider, untreated
3¼ c. sugar
1   Campden tablet
½   pack all-purpose wine yeast

Directions:

1. Mix all ingredients.
2. Ferment under fermentation lock.
3. Rack when fermentation slows and sediment forms in bottom of jug.
4. Allow fermentation to finish, and rack until wine is clear.
5. Age as long as possible.
6. This wine is normally drinkable after 3 months, better after 6 months, and outstanding after 12 months.
7. Note: For a sweet wine use 4 cups sugar.

Cran-Apple Spiced Liqueur

The cranberries give this liqueur a change of pace.
Save soaked apples and cranberries to serve over ice cream or
pound cake.

Ingredients:

- 4 med. Granny Smith apples, peeled, cored
- 2 c. white wine, divided
- 2 cinnamon sticks
- 1 tsp. whole cloves
- 2 c. sugar
- 1 pkg. cranberries (12 oz.), coarsely chopped
- 2 c. brandy
- 1 tsp. grated orange peel

Directions:

1. Cut apples into eighths; combine in large bowl with ½ cup wine, cinnamon, and cloves.
2. Cook on high heat 8 minutes, stirring occasionally; add sugar and dissolve, about 4 minutes.
3. Add cranberries, brandy, orange peel, and remaining wine; mix well, and pour into 2-quart glass container.
4. Cover tightly; store in cool, dark place 3 weeks, shaking occasionally.
5. Strain through double-thickness cheesecloth; repeat until liquid is clear, then pour into 1-quart bottle or decanter.
6. Cover tightly; store in cool, dark place for 2 weeks before serving or gift-giving.

Yields: 1 quart.

Fruit Sangria with Cloved Apples

Here is a wonderful summertime or actually anytime beverage.

Ingredients:

1 bottle red wine (750 ml.)
½ c. rum
1 lemon, sliced
1 orange, sliced
1 lime, sliced
1 pint strawberries, washed, hulled, sliced
1 apple, cored, cut into 8 wedges
8 whole cloves
1 liter lemon-lime carbonated beverage

Directions:

1. In large jar or pitcher, combine wine and rum with lemon, orange, lime, and strawberries.
2. Push cloves into apple wedges, and add to mixture.
3. Cover, and refrigerate for at least 4 hours or overnight–as long as possible.
4. To serve, fill tall, chilled glass half full of wine mixture; fill rest of glass with soda, and stir gently.
5. Remove cloves from apple slices, and garnish drinks by spooning some marinated fruit into each glass.

Yields: 8 servings.

Did You Know? . . . .

Did you know that the wands of Druids were made from either yew or apple wood?

Hot Spiked Cider

Hot cider is always a favorite, especially during those fall and winter months when the air turns crispy and cool.

Ingredients:

- 1 gal. apple cider
- ½ c. maple syrup
- 1 c. rum, brandy, or bourbon
- ½ c. butter, softened
- ½ tsp. ground cinnamon
- ½ tsp. ground nutmeg
- 1 tsp. ground allspice

Directions:

1. Heat apple cider, maple syrup, and liquor.
2. Mix butter and spices together; use ½ teaspoon, or to taste, per cup of hot cider.
3. Serve in warmed mugs.
4. Cinnamon sticks and peppermint candy canes make a nice addition to each mug.

Yields: 10 servings.

Spicy Apple Eggnog

This is a delicious drink, especially for the holidays. It catches your attention with the surprising added apple flavor.

Ingredients:

- 2 eggs, beaten
- 3 c. milk
- 2 c. light cream
- ⅓ c. sugar
- ½ tsp. ground cinnamon
- 1 dash salt

¾ c. apple brandy
ground nutmeg

Directions:

1. In saucepan combine eggs, milk, cream, sugar, cinnamon, and salt.
2. Cook and stir over medium heat until slightly thickened and heated through.
3. Remove from heat; stir in brandy.
4. Sprinkle with nutmeg; serve while hot.

Yields: 6 servings.

Apple Wine Cooler with Cinnamon Tea

This is a wonderful drink to share with a friend on a quiet afternoon or early evening.

Ingredients:

1½ c. boiling water
6   cinnamon-flavored apple tea bags
⅓   c. sugar
1½ c. cold water
1   c. white wine
2   tsp. lemon juice
    club soda, chilled
    ice
    lemon slices for garnish

Directions:

1. In teapot pour boiling water over tea bags; cover and brew 5 minutes.
2. Remove tea bags; stir in sugar and cool.
3. In pitcher combine tea, cold water, wine, and lemon juice.
4. Serve in ice filled glasses with a splash of club soda; garnish, if desired, with lemon slices.

Yields: 4 servings.

Spicy Fruit Wine

This is an excellent wine to curl up with in front of a fire or to share on a crisp, fall day.

Ingredients:

1 c. water
1 c. brown sugar, firmly packed
2 c. pineapple juice
2 oranges, juiced, reserve rind
6 whole cloves
3 whole allspice berries
2 cinnamon sticks
2 orange rinds, cut in small strips
½ tsp. salt
4 c. red wine
8 cinnamon sticks for garnish

Directions:

1. In large, nonreactive saucepan combine water, brown sugar, pineapple juice, and orange juice.
2. Season with cloves, allspice, 2 cinnamon sticks, orange rind, and salt.
3. Bring to a boil, reduce heat, and let simmer for 15 minutes.
4. Pour in wine, heat to just boiling, and remove from heat.
5. Serve hot with cinnamon stick for garnish.

Yields: 8 servings.

Did You Know? . . . .

Did you know that apple varieties range in size from a little larger than a cherry to as large as a grapefruit?

Festival Information

Following is a list of just a few of the apple festivals throughout the country each year. You may use the following contact information or contact the local Chamber of Commerce or Visitor's Information Bureau of each town to find out the exact dates on which the festivals are held in each community.

Arkansas Apple Festival
October of each year
Lincoln, AR
www.arkansasapplefestival.org

Bayfield Apple Festival
October of each year
Bayfield, WI
800-447-4094
www.bayfield.org

Fort Wayne Johnny Appleseed Festival
September of each year
Fort Wayne, IN
www.johnnyappleseedfest.com

Apple Harvest Festival
October of each year
Ithaca, NY
607-277-8679
www.downtownithaca.com

Unicoi County Apple Festival
October of each year
Erwin, TN
423-743-3000
www.unicoicounty.org/applefestival.html

Georgia Apple Festival
October of each year
Ellijay, GA
www.georgiaapplefestival.org

Applebutterfest
October of each year
Grand Rapids, OH
www.applebutterfest.org

South Carolina Apple Festival
September of each year
Westminster, SC
www.westminstersc.com/festival.htm

Washington State Apple Harvest Festival
September of each year
Wenatchee, WA
509-662-2116
www.wenatchee.org

Springville Apple Festival
October of each year
Springville, CA
559-539-0619
www.springville.ca.us/applefest

Apple Associations and Commissions

In the United States, apples are grown commercially in 36 states. Following is a selection of the many associations or commissions available for apple growers.

Arizona Apple Growers Association
27207 S. Brookerson Road
Willcox, AZ 85643
Phone: 520-384-6099
eggersfarms@starband.net

California Apple Commission
770 East Shaw, Suite 220
Fresno, CA 93710
Phone: 559-225-3000
www.calapple.org

Wisconsin Apple Growers Association
211 Canal Road
Waterloo, WI 53594
Phone: 920-478-4277

Vermont Apple Marketing Board
116 State Street
Montpelier, VT 05620
Phone: 802-828-3827
www.vermontapples.org

Georgia Commodity Commission for Apples
326 Agricultural Building
Capitol Square
Atlanta, GA 30334
Phone: 404-656-3678

Hood River Grower-Shipper Association
P.O. Box 168
Odell, OR 97044-0168
Phone: 541-387-4769

Idaho Apple Commission
P.O. Box 909
Parma, ID 83660-0909
208-722-5111
idapple@widaho.com

Illinois State Horticultural Society
RR 13, Box 36A
Bloomington, IL 61704
Phone: 309-828-8929

Indiana Horticultural Society
Department of Horticulture
1165 Horticulture Building
Purdue University
West Lafayette, IN 47907
Phone: 765-463-6587

Iowa Fruit and Vegetable Growers Association
1701 Willis Avenue
Perry, IA 50220
Phone: 515-465-5992

Maryland Apple Promotion Board
P.O. Box 917
Hagerstown, MD 21741
Phone: 301-733-8777
www.marylandapples.org

Washington Apple Commission
2900 Euclid Avenue
P.O. Box 18
Wenatchee, WA 98807
Phone: 509-663-9600
Email: info@waapple.org

U.S. and Metric Measurement Charts

Here are some measurement equivalents to help you with exchanges. There was a time when many people thought the entire world would convert to the metric scale. While most of the world has, America still has not. Metric conversions in cooking are vitally important to preparing a tasty recipe. Here are simple conversion tables that should come in handy.

U.S. Measurement Equivalents

A few grains/pinch/dash, (dry) = Less than ⅛ teaspoon
A dash (liquid) = A few drops
3 teaspoons = 1 tablespoon
½ tablespoon = 1½ teaspoons
1 tablespoon = 3 teaspoons
2 tablespoons = 1 fluid ounce
4 tablespoons = ¼ cup
5⅓ tablespoons = ⅓ cup
8 tablespoons = ½ cup
8 tablespoons = 4 fluid ounces
10⅔ tablespoons = ⅔ cup
12 tablespoons = ¾ cup
16 tablespoons = 1 cup
16 tablespoons = 8 fluid ounces
⅛ cup = 2 tablespoons
¼ cup = 4 tablespoons
¼ cup = 2 fluid ounces
⅓ cup = 5 tablespoons plus 1 teaspoon
½ cup = 8 tablespoons
1 cup = 16 tablespoons
1 cup = 8 fluid ounces
1 cup = ½ pint
2 cups = 1 pint
2 pints = 1 quart
4 quarts (liquid) = 1 gallon
8 quarts (dry) = 1 peck
4 pecks (dry) = 1 bushel
1 kilogram = approximately 2 pounds
1 liter=approximately 4 cups or 1quart

Approximate Metric Equivalents by Volume

U.S.	Metric
¼ cup	= 60 milliliters
½ cup	= 120 milliliters
1 cup	= 230 milliliters
1¼ cups	= 300 milliliters
1½ cups	= 360 milliliters
2 cups	= 460 milliliters
2½ cups	= 600 milliliters
3 cups	= 700 milliliters
4 cups (1 quart)	= .95 liter
1.06 quarts	= 1 liter
4 quarts (1 gallon)	= 3.8 liters

Approximate Metric Equivalents by Weight

U.S.	Metric
¼ ounce	= 7 grams
½ ounce	= 14 grams
1 ounce	= 28 grams
1¼ ounces	= 35 grams
1½ ounces	= 40 grams
2½ ounces	= 70 grams
4 ounces	= 112 grams
5 ounces	= 140 grams
8 ounces	= 228 grams
10 ounces	= 280 grams
15 ounces	= 425 grams
16 ounces (1 pound)	= 454 grams

Glossary

Aerate: A synonym for sift; to pass ingredients through a fine-mesh device to break up large pieces and incorporate air into ingredients to make them lighter.

Al dente: "To the tooth," in Italian. The pasta is cooked just enough to maintain a firm, chewy texture.

Baste: To brush or spoon liquid fat or juices over meat during roasting to add flavor and prevent drying out.

Bias-slice: To slice a food crosswise at a 45-degree angle.

Bind: To thicken a sauce or hot liquid by stirring in ingredients such as eggs, flour, butter, or cream until it holds together.

Blackened: Popular Cajun-style cooking method. Seasoned foods are cooked over high heat in a super-heated heavy skillet until charred.

Blanch: To scald, as in vegetables being prepared for freezing; as in almonds so as to remove skins.

Blend: To mix or fold two or more ingredients together to obtain equal distribution throughout the mixture.

Braise: To brown meat in oil or other fat, and then cook slowly in liquid. The effect of braising is to tenderize the meat.

Bread: To coat food with crumbs (usually with soft or dry bread crumbs), sometimes seasoned.

Brown: To quickly sauté, broil, or grill either at the beginning or at the end of meal preparation, often to enhance flavor, texture, or eye appeal.

Brush: To use a pastry brush to coat a food such as meat or pastry with melted butter, glaze, or other liquid.

Beurre Manié: French for "kneaded butter." A dough, consisting of equal parts of soft butter and flour, used to thicken soups and sauces.

Butterfly: To cut open a food such as pork chops down the center without cutting all the way through, and then spread apart.

Caramelize: To brown sugar over a flame, with or without the addition of some water to aid the process. The temperature range in which sugar caramelizes is approximately 320 to 360 degrees F.

Clarify: To remove impurities from butter or stock by heating the liquid, then straining or skimming it.

Coddle: A cooking method in which foods (such as eggs) are put in separate containers and placed in a pan of simmering water for slow, gentle cooking.

Confit: To slowly cook pieces of meat in their own gently rendered fat.

Core: To remove the inedible center of fruits such as pineapples.

Cream: To beat vegetable shortening, butter, or margarine, with or without sugar, until light and fluffy. This process traps in air bubbles, later used to create height in cookies and cakes.

Crème Fraîche: A heavy cream slightly soured with bacterial culture but not as sour or as thick as sour cream. Crème fraîche is pronounced "krem fresh."

Crimp: To create a decorative edge on a pie crust. On a double pie crust, this also seals the edges together.

Curd: A custard-like pie or tart filling flavored with juice and zest of citrus fruit, usually lemon, although lime and orange may also be used.

Curdle: To cause semisolid pieces of coagulated protein to develop in food, usually as a result of the addition of an acid substance, or the overheating of milk or egg-based sauces.

Custard: A mixture of beaten egg, milk, and possibly other ingredients such as sweet or savory flavorings, which are cooked with gentle heat, often in a water bath or double boiler. As pie filling, the custard is frequently cooked and chilled before being layered into a baked crust.

Deglaze: To add liquid to a pan in which foods have been fried or roasted, in order to dissolve the caramelized juices stuck to the bottom of the pan.

Dot: To sprinkle food with small bits of an ingredient such as butter to allow for even melting.

Dredge: To sprinkle lightly and evenly with sugar or flour. A dredger has holes pierced on the lid to sprinkle evenly.

Drippings: The liquids left in the bottom of a roasting or frying pan after meat is cooked. Drippings are generally used for gravies and sauces.

Drizzle: To pour a liquid such as a sweet glaze or melted butter in a slow, light trickle over food.

Dust: To sprinkle food lightly with spices, sugar, or flour for a light coating.

Egg Wash: A mixture of beaten eggs (yolks, whites, or whole eggs) with either milk or water. Used to coat cookies and other baked goods to give them a shine when baked.

Emulsion: A mixture of liquids, one being a fat or oil and the other being water based so that tiny globules of one are suspended in the other. This may involve the use of stabilizers, such as egg or custard. Emulsions may be temporary or permanent.

Entrée: A French term that originally referred to the first course of a meal, served after the soup and before the meat courses. In the United States, it refers to the main dish of a meal.

Fillet: To remove the bones from meat or fish for cooking.

Filter: To remove lumps, excess liquid, or impurities by passing through paper or cheesecloth.

Firm-Ball Stage: In candy making, the point at which boiling syrup dropped in cold water forms a ball that is compact yet gives slightly to the touch.

Flambé: To ignite a sauce or other liquid so that it flames.

Flan: An open pie filled with sweet or savory ingredients; also, a Spanish dessert of baked custard covered with caramel.

Flute: To create a decorative scalloped or undulating edge on a pie crust or other pastry.

Fricassee: Usually a stew in which the meat is cut up, lightly cooked in butter, and then simmered in liquid until done.

Frizzle: To cook thin slices of meat in hot oil until crisp and slightly curly.

Ganache: A rich chocolate filling or coating made with chocolate, vegetable shortening, and possibly heavy cream. It can coat cakes or cookies and be used as a filling for truffles.

Glaze: A liquid that gives an item a shiny surface. Examples are fruit jams that have been heated or chocolate thinned with melted vegetable shortening. Also, to cover a food with such a liquid.

Granita: A semi-frozen dessert of sugar, water, and flavorings from Sicily, Italy.

Gratin: To bind together or combine food with a liquid such as cream, milk, béchamel sauce, or tomato sauce in a shallow dish. The mixture is then baked until cooked and set.

Grenadine Syrup: Traditionally a red syrup that is used as an ingredient in cocktails. Grenadine, the French word for pomegranate, was originally prepared from pomegranate juice and sugar.

Hard-Ball Stage: In candy making, the point at which syrup has cooked long enough to form a solid ball in cold water.

Hull (also husk): To remove the leafy parts of soft fruits, such as strawberries or blackberries.

Infusion: To extract flavors by soaking them in liquid heated in a covered pan. The term also refers to the liquid resulting from this process.

Jerk or Jamaican Jerk Seasoning: A dry mixture of various spices such as chilies, thyme, garlic, onions, and cinnamon or cloves used to season meats such as chicken or pork.

Julienne: To cut into long, thin strips.

Jus: The natural juices released by roasting meats.

Kielbasa: A Polish word for traditional Polish sausage.

Larding: To inset strips of fat into pieces of meat, so that the braised meat stays moist and juicy.

Marble: To gently swirl one food into another.

Marinate: To combine food with aromatic ingredients to add flavor.

Meringue: Egg whites beaten until they are stiff, then sweetened. It can be used as the topping for pies or baked as cookies.

Muddle: To mash or crush ingredients with a spoon or a muddler (a rod with a flattened end). Usually identified with the preparation of mixed drinks.

Mull: To slowly heat cider with spices and sugar.

Nonreactive Pan: Cookware that does not react chemically with foods, primarily acidic foods. Glass, stainless steel, enamel, anodized aluminum, and permanent nonstick surfaces are basically nonreactive. Shiny aluminum is reactive.

Parboil: To partly cook in a boiling liquid.

Peaks: The mounds made in a mixture. For example, egg white that has been whipped to stiffness. Peaks are "stiff" if they stay upright or "soft" if they curl over.

Pesto: A sauce usually made of fresh basil, garlic, olive oil, pine nuts, and cheese. The ingredients are finely chopped and then mixed, uncooked, with pasta. Generally, the term refers to any uncooked sauce made of finely chopped herbs and nuts.

Pipe: To force a semisoft food through a bag (either a pastry bag or a plastic bag with one corner cut off) to decorate food.

Pressure Cooking: To cook using steam trapped under a locked lid to produce high temperatures and achieve fast cooking time.

Purée: To mash or sieve food into a thick liquid.

Ramekin: A small baking dish used for individual servings of sweet and savory dishes.

Reduce: To cook liquids down so that some of the water evaporates.

Refresh: To pour cold water over freshly cooked vegetables to prevent further cooking and to retain color.

Roux: A cooked paste usually made from flour and butter used to thicken sauces.

Sauté: To cook foods quickly in a small amount of oil in a skillet or sauté pan over direct heat.

Scald: To heat a liquid, usually a dairy product, until it almost boils.

Sear: To seal in a meat's juices by cooking it quickly using very high heat.

Seize: To form a thick, lumpy mass when melted (usually applies to chocolate).

Sift: To remove large lumps from a dry ingredient such as flour or confectioners' sugar by passing it through a fine mesh. This process also incorporates air into the ingredients, making them lighter.

Simmer: To cook food in a liquid at a low enough temperature that small bubbles begin to break the surface.

Steam: To cook over boiling water in a covered pan. This method keeps foods' shape, texture, and nutritional value intact better than methods such as boiling.

Steep: To soak dry ingredients (tea leaves, ground coffee, herbs, spices, etc.) in liquid until the flavor is infused into the liquid.

Stewing: To brown small pieces of meat, poultry, or fish, then simmer them with vegetables or other ingredients in enough liquid to cover them, usually in a closed pot on the stove, in the oven, or with a slow cooker.

Thin: To reduce a mixture's thickness with the addition of more liquid.

Truss: To use string, skewers, or pins to hold together a food to maintain its shape while it cooks (usually applied to meat or poultry).

Unleavened: Baked goods that contain no agents to give them volume, such as baking powder, baking soda, or yeast.

Vinaigrette: A general term referring to any sauce made with vinegar, oil, and seasonings.

Zest: The thin, brightly colored outer part of the rind of citrus fruits. It contains volatile oils, used as a flavoring.

Recipe Index

314

315

Reader Feedback Form

Dear Reader,

We are very interested in what our readers think. Please fill in the form below and return it to:

Whispering Pine Press International, Inc.
c/o Apple Delights Cookbook
507 N. Sullivan Road Suite LL-5, Spokane Valley, WA 99037-8576
Phone: (509) 928-8700 | Fax: (509) 922-9949
Publisher Websites: www.whisperingpinepress.com www.whispering-pinepressbookstore.com
Blog: www.whisperingpinepressblog.com
Email: sales@whisperingpinepress.com

Name: _____

Address: _____

City, St., Zip: _____

Phone/Fax: (____) _____ | (____) _____

Email: _____

Comments/Suggestions: _____

_____

_____

_____

_____

A great deal of care and attention has been exercised in the creation of this book. Designing a great cookbook that is original, fun, and easy to use has been a job that required many hours of diligence, creativity, and research. Although we strive to make this book completely error free, errors and discrepancies may not be completely excluded. If you come across any errors or discrepancies, please make a note of them and send them to our publishing office. We are constantly updating our manuscripts, eliminating errors, and improving quality.

Please contact us at the address above.

About the Cookbook Delights Series

The *Cookbook Delights Series* includes many different topics and themes. If you have a passion for food and wish to know more information about different foods, then this series of cookbooks will be beneficial to you. Each book features a different type of food, such as avocados, strawberries, huckleberries, salmon, vegetarian, lentils, almonds, cherries, coconuts, lemons, and many, many more.

The *Cookbook Delights Series* not only includes cookbooks about individual foods but also includes several holiday-themed cookbooks. Whatever your favorite holiday may be, chances are we have a cookbook with recipes designed with that holiday in mind. Some examples include *Halloween Delights, Thanksgiving Delights, Christmas Delights, Valentine Delights, Mother's Day Delights, St. Patrick's Day Delights,* and *Easter Delights.*

Each cookbook is designed for easy use and is organized into alphabetical sections. Over 250 recipes are included along with other interesting facts, folklore, and history of the featured food or theme. Each book comes with a beautiful full-color cover, ordering information, and a list of other upcoming books in the series.

Note cards, bookmarks, and a daily journal have been printed and are available to go along with each cookbook. You may view the entire line of cookbooks, journals, cards, posters, puzzles, and bookmarks by visiting our website at and www.appledelights. com, or you can email us with your questions and comments to: sales@whisperingpinepress.com.

Please ask your local bookstore to carry these sets of books.

To order, please contact:

Whispering Pine Press International, Inc.
c/o Apple Delights Cookbook
507 N. Sullivan Road Suite LL-5
Spokane Valley, WA 99037-8576
Phone: (509) 928-8700 | Fax: (509) 922-9949
Publisher Websites: www.whisperingpinepress.com
www.whisperingpinepressbookstore.com
Blog: www.whisperingpinepressblog.com
Email: sales@whisperingpinepress.com
SAN 253-200X

We Invite You to Join the
Whispering Pine Press International, Inc.
Book Club!

Whispering Pine Press International, Inc.
c/o Apple Delights Cookbook
507 N. Sullivan Road Suite LL-5, Spokane Valley, WA 99037-8576
Phone: (509) 928-8700 | Fax: (509) 922-9949
Publisher Websites: www.whisperingpinepress.com
www.whisperingpinepressbookstore.com
Blog: www.whisperingpinepressblog.com
Email: sales@whisperingpinepress.com

Buy 11 books and get the next one free, based on the average price of the first eleven purchased.

How the club works:

Simply use the order form below and order books from our catalog. You can buy just one at a time or all eleven at once. After the first eleven books are purchased, the next one is free. Please add shipping and handling as listed on this form. There are no purchase requirements at any time during your membership. Free book credit is based on the average price of the first eleven books purchased.

Join today! Pick your books and mail in the form today!

Yes! I want to join the Whispering Pine Press International, Inc., Book Club! Enroll me and send the books indicated below.

Title	Price
1.	
2.	
3.	
4.	
5.	
6.	
7.	
8.	
9.	
10.	
11.	

Free Book Title: _____

Free Book Price: _____ Avg. Price: _____ Total Price: _____

Credit for the free book is based on the average price of the first 11 books purchased.

(Circle one) Check | Visa | MasterCard | Discover | American Express

Credit Card #: _____ Expiration Date: _____

Name: _____

Address: _____

City: _____ State: _____ Country: _____

Zip/Postal: _____ Phone: (_____) _____

Email: _____

Signature_____

318

Whispering Pine Press International, Inc. Fundraising Opportunities

Fundraising cookbooks are proven moneymakers and great keepsake providers for your group. Whispering Pine Press International, Inc., offers a very special personalized cookbook fundraising program that encourages success to organizations all across the USA.

Our prices are competitive and fair. Currently, we offer a special of 100 books with many free features and excellent customer service. Any purchase you make is guaranteed first-rate.

Flexibility is not a problem. If you have special needs, we guarantee our cooperation in meeting each of them. Our goal is to create a cookbook that goes beyond your expectations. We have the confidence and a record that promises continual success.

Another great fundraising program is the *Cookbook Delights Series* Program. With cookbook orders of 50 copies or more, your organization receives a huge discount, making for a prompt and lucrative solution.

We also specialize in assisting group fundraising – Christian, community, nonprofit, and academic among them. If you are struggling for a new idea, something that will enhance your success and broaden your appeal, Whispering Pine Press International, Inc., can help.

For more information, write, phone, or fax to:

Whispering Pine Press International, Inc.
507 N. Sullivan Road Suite LL-5
Spokane Valley, WA 99037-8576
Phone: (509) 928-8700 | Fax: (509) 922-9949
Publisher Websites: www.whisperingpinepress.com
www.whisperingpinepressbookstore.com
Blog: www.whisperingpinepressblog.com
Email: sales@whisperingpinepress.com
Book Website: www.appledelights.com
SAN 253-200X

Personalized and/or Translated Order Form for Any Book by Whispering Pine Press International, Inc.

Dear Readers:

   If you or your organization wishes to have this book or any other of our books personalized, we will gladly accommodate your needs. For instance, if you would like to change the names of the characters in a book to the names of the children in your family or Sunday school class, we would be happy to work with you on such a project. We can add more information of your choosing and customize this book especially for your family, group, or organization.

   We are also offering an option of translating your book into another language. Please fill out the form below telling us exactly how you would like us to personalize your book.

Please send your request to:

Whispering Pine Press International, Inc.
507 N. Sullivan Road Suite LL-5, Spokane Valley, WA 99037-8576
Phone: (509) 928-8700 | Fax: (509) 922-9949
Publisher Websites: www.whisperingpinepress.com
www.whisperingpinepressbookstore.com
Blog: www.whisperingpinepressblog.com
Email: sales@whisperingpinepress.com

Person/Organization placing request: _____

Date_____ Phone: (____) _____

Address_____ Fax: (____) _____

City_____ State_____ Zip: _____

Language of the book: _____

Please explain your request in detail: _____

_____

_____

_____

_____

_____

_____

Gifts and Gift Baskets Order Form

Apple Delights Cookbook
A Collection of Apple Recipes, Cookbook Delights Series
ISBN: 978-1-59649-402-2   case bound $ 29.95 plus S&H
ISBN: 978-1-59210-542-7   perfect bound $ 19.95 plus S&H
ISBN: 978-1-59649-231-8   spiral bound $ 21.95 plus S&H
ISBN: 978-1-59210-695-0   comb bound $ 22.95 plus S&H
ISBN: 978-1-59434-799-3   large print edition $ 29.95 plus S&H
ISBN: 978-1-59210-697-4   printable cd $ 15.95 plus S&H
ISBN: 978-1-59649-060-4   E-PDF $ 9.99 elec dwnld
ISBN: 978-1-59210-360-7   E-PUB $ 9.99 elec dwnld
Apple Delights Menu Cookbook
A Collection of Apple-Themed Menus, Menu Cookbook Delights Series
Available in same bindings and prices as Delights Cookbooks listed above.

Apple Delights Journal
A Daily Journal
ISBN: 978-1-59649-627-9   spiral bound $ 19.95 plus S&H
ISBN: 978-1-59649-550-0   comb bound $ 20.95 plus S&H
ISBN: 978-1-59434-322-3   E-PDF $ 9.99 elec dwnld
ISBN: 978-1-59210-424-6   E-PUB $ 9.99 elec dwnld

Apple Delights Apron, Red Apples
ITEM: BFAPRAPAPL   apron $ 14.95 plus S&H
Apple Delights Apron, Yellow Apples
ITEM: BFAPYLAAPL   apron $ 14.95 plus S&H
Apple Delights Apron, Apple Pie
ITEM: BFAPAPIAPL   apron $ 14.95 plus S&H
Apple Delights Apron, Fallen Apples
ITEM: BFAPFLNAPL   apron $ 14.95 plus S&H
Apple Delights Bookmark, Red Apples
ITEM: BMRAPAPL   bookmark $ 3.95 plus S&H
Apple Delights Bookmark, Yellow Apples
ITEM: BMYLAAPL   bookmark $ 3.95 plus S&H
Apple Delights Bookmark, Apple Pie
ITEM: BMAPIAPL   bookmark $ 3.95 plus S&H
Apple Delights Bookmark, Fallen Apples
ITEM: BMFLNAPL   bookmark $ 3.95 plus S&H
Apple Delights Gift Baskets
A collection of customized gift baskets to choose from in which to place
your choice of gift items selected.
ITEM: GBXSMAPL   extra small $ 4.95 plus S&H
ITEM: GBSMLAPL   small $ 9.95 plus S&H
ITEM: GBMEDAPL   medium $ 14.95 plus S&H
ITEM: GBLGEAPL   large $ 19.95 plus S&H
ITEM: GBXLGAPL   extra large $ 24.95 plus S&H
Apple Delights Greeting Card, Red Apples
ITEM: GC55X85RAPAPL   size: 5½" x 8½" $ 3.95 plus S&H
ITEM: GC85X55RAPAPL   size: 8½" x 5½" $ 3.95 plus S&H
Apple Delights Greeting Card, Yellow Apples
ITEM: GC55X85YLAAPL   size: 5½" x 8½" $ 3.95 plus S&H
ITEM: GC85X55YLAAPL   size: 8½" x 5½" $ 3.95 plus S&H
Apple Delights Greeting Card, Apple Pie
ITEM: GC55X85APIAPL   size: 5½" x 8½" $ 3.95 plus S&H

ITEM: GC85X55APIAPL   size: 8½" x 5½" $ 3.95 plus S&H
Apple Delights Greeting Card, Fallen Apples
ITEM: GC55X85FLNAPL   size: 5½" x 8½" $ 3.95 plus S&H
ITEM: GC85X55FLNAPL   size: 8½" x 5½" $ 3.95 plus S&H
Apple Delights Mouse Pad
ITEM: MPBLKAPL   black pad $ 14.95 plus S&H
ITEM: MPCBAPL   cobalt blue pad $ 14.95 plus S&H
ITEM: MPNAVAPL   navy pad $ 14.95 plus S&H
ITEM: MPREDAPL   red pad $ 14.95 plus S&H
ITEM: MPBURAPL   burgundy pad $ 14.95 plus S&H
Apple Delights Note Card, Red Apples
ITEM: NCRAPAPL   size: 4½" x 6" $ 3.95 plus S&H
Apple Delights Note Card, Yellow Apples
ITEM: NCYLAAPL   size: 4½" x 6" $ 3.95 plus S&H
Apple Delights Note Card, Apple Pie
ITEM: NCAPIAPL   size: 4½" x 6" $ 3.95 plus S&H
Apple Delights Note Card, Fallen Apples
ITEM: NCFLNAPL   size: 4½" x 6" $ 3.95 plus S&H
Apple Delights Note Card, Frameable, Red Apples
ITEM: FNCRAPAPL   size: 8½" x 11" $ 19.95 plus S&H
Apple Delights Note Card, Frameable, Yellow Apples
ITEM: FNCYLAAPL   size: 8½" x 11" $ 19.95 plus S&H
Apple Delights Note Card, Frameable, Apple Pie
ITEM: FNCAPIAPL   size: 8½" x 11" $ 19.95 plus S&H
Apple Delights Note Card, Frameable, Fallen Apples
ITEM: FNCFLNAPL   size: 8½" x 11" $ 19.95 plus S&H
Apple Delights Postcard, Red Apples
ITEM: PCRAPAPL   postcard $ 3.95 plus S&H
Apple Delights Postcard, Yellow Apples
ITEM: PCYLAAPL   postcard $ 3.95 plus S&H
Apple Delights Postcard, Apple Pie
ITEM: PCAPIAPL   postcard $ 3.95 plus S&H
Apple Delights Postcard, Fallen Apples
ITEM: PCFLNAPL   postcard $ 3.95 plus S&H
Apple Delights Poster, Red Apples
ITEM: P11X17RAPAPL   size: 11" x 17" $ 9.95 plus S&H
ITEM: P18X24RAPAPL   size: 18" x 24" $ 25.95 plus S&H
ITEM: P24X36RAPAPL   size: 24" x 36" $ 29.95 plus S&H
Apple Delights Poster, Yellow Apples
ITEM: P11X17YLAAPL   size: 11" x 17" $ 9.95 plus S&H
ITEM: P18X24YLAAPL   size: 18" x 24" $ 25.95 plus S&H
ITEM: P24X36YLAAPL   size: 24" x 36" $ 29.95 plus S&H
Apple Delights Poster, Apple Pie
ITEM: P11X17APIAPL   size: 11" x 17" $ 9.95 plus S&H
ITEM: P18X24APIAPL   size: 18" x 24" $ 25.95 plus S&H
ITEM: P24X36APIAPL   size: 24" x 36" $ 29.95 plus S&H
Apple Delights Poster, Fallen Apples
ITEM: P11X17FLNAPL   size: 11" x 17" $ 9.95 plus S&H
ITEM: P18X24FLNAPL   size: 18" x 24" $ 25.95 plus S&H
ITEM: P24X36FLNAPL   size: 24" x 36" $ 29.95 plus S&H
Apple Delights Puzzle, Red Apples
ITEM: PUZRAPAPL   8½" x 11" puzzle $ 19.95 plus S&H
Apple Delights Puzzle, Yellow Apples
ITEM: PUZYLAAPL   8½" x 11" puzzle $ 19.95 plus S&H

Apple Delights Puzzle, Apple Pie
ITEM: PUZAPIAPL   8½" x 11" puzzle $ 19.95 plus S&H
Apple Delights Puzzle, Fallen Apples
ITEM: PUZFLNAPL   8½" x 11" puzzle $ 19.95 plus S&H
Apple Delights Refrigerator Magnet, Red Apples
ITEM: KRFMRAPAPL   refrigerator magnet $ 6.95 plus S&H
Apple Delights Refrigerator Magnet, Yellow Apples
ITEM: KRFMYLAAPL   refrigerator magnet $ 6.95 plus S&H
Apple Delights Refrigerator Magnet, Apple Pie
ITEM: KRFMAPIAPL   refrigerator magnet $ 6.95 plus S&H
Apple Delights Refrigerator Magnet, Fallen Apples
ITEM: KRFMFLNAPL   refrigerator magnet $ 6.95 plus S&H
Apple Delights T-shirt
SIZES: Children SM, M, L and Adult SM, M, L, XL, XXL and XXXL
ITEM: BFCSAPLTS   children SM $ 15.95 plus S&H
ITEM: BFCMAPLTS   children M $ 15.95 plus S&H
ITEM: BFCLAPLTS   children L $ 15.95 plus S&H
ITEM: BFASAPLTS   adult SM $ 15.95 plus S&H
ITEM: BFAMAPLTS   adult M $ 15.95 plus S&H
ITEM: BFALAPLTS   adult L $ 15.95 plus S&H
ITEM: BFAXLAPLTS   adult XL $ 15.95 plus S&H
ITEM: BFAXXLAPLTS   adult XXL $ 20.95 plus S&H
ITEM: BFAXXXLAPLTS   adult XXXL $ 20.95 plus S&H

  Please specify color when ordering T-shirts. Choose from burgundy,
navy, pink, white, light green, purple, light blue, or forest green.
Apple Delights Tote Bag, Red Apples
ITEM: BFTBRAPAPL   tote bag $ 12.95 plus S&H
Apple Delights Tote Bag, Yellow Apples
ITEM: BFTBYLAAPL   tote bag $ 12.95 plus S&H
Apple Delights Tote Bag, Apple Pie
ITEM: BFTBAPIAPL   tote bag $ 12.95 plus S&H
Apple Delights Tote Bag, Fallen Apples
ITEM: BFTBFLNAPL   tote bag $ 12.95 plus S&H

       Title   Price
1. _____

2. _____

3. _____

4. _____

(Please circle one) Check | Visa | MasterCard | Discover | American Express

Credit Card #: _____Expiration Date: _____

Name: _____

Address: _____

City: _____State: _____Country: _____

Zip/Postal: _____ Phone: (_____) _____

Email: _____

Signature: _____

Whispering Pine Press International, Inc.
c/o Apple Delights Cookbook
507 N. Sullivan Road Suite LL-5, Spokane Valley, WA 99037-8576
Phone: (509) 928-8700 | Fax: (509) 922-9949
Email: sales@whisperingpinepress.com

Apple Delights Cookbook

A Collection of Apple Recipes

How to Order

Get your additional copies of this book by returning an order form and your check, money order, or credit card information to:

Whispering Pine Press International, Inc.
507 N. Sullivan Road Suite LL-5, Spokane Valley, WA 99037-8576
Phone: (509) 928-8700 | Fax: (509) 922-9949
Publisher Websites: www.whisperingpinepress.com
www.whisperingpinepressbookstore.com
Blog: www.whisperingpinepressblog.com
Email: sales@whisperingpinepress.com

Customer Name: _____

Address: _____

City, St., Zip: _____

Phone/Fax: _____

Email: _____

- -

Please send me _____ copies of _____

_____ at $_____ per copy and $4.95 for shipping and handling per book, plus $2.95 each for additional books. Enclosed is my check, money order, or charge my account for $_____.

☐ Check   ☐ Money Order   ☐ Credit Card

(*Circle One*) MasterCard | Discover | Visa | American Express
☐☐☐☐   ☐☐☐☐   ☐☐☐☐   ☐☐☐☐

Expiration Date: _____

_____
Signature

_____
Print Name

324

Whispering Pine Press International, Inc.

P.O. Box 668 Spokane Valley, WA 99037-0668 USA
507 North Sullivan Road Suite A-9 Spokane Valley, WA 99037-8531 USA
Phone: (509) 924-2124• Fax: (509) 924-2134
E-mail: sales@whisperingpinepress.com
Website: www.whisperingpinepress.com

Book Catalog Website: www.bookcatalog.info | E-mail: sales@bookcatalog.info

Shop Online:

www.whisperingpinepress.com
Fax orders to: 1 (509) 924-2134

Gift-wrapping, Autographing and Inscription

We are proud to offer personal autographing by the author For a limited time this service is absolutely free!
Gift-wrapping is also available for $3.95 per item.

1. Sold To

Name: _____
Street/Route: _____
_____
City: _____
State: _____ Zip: _____
Country: _____
Gift message: _____
_____
E-mail address: _____
Daytime Phone: (_ _) _ _ _-_ _ _ _
 *Necessary for verifying orders
Home Phone: (_ _) _ _ _-_ _ _ _
Fax: (_ _) _ _ _-_ _ _ _

2. Ship To

☐ Is this a new or corrected address?
☐ Alternative Shipping Address
☐ Mailing Address

Name: _____
Address: _____
_____
City: _____
State: _____ Zip: _____
Country: _____
E-mail address: _____

3. Items Ordered

ISBN # /Item #	Size	Color	Qty.	Title or Description	Price	Total

4. Method Of Payment

☐ Visa ☐ MasterCard ☐ Discover ☐ American Express
☐ Check/Money Order Please make it payable to Whispering Pine Press
International, Inc. (No Cash or COD's)

Expiration Date

Account Number ____ /____
Month Year

[ ][ ][ ][ ] [ ][ ][ ][ ] [ ][ ][ ][ ] [ ][ ][ ][ ]

Signature_____
Cardholder's signature
Printed Name_____
Please print name of cardholder
Address of Cardholder_____
_____

5. Shipping & Handling

Continental US
US Postal Ground: Please add for first book $4.50
and each additional book add $2.00. Please allow 1-4
weeks for delivery.
US Postal Air: Please add $10.00 shipping and
handling. Please allow 1-3 days for delivery.

Alaska, Hawaii and the US Territories
By Ship: Please add 10% shipping and handling
(minimum charge $7.00) Please allow 6-12 weeks for
delivery.
By Air: Please add 12% shipping and handling
(minimum charge $9.00) Please allow 2-6 weeks for
delivery.

International
By Ship: Please add 10% shipping and handling (minimum shipping charge $7.00) Please allow 6-12 weeks for
delivery.
By Air: Please add 12% shipping and handling (minimum charge $9.00) Please allow 2-6 weeks delivery
Fed Ex Shipments: Add $5.00 to the above annual charges for overnight delivery

Subtotal	
Gift wrap $3.95 Each	
For delivery in WA add 8.6% sales tax.	
Regular shipping See chart at left	
6. Total	

Whispering Pine Press International, Inc.
P.O. Box 668 Spokane Valley, WA 99037-0668 USA
507 North Sullivan Road Suite A-9 Spokane Valley, WA 99037-8531 USA
Phone: (509) 924-2124• Fax: (509) 924-2134
E-mail: sales@whisperingpinepress.com
Website: www.whisperingpinepress.com
Book Catalog Website: www.bookcatalog.info | E-mail: sales@bookcatalog.info

Shop Online:

www.whisperingpinepress.com
Fax orders to: 1 (509) 924-2134

Gift-wrapping, Autographing and Inscription
We are proud to offer personal autographing by the author For a limited time this service is absolutely free!
Gift-wrapping is also available for $3.95 per item.

1. Sold To

Name: _____
Street/Route: _____
_____
City: _____
State: _____ Zip: _____
Country: _____
Gift message: _____
_____
E-mail address: _____
Daytime Phone: (_ _) _ _ _ - _ _ _ _
  *Necessary for verifying orders
  Home Phone: (_ _) _ _ _ - _ _ _ _
  Fax: (_ _) _ _ - _ _ _ _

2. Ship To

☐ Is this a new or corrected address?
☐ Alternative Shipping Address
☐ Mailing Address

Name: _____
Address: _____
_____
City: _____
State: _____ Zip: _____
Country: _____
E-mail address: _____

3. Items Ordered

ISBN # /Item #	Size	Color	Qty.	Title or Description	Price	Total

4. Method Of Payment

☐ Visa ☐ MasterCard ☐ Discover ☐ American Express
☐ Check/Money Order   Please make it payable to Whispering Pine Press
International, Inc. (No Cash or COD's)

                                 Expiration Date

Account Number   _____/_____
                               Month   Year

☐☐☐☐ ☐☐☐☐ ☐☐☐☐ ☐☐☐☐

Signature_____
               Cardholder's signature
Printed Name_____
               Please print name of cardholder
Address of Cardholder_____
_____

5. Shipping & Handling

Continental US
US Postal Ground: Please add for first book $4.50
and each additional book add $2.00. Please allow 1-4
weeks for delivery.
US Postal Air: Please add $10.00 shipping and
handling. Please allow 1-3 days for delivery.

Alaska, Hawaii and the US Territories
By Ship: Please add 10% shipping and handling
(minimum charge $7.00) Please allow 6-12 weeks for
delivery.
By Air: Please add 12% shipping and handling
(minimum charge $9.00) Please allow 2-6 weeks for
delivery.

International
By Ship: Please add 10% shipping and handling (minimum shipping charge $7.00) Please allow 6-12 weeks for
delivery.
By Air: Please add 12% shipping and handling (minimum charge $9.00) Please allow 2-6 weeks delivery
Fed Ex Shipments: Add $5.00 to the above airmail charges for overnight delivery.

Subtotal	
Gift wrap $3.95 Each	
For delivery in WA add 8.6% sales tax.	
Regular shipping See chart at left	
6. Total	

About the Author and Cook

Karen Jean Matsko Hood has always enjoyed cooking, baking, and experimenting with recipes. At this time Hood is working to complete a series of cookbooks that blends her skills and experience in cooking and entertaining. Hood entertains large groups of people and especially enjoys designing creative menus with holiday, international, ethnic, and regional themes.

Hood is publishing a cookbook series entitled the *Cookbook Delights Series*, in which each cookbook emphasizes a different food ingredient or theme. The first cookbook in the series is *Apple Delights Cookbook*. Hood is working to complete another series of cookbooks titled *Hood and Matsko Family Cookbooks*, which includes many recipes handed down from her family heritage and others that have emerged from more current family traditions. She has been invited to speak on talk radio shows on various topics, and favorite recipes from her cookbooks have been prepared on local television programs.

Hood was born and raised in Great Falls, Montana. As an undergraduate, she attended the College of St. Benedict in St. Joseph, Minnesota, and St. John's University in Collegeville, Minnesota. She attended the University of Great Falls in Great Falls, Montana. Hood received a B.S. Degree in Natural Science from the College of St. Benedict and minored in both Psychology and Secondary Education. Upon her graduation, Hood and her husband taught science and math on the island of St. Croix in the U.S. Virgin Islands. Hood has completed postgraduate classes at the University of Iowa in Iowa City, Iowa. In May 2001, she completed her Master's Degree in Pastoral Ministry at Gonzaga University in Spokane, Washington. She has taken postgraduate classes at Lewis and Clark College on the North Idaho college campus in Coeur d'Alene, Idaho, and Taylor University in Fort Wayne, Indiana. Hood is working on research projects to complete her Ph.D. in Leadership Studies at Gonzaga University in Spokane, Washington.

Hood resides in Greenacres, Washington, along with her husband, sixteen children, and foster children. Her interests include writing, teaching, and volunteering as a court advocate in the juvenile court system for abused and neglected children. Hood is a literary advocate for youth and adults. Her hobbies include cooking, baking, collecting, photography, indoor and outdoor gardening, and the cultivation of unusual flowering plants and orchids. She enjoys raising several specialty breeds of animals including Icelandic horses, bichons frisés, cockapoos, Icelandic sheepdogs, and a few rescue cats. Hood also enjoys bird-watching and finds all aspects of nature precious.

She demonstrates a passionate appreciation of the environment and a respect for all life. Karen welcomes you to blog with her at www.karensblog.net. She also invites you to visit her websites at www.karenjeanmatskohood.com and www.karensbookstore.com.

www.hoodfamilyblog.com

www.ingramcontent.com/pod-product-compliance
Lightning Source LLC
Chambersburg PA
CBHW031234090426
42742CB00007B/198